Ivy Global

New SAT 4 Practice Tests
Edition 1.1

$$100(1.07)^n = 200$$
$$(1.07)^n = 2$$

Resources & Downloads:

IVYGLOBAL.COM/STUDY

NEW SAT 4 PRACTICE TESTS

This publication was written and edited by the team at Ivy Global.

Editor-in-Chief: Sarah Pike

Producers: Lloyd Min and Junho Suh

Editors: Sacha Azor, Corwin Henville, Nathan Létourneau, and Kristin Rose.

Contributors: Ethan Abramson, Ian Billinge, Stephanie Bucklin, Alexandra Candib, Shavumiyaa Chandrabalan, Natalia Cole, Shayna Darling, Rushama De, Nathaniel Dolquist, Jacqueline Fedida, Yvonne Greenen, Elizabeth Hilts, Lei Huang, Ricki Korff, Jordan Marzouk, Mark Mendola, Ward Pettibone, Yolanda Song, Camille Wong, and Nicole Young.

This product was developed by Ivy Global, a pioneering education company that delivers a wide range of educational services.

E-mail: publishing@ivyglobal.com
Website: http://www.ivyglobal.com

CONTENTS

Chapter 1
Introduction

ABOUT THIS BOOK
PART 1

Welcome, students and parents! The New SAT Practice Tests in this book were created to help you prepare for the newly redesigned SAT. In this book, you'll find tips for getting the most out of your studying and doing your best on test day. Most importantly, you'll find four realistic, full-length practice tests that will help you assess and develop your skills.

If you would like more in-depth review of the concepts on the SAT, as well as even more practice in applying your knowledge, you can also check out Ivy Global's New SAT Guide. It contains hundreds of pages of lessons, strategies, and questions that will help improve your skills and familiarize you with the format of the test. For more information or to purchase the New SAT Guide, please visit us at sat.ivyglobal.com.

Also be sure to check out ivyglobal.com/study for bonuses related to this book. As an owner of Ivy Global's New SAT 4 Practice Tests, you can access additional resources to support your studying, including extra scoring sheets and detailed answer explanations.

The tests in this book are designed to prepare you for the new SAT, which will first be administered in March 2016. If you are planning on taking the SAT before that, you will be taking a substantially different test and should prepare accordingly.

If you have any questions or feedback, we would love to hear from you. Send us an email anytime at publishing@ivyglobal.com.

SAT BASICS

PART 2

WHAT IS THE SAT?

The SAT is a standardized test written and administered by the College Board. It is designed to assess students' skills in critical reading, writing, and mathematics to measure college- and career-readiness. Many American colleges and universities require SAT scores as part of the application process. It is considered a valuable tool for evaluating whether students are equipped with the skills necessary for success at the college level.

Of course, SAT scores aren't the only things that colleges consider when assessing applicants. Your high school grades, course selection, extracurricular activities, recommendation letters, and application essays are all factors that the colleges you apply to will use to decide whether you are a good fit. However, studying for the SAT will ensure that you present your best self to the people looking at these materials.

Moreover, the skills you will strengthen as you prepare for the test will be useful when you begin your college education. College-level work will rarely consist of multiple-choice questions, but it will often demand close attention to the details of a text, a strong command of standard written English, and fluency in foundational math skills—all things that the SAT tests.

TAKING THE TEST

Students generally take the SAT during 11th grade or early in the year during 12th grade. Most colleges will accept scores received through December of your 12th grade year, although if you're applying to any colleges through Early Admission you'll need to take the SAT by November of 12th grade at the latest. If you are dissatisfied with your score, you can take the test again. Therefore, you might want to pick your first test date far enough in advance that you can retake if you wish without missing any deadlines.

The easiest way to register to take the SAT is online through the official College Board website: sat.collegeboard.org. You'll need to fill out a personal profile form and upload a recognizable photo, which will be included on your admission ticket. You can also register by mail if you ask your school counselor for a copy of *The Student Registration Guide and SAT Subject Tests*. More information about registering—including test dates, deadlines, fees, and getting your scores to schools—can be found on the College Board site.

SAT Breakdown

PART 3

The SAT is three hours long, not including the optional Essay, which adds another 50 minutes. It consists of the following sections, administered in this order:

- 100-minute Evidence-based Reading and Writing section
  - Reading Test (65 minutes, 52 questions)
  - Writing and Language Test (35 minutes, 44 questions)
- 80-minute Math Test
  - Calculator Not Permitted section (25 minutes, 20 questions)
  - Calculator Permitted section (55 minutes, 38 questions)
- Essay Test (50 minutes, 1 essay task, optional)

With the exception of a few math questions and the Essay, all questions on the SAT are multiple choice, meaning that you will select the best answer from four possible options. Below, you'll find brief summaries of these sections, as well as information on how they'll be scored. This is not an exhaustive list of the topics covered on each test; for more detailed information, you can look at the College Board's site, which outlines the parameters of each section, and check out Ivy Global's New SAT Guide, which gives detailed explanations of, and strategies for, the types of questions you'll see on each part of the test.

Reading Test

On the SAT Reading Test, you'll read four single passages and one set of paired passages. Each passage or pair will be followed by a set of ten or eleven questions, for a total of five question sets and 52 questions. The passages will fall under the following domains:

- *Literature*: One passage will be taken from classic or contemporary literature from the United States and around the world.
- *Science*: Two passages will cover both basic concepts and recent developments in the natural sciences, including Earth science, biology, chemistry, and physics.
- *History/Social Studies*: One passage will be drawn from or discuss the fields of history and the social sciences including anthropology, communication studies, economics, education, human geography, law, linguistics, political science, psychology, and sociology.

- *Founding Documents/Great Global Conversation*: One passage will be drawn either from historically important, foundational texts from the United States, or from other historically and culturally important works dealing with issues at the heart of civic and political life.

Two passages—one Science passage and one History/Social Studies passage—will be accompanied by graphics displaying relevant data or other quantitative information. Although you will be asked to interpret them on their own and in the context of the passage, you will not be asked to perform mathematical calculations on the Reading Test.

The questions on the Reading Test ask you to read high-quality previously published texts closely. Some questions will ask you about the information presented in the passage to ensure that you have read it accurately. Other questions will ask you to examine the purpose of particular choices of words or phrases, as well as their effects. Passages with graphics will always have a few questions asking about the graphic and its relationship to the passage, and paired passages will always have a few questions asking about the relationship between the two passages.

WRITING TEST

On the SAT Writing Test, you'll read four passages written specifically for the test. Each passage will be accompanied by eleven questions, for a total of forty-four questions. Unlike on the Reading Test, the questions are presented alongside the passages instead of all at the end; this means you can work on the questions as you are reading. Questions correspond to numbers placed in the text, usually next to underlined portions that specify which word or words the question is referring to.

Some of the questions on the Writing Test will ask you to decide whether there is a grammatical or other error in the passage, such as a lack of subject-verb agreement or a word used incorrectly. Others will ask you to improve the expression of the writer's ideas. This might include deciding whether and why to delete or keep a particular sentence, moving a sentence or a paragraph so that the passage makes more logical sense, or rewording a sentence which is grammatically correct but confusing or redundant.

MATH TEST

The SAT Math Test has two parts that mostly test similar concepts; the major difference is that one allows you to use a calculator and one does not. They both consist of a mix of multiple choice and student-produced response questions. Student-produced response questions ask you to come up with the answer to a problem without selecting from a set of options; you will have to fill in the digits of your answer in a grid on your answer sheet.

The Calculator Not Permitted section consists of fifteen multiple-choice questions and five student-produced response questions, for a total of twenty questions; the Calculator Permitted section consists of thirty multiple-choice questions and eight student-produced questions, for a total of thirty-eight questions. The two sections are consecutive but separate, so you cannot work at them at the same time.

The concepts tested on both sections of the Math Test include basic algebra concepts, such as algebraic expressions, linear equations, inequalities, functions, and systems of equations; more advanced algebra concepts, such as factoring and performing operations on polynomial expressions, quadratic equations, and exponential functions; and a handful of other math topics, such as trigonometric ratios, the Pythagorean theorem, arc length and other circle problems, congruence of geometric figures, and complex numbers.

In addition to these topics, the Calculator Permitted section will also include a number of questions related to problem-solving and data analysis. These will include topics such as unit conversions, properties of data, visual representations of data such as graphs, statistics and probability, modeling and evidence-related uses of data, and measurements applicable to data sets such as mean, mode, median, and standard deviation.

ESSAY

On the SAT Essay, you will receive a prompt in the form of a previously published, contemporary piece written for an educated public audience. Your task will not be to agree or disagree with the argument presented by the author of the prompt, but rather to analyze how the author of the prompt constructs her argument. This will entail looking at the evidence used in the source text, as well as discussing other relevant features such as rhetorical devices employed by the author, or pertinent organizational strategies.

Essay graders will be looking for an organized and well-written essay with a strong thesis that fulfills the particular task of analyzing an author's argument. They will also be looking for your own Essay to demonstrate that you have thoroughly comprehended the source text.

The Essay portion of the SAT is optional. However, many schools will require it, so it's recommended that you choose to take it. Either way, you need to make this decision at the time of registration.

SCORING

The Reading Test, Writing Test, and the two combined sections of the Math Test will each receive a test score on a scale from 10-40. The Reading Test and Writing Test will be scored together as Evidence-Based Reading and Writing on a scale from 200-800; the Math Test by itself will also be scored on a scale from 200-800. Those two area scores will be added together for a composite score from 400 to 1600, the same scale that will be used by the new SAT.

In addition, the new SAT will feature a set of subscores measuring your achievement in certain areas across the different sections of the test. Some of these will focus on your ability to engage with certain types of content, such as Science or History/Social Studies, while others will look at particular skills used on the Reading and Writing Tests and the two Math Test sections. As of our publication date, the College Board had not released information about how subscores will be calculated.

The Essay will be scored separately, and it will not factor into the composite score. Essays will be assessed by two graders in the categories of Reading, Analysis, and Writing, each scored on a scale from 1-4 by each grader; that means that the total score for each category will range from 2 to 8.

Approaching the SAT

The information in this section applies to the real SAT, but you should be familiar with it before you take your first practice test so that you can treat your test as realistically as possible. We'll also go over some general advice for SAT preparation, as well as how to get the most out of the tests in this book.

Know the Test

The first thing to understand about the SAT is the style and structure of the test itself. The SAT is a standardized test, which means that although the specific questions will change from year to year, the format is always the same. The SAT is scored not by a human, but by a computer that "reads" your answer sheet. This means that filling in your answer bubbles neatly and completely is essential, since a computer can't tell that you got the right answer but didn't fill the bubble in completely. Bubbling correctly is a habit you can practice with the tests in this book.

It also means there's no partial credit for knowing how to solve a problem but making a computation error. Checking your work is always a good idea, but it's especially important on a standardized test. Try to budget your time to leave a few minutes at the end to double-check your answers so you don't miss a question you understood but entered incorrectly into your calculator.

Each question on the SAT is worth one point regardless of how hard or easy it is. The new SAT also has no penalty for wrong answers, so you should always guess without worrying that you might hurt your score.

Study Tips

When you study for the SAT, make your space as calm and free of distractions as possible. Leave your phone and other electronics out of reach, so you won't be tempted to look at them. If you're timing yourself on a practice test, set a loud alarm instead of looking at your phone or computer screen.

Don't try to do too much at once. It's hard to learn much by the end of a four-hour study session, especially if you're already tired from a day at school. It's also difficult to master several new concepts at once. Set aside moderate amounts of time during which you plan to focus on one or two concepts, and then build in a review day every other week. This means you want to start well in advance so that you have plenty of time to practice slowly and steadily instead of stressing and cramming in the few weeks before the test.

Never stay up late studying. In addition to making you feel tired in the morning, losing sleep can harm your health over the long run. Sleep is also when your brain solidifies new information, so it's a crucial part of the learning process.

USING THIS BOOK

This book contains four full-length practice tests for the new SAT. We recommend that you start by taking one of them as a diagnostic test, to help you assess how your current skills have prepared you for the SAT and what areas you can improve on the most.

Practice tests are most effective when taken in realistic conditions, so use a pencil to bubble in your answers and set a timer for each section. Taking the practice test in one sitting, with a short break halfway through, is ideal; however, if you're a busy student you can also split up the test and work on one section each night.

If you run out of time before the end of a section, you can use the remaining questions as practice, but mark where you ran out of time so you have more information about your performance. There is no penalty for wrong answers, so you should always guess to build the habit; however, you should circle which questions you had to guess on and include them as wrong answers when you review your work.

Review is crucial to the studying process. Practicing will help you get familiar with the test, but the real value of taking a practice test is in going over your answers and seeing what went wrong. If you're not sure why you missed a question, you can go to sat.ivyglobal.com for Ivy Global's answer explanations. Instead of marking down wrong answers and moving on, you should be able to explain to someone else what your mistake was and how to get the right answer; if you can't do this, you should review the material the question is testing.

Look for patterns in your diagnostic test. If you got almost all algebra questions right, but missed half of the questions about data analysis, you can spend less time reviewing algebra and more time practicing reading graphs and analyzing quantitative data. If you got questions about the development of ideas correct but missed those relating to verb tense or pronoun agreement, you can devote your writing study to reviewing the conventions of standard written English.

Take time between practice tests to let new concepts sink in and practice what you need to work on. Celebrate if you begin to master question types you initially struggled with, and don't beat yourself up if some concepts continue to be difficult. You might be able to ask your English or math teachers for help or advice on where to find more support if this is the case.

TEST DAY

PART 5

On the day of the SAT, you want to maximize your chances of success. Here are some general tips to make sure you can do your best.

BEFORE THE TEST

On the night before your test, study only lightly, if at all. You won't be able to fully learn anything new at this point. Review up to three tricky areas if you want, but the most important thing you can do the night before the SAT—or any big test—is give yourself a solid night of sleep.

Lay out your clothes for the next day so that getting dressed goes smoothly. It's a good idea to wear layers so you can adjust to the room's temperature. Also lay out the bag you'll take, making sure to bring:

- Admission Ticket
- Approved Photo ID
- No. 2 pencils and erasers
- Calculator with new batteries and back-up batteries
- A watch
- Snack and water bottle
- Directions to the test center and instructions for finding the entrance

Set your alarm, and determine the time at which you will leave, allowing extra time in case of any delays. In the morning, make sure you eat a healthy breakfast—you don't want to be stuck past the two-hour mark with an empty stomach!

Many students also find that it helps to do some problems before you get to the test center. These don't need to be especially hard, or related to particular areas you've been practicing; you're probably not going to learn anything new on the morning of the test. You don't even need to check whether you got them right or not. The idea is to give your brain a warm-up, the way athletes stretch before games; this way, the test isn't the first challenging thing your brain is doing that day, and you're already in thinking mode.

MANAGING YOUR TIME

The SAT is 3 hours long—50 minutes longer if you're doing the Essay. Remember that time between sections isn't transferable; you're given a set amount of time for each section and you can't proceed to the next section if you finish early. When you take the practice tests in this book, be sure to time yourself so you can get a sense for how long each section takes to complete. This will come in handy on the real test, so you can gauge whether you are on track to finish on time or whether you need to speed up.

It's important not to get too stuck on any single question and to move through the test at a steady pace. Don't waste 10 minutes on a question that stumps you only to find that you don't have enough time to answer the things you know inside out. Each question is worth just one point, no matter how hard it is. If you're stuck on a problem, make your best guess and move on. Circle the problem in your question booklet so you can go back to it if you have time at the end to check your answers. Remember not to make any stray marks on your answer sheet, even when you guess.

AFTER THE TEST

Give yourself a pat on the back! You've just completed a major step in your educational journey. If you can, plan ahead to spend the rest of the day doing something fun, like celebrating with your friends who also took the test or watching a favorite movie.

Your score report will become available to you about two to four weeks after the test. If you do receive a score you're not happy with, you can always take the test again, armed now with more knowledge of how you respond in a real testing situation. However, you should be proud of your effort regardless of your score; you're working hard to further your education, and that's a wonderful thing.

Chapter 2
PRACTICE TESTS

Practice Test 1

SAT

Directions

- Work on just one section at a time.
- If you complete a section before the end of your allotted time, use the extra minutes to check your work on that section only. Do NOT use the time to work on another section.

Using Your Test Booklet

- No credit will be given for anything written in the test booklet. You may use the test booklet for scratch paper.
- You are not allowed to continue answering questions in a section after the allotted time has run out. This includes marking answers on your answer sheet that you previously noted in your test booklet.
- You are not allowed to fold pages, take pages out of the test booklet, or take any pages home.

Answering Questions

- Each answer must be marked in the corresponding row on the answer sheet.
- Each bubble must be filled in completely and darkly within the lines.

  Correct   Incorrect

- Be careful to bubble in the correct part of the answer sheet.
- Extra marks on your answer sheet may be marked as incorrect answers and lower your score.
- Make sure you use a No. 2 pencil.

Scoring

- You will receive one point for each correct answer.
- Incorrect answers will NOT result in points deducted. Even if you are unsure about an answer, you should make a guess.

DO NOT BEGIN THIS TEST
UNTIL YOUR PROCTOR TELLS YOU TO DO SO

Download printable answer sheets, answer keys, and Excel scoring sheets from:

ivyglobal.com/study

Section 1

#	A B C D	#	A B C D	#	A B C D	#	A B C D	#	A B C D
1	○ ○ ○ ○	12	○ ○ ○ ○	23	○ ○ ○ ○	34	○ ○ ○ ○	45	○ ○ ○ ○
2	○ ○ ○ ○	13	○ ○ ○ ○	24	○ ○ ○ ○	35	○ ○ ○ ○	46	○ ○ ○ ○
3	○ ○ ○ ○	14	○ ○ ○ ○	25	○ ○ ○ ○	36	○ ○ ○ ○	47	○ ○ ○ ○
4	○ ○ ○ ○	15	○ ○ ○ ○	26	○ ○ ○ ○	37	○ ○ ○ ○	48	○ ○ ○ ○
5	○ ○ ○ ○	16	○ ○ ○ ○	27	○ ○ ○ ○	38	○ ○ ○ ○	49	○ ○ ○ ○
6	○ ○ ○ ○	17	○ ○ ○ ○	28	○ ○ ○ ○	39	○ ○ ○ ○	50	○ ○ ○ ○
7	○ ○ ○ ○	18	○ ○ ○ ○	29	○ ○ ○ ○	40	○ ○ ○ ○	51	○ ○ ○ ○
8	○ ○ ○ ○	19	○ ○ ○ ○	30	○ ○ ○ ○	41	○ ○ ○ ○	52	○ ○ ○ ○
9	○ ○ ○ ○	20	○ ○ ○ ○	31	○ ○ ○ ○	42	○ ○ ○ ○		
10	○ ○ ○ ○	21	○ ○ ○ ○	32	○ ○ ○ ○	43	○ ○ ○ ○		
11	○ ○ ○ ○	22	○ ○ ○ ○	33	○ ○ ○ ○	44	○ ○ ○ ○		

Section 2

#	A B C D	#	A B C D	#	A B C D	#	A B C D	#	A B C D
1	○ ○ ○ ○	10	○ ○ ○ ○	19	○ ○ ○ ○	28	○ ○ ○ ○	37	○ ○ ○ ○
2	○ ○ ○ ○	11	○ ○ ○ ○	20	○ ○ ○ ○	29	○ ○ ○ ○	38	○ ○ ○ ○
3	○ ○ ○ ○	12	○ ○ ○ ○	21	○ ○ ○ ○	30	○ ○ ○ ○	39	○ ○ ○ ○
4	○ ○ ○ ○	13	○ ○ ○ ○	22	○ ○ ○ ○	31	○ ○ ○ ○	40	○ ○ ○ ○
5	○ ○ ○ ○	14	○ ○ ○ ○	23	○ ○ ○ ○	32	○ ○ ○ ○	41	○ ○ ○ ○
6	○ ○ ○ ○	15	○ ○ ○ ○	24	○ ○ ○ ○	33	○ ○ ○ ○	42	○ ○ ○ ○
7	○ ○ ○ ○	16	○ ○ ○ ○	25	○ ○ ○ ○	34	○ ○ ○ ○	43	○ ○ ○ ○
8	○ ○ ○ ○	17	○ ○ ○ ○	26	○ ○ ○ ○	35	○ ○ ○ ○	44	○ ○ ○ ○
9	○ ○ ○ ○	18	○ ○ ○ ○	27	○ ○ ○ ○	36	○ ○ ○ ○		

Section 3 (No calculator)

	A B C D		A B C D		A B C D		A B C D		A B C D
1	○ ○ ○ ○	4	○ ○ ○ ○	7	○ ○ ○ ○	10	○ ○ ○ ○	13	○ ○ ○ ○
2	○ ○ ○ ○	5	○ ○ ○ ○	8	○ ○ ○ ○	11	○ ○ ○ ○	14	○ ○ ○ ○
3	○ ○ ○ ○	6	○ ○ ○ ○	9	○ ○ ○ ○	12	○ ○ ○ ○	15	○ ○ ○ ○

Only answers that are gridded will be scored. You will not receive credit for anything written in the boxes.

16 · 17 · 18 · 19 · 20

(Grid-in bubbles for questions 16–20, digits 0–9 with fraction bar and decimal point options)

Section 4 (Calculator)

	A B C D		A B C D		A B C D		A B C D		A B C D
1	○ ○ ○ ○	7	○ ○ ○ ○	13	○ ○ ○ ○	19	○ ○ ○ ○	25	○ ○ ○ ○
2	○ ○ ○ ○	8	○ ○ ○ ○	14	○ ○ ○ ○	20	○ ○ ○ ○	26	○ ○ ○ ○
3	○ ○ ○ ○	9	○ ○ ○ ○	15	○ ○ ○ ○	21	○ ○ ○ ○	27	○ ○ ○ ○
4	○ ○ ○ ○	10	○ ○ ○ ○	16	○ ○ ○ ○	22	○ ○ ○ ○	28	○ ○ ○ ○
5	○ ○ ○ ○	11	○ ○ ○ ○	17	○ ○ ○ ○	23	○ ○ ○ ○	29	○ ○ ○ ○
6	○ ○ ○ ○	12	○ ○ ○ ○	18	○ ○ ○ ○	24	○ ○ ○ ○	30	○ ○ ○ ○

Only answers that are gridded will be scored. You will not receive credit for anything written in the boxes.

31 32 33 34 35

Only answers that are gridded will be scored. You will not receive credit for anything written in the boxes.

36 37 38

Section 5 (Optional)

Important: Use a No. 2 pencil. Write inside the borders.

You may use the space below to plan your essay, but be sure to write your essay on the lined pages. Work on this page will not be scored.

Use this space to plan your essay.

START YOUR ESSAY HERE.

_____

_____

_____

_____

_____

_____

_____

_____

_____

_____

_____

_____

_____

_____

_____

_____

_____

_____

_____

_____

_____

_____

_____

_____

_____

Continue on the next page.

_____

_____

_____

_____

_____

_____

_____

_____

_____

_____

_____

_____

_____

_____

_____

_____

_____

_____

_____

_____

_____

_____

_____

_____

Continue on the next page.

Continue on the next page.

_____

_____

_____

_____

_____

_____

_____

_____

_____

_____

_____

_____

_____

_____

_____

_____

_____

_____

_____

_____

_____

_____

_____

_____

STOP.

Section 1

Reading Test

65 MINUTES, 52 QUESTIONS

Turn to Section 1 of your answer sheet to answer the questions in this section.

DIRECTIONS

Every passage or paired set of passages is accompanied by a number of questions. Read the passage or paired set of passages, then use what is said or implied in what you read and in any given graphics to choose the best answer to each question.

Questions 1-11 are based on the following passage.

This passage is adapted from Atul Grover, "Should Hospital Residency Programs Be Expanded to Increase the Number of Doctors?" © 2013 Dow Jones & Company.

Thanks to baby boomers, the population over 65 will have doubled between 2000 and 2030. And when the Affordable Care Act takes full effect, up to
Line 32 million new patients will seek access to medical
5 care, many of whom will need treatment for ailments that have gone undiagnosed for years, such as cancer, diabetes, arthritis and heart disease. This surge in demand means the U.S. will have a shortfall of at least 90,000 doctors by the end of the decade,
10 according to the Association of American Medical Colleges Center for Workforce Studies. Many parts of the country have too few doctors already.

A small, vocal minority of researchers suggest we don't need more doctors. That minority clearly is
15 having an impact: many clinicians and policy makers say there is 20% to 30% "waste" in our health-care system. Elliott Fisher, a Dartmouth professor, says those numbers are backed up by Dartmouth research.

20 The Dartmouth studies base their conclusions about waste on comparisons of health-care spending in different geographic areas. But other studies have shown that differences in the health status of patients In the different regions explain the majority of
25 variations in spending. In other words, urban areas, with their high concentrations of poor people, tend to have a higher disease burden and thus higher medical needs. Sicker patients, along with high labor costs, explain the higher levels of spending found in
30 these urban areas—not too many doctors.

There is no question that delivery of care needs to be better organized, and that some current reforms are likely to improve patient outcomes. That's true, for example, with experiments in team-based care.
35 However, these improvements in patient care have not translated to any reduction in the need for physician time.

Another new experiment—accountable-care organizations, which allow groups of providers to
40 share any savings gained by keeping their patients healthy—also hasn't been shown to reduce the number of physicians needed. Indeed, there is a lot of wishful thinking associated with ACOs, just as there was with HMOs[1] in the 1990s—that everyone

---

[1] Health maintenance organizations

CONTINUE

45 would be cared for in a way that would cost less and
would prevent people from ever getting sick.
Unfortunately, that didn't turn out to be the reality.

Primary care and prevention will increase the
need for doctors. An 8-year-old girl with acute
50 leukemia today has an 80% chance of survival. If
she survives, in the years that follow, she is likely to
get a vaccine to avoid cervical cancer, take
cholesterol-lowering drugs and undergo multiple
screenings for breast cancer. She may still develop
55 heart disease or cancer. And as she and millions of
other people continue to age, their risk for other
conditions like Alzheimer's will increase
dramatically. But she, like everyone else, deserves
first-rate care every step of the way. We need more
60 doctors, not fewer. ↑ docs

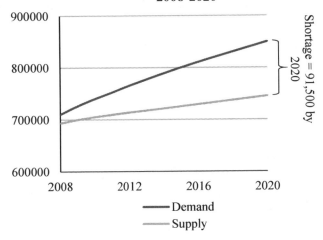

Projected Supply and Demand, Physicians,
2008-2020

1

Which of the following provides the best summary
of the passage's main idea?

A) The US health care system is about to suffer a
significant collapse, and hundreds of hospitals
will have to be shut down.

B) There is too much wasteful spending in the
current health care system, which additional
doctors cannot correct.

C) The US needs to prepare for increasing health
care demands by training more doctors.

D) Accountable-care organizations (ACOs) will
improve the current health care system and
reduce unnecessary care.

2

The author argues that the US will experience a
shortfall of doctors because

A) a large portion of doctors are choosing to retire
early.

B) new legislation and an aging population will
increase the demand for healthcare.

C) many doctors waste too much of their time on
non-essential treatments rather than more
important ailments.

D) many medical programs have closed and fewer
doctors are being trained.

3

Which choice provides the best evidence for the
answer to the previous question?

A) Lines 7-11 ("This surge … Studies")

B) Lines 14-17 ("That minority … system")

C) Lines 25-28 ("In other … needs")

D) Lines 50-55 ("If she … cancer")

CONTINUE

4

The passage most strongly suggests that

A) primary care and prevention, while important, will not solve the issue of a doctor shortage.

B) preventing diseases via primary care will help reduce costs for healthcare by reducing early death.

C) relocating doctors from urban to rural areas will reduce US medical costs.

D) the first step in resolving the doctor shortage is conducting more extensive research on its causes.

5

Which choice provides the best evidence for the answer to the previous question?

A) Lines 22-25 ("But other … spending")

B) Lines 28-30 ("Sicker patients … doctors")

C) Lines 35-37 ("However these … time")

D) Lines 48-49 ("Primary care … doctors")

6

As used in line 13, "vocal" most nearly means

A) blunt.

B) outspoken.

C) out loud.

D) forthright.

7

The passage suggests that the 20%-30% "waste" mentioned in lines 14-19 is

A) likely to result in a reduction in the demand for physician time.

B) a significant expense, but still less expensive than the cost of training enough new doctors.

C) mostly explained by differences in patient health, rather than wasteful spending.

D) best explained by the fact that affluent patients tend to spend more on healthcare.

8

The primary purpose of the fifth paragraph (lines 38-47) is to

A) discuss another potential option to mitigate the coming shortage of physicians.

B) offer a historical account of physicians' various organizations.

C) provide evidence that the government is coming up with clever options to address problems in healthcare.

D) support the author's claim that new experiments in patient care will not solve the coming doctor shortage.

9

As used in line 49, "acute" most nearly means

A) critical.

B) keen.

C) severe.

D) sharp.

CONTINUE

10

Which of the following best expresses the main point of the final paragraph (lines 48-60)?

A) Even though patients may live longer, primary and preventative care still offer savings.

B) We must provide the highest quality of care possible, in order to reduce costs.

C) The shortage of physicians is best explained by an excessive amount of primary care.

D) Although we have a responsibility to provide high-quality care, we should not expect for that to decrease medical costs.

11

Which of the following claims is best supported by the graph?

A) There will be more doctors in 2020 than at any time since 2008, and a greater shortage of doctors.

B) The doctor shortage will continue to grow until there are 91,500 fewer doctors in 2020 than there were in 2008.

C) By 2015, around 850,000 patients will need a doctor, but only about 750,000 will receive any form of treatment.

D) An increase in the supply of doctors over time will cause an even greater increase in the demand.

Questions 12-22 are based on the following passages.

The following passages are adapted from Chensheng Lu and Janet H. Silverstein, "Would Americans Be Better Off Eating an Organic Diet?" © 2014 by Dow Jones & Company.

Passage 1

Is there definitive scientific proof that an organic diet is healthier? Not yet. Robust scientific studies comparing food grown organically and food grown
Line conventionally don't exist, thanks to a lack of
5 funding for this kind of research in humans.

But let's be clear: some convincing scientific work does exist to suggest that an organic diet has its benefits. What's more, it only makes sense that food free of pesticides and chemicals is safer and
10 better for us than food containing those substances, even at trace levels. This was illustrated in a study published in the journal Environmental Health Perspectives in 2006. That study, which I led, showed that within five days of substituting mostly
15 organic produce in children's diets for conventional produce, pesticides disappeared from the children's urine.

Many say the pesticides found in our food are nothing to fear because the levels fall well below
20 federal safety guidelines and thus aren't dangerous. Similarly, they say the bovine growth hormone used to increase cows' milk yield is perfectly safe. But federal guidelines don't take into account what effect repeated exposure to low levels of chemicals
25 might have on humans over time. And many pesticides were eventually banned or restricted by the federal government after years of use when they were discovered to be harmful to the environment or human health.
30 Organic skeptics like to cite a meta-analysis study published in the Annals of Internal Medicine last year that suggested organic foods are neither healthier nor more nutritious than their conventional counterparts. Left out of that analysis, however,
35 were recent field studies showing that organic

CONTINUE

32   PRACTICE TEST 1 | Ivy Global

produce, such as strawberries, leafy vegetables, and wheat, not only tastes better but contains much higher levels of phenolic acids than conventional produce. Phenolic acids are secondary plant
40 metabolites that can be absorbed easily through the walls of the intestinal tract, and can act as potent antioxidants that prevent cellular damage, and therefore offer some protection against oxidative stress, inflammation, and cancer. Knowing that we
45 could reduce our exposure to pesticides and increase our exposure to antioxidants by eating organic food, it makes great common sense to consume more of it.

Passage 2

There is no definitive evidence that organic food is more nutritious or healthier than conventional
50 food, but there is proof that eating more fruits and vegetables and less processed food is.

Therefore, our focus as a society should be to eat as much fresh food and whole grains as possible— regardless of whether it is organically grown or not.
55 It is difficult to compare the nutritional value of organic versus conventional food because the soil, climate, timing of harvest, and storage conditions all affect the composition of produce. Still, published studies have found no significant differences in
60 nutritional quality between organic and nonorganic produce or milk. Similarly, there is no evidence that giving bovine growth hormone (BGH) to cows changes the composition of milk or affects human health. BGH is inactive in humans and degrades in
65 the acidic environment of the stomach.

As for pesticide exposure, the U.S. in 1996 established maximum permissible levels for pesticide residues in food to ensure food safety. Many studies have shown that pesticide levels in
70 conventional produce fall well below those guidelines. While it's true that organic fruits and vegetables in general contain fewer traces of these chemicals, we can't draw conclusions about what that means for health as there haven't been any long-
75 term studies comparing the relationship between exposure to pesticides from organic versus

nonorganic foods and adverse health outcomes. It may seem like "common sense" to reduce exposure to these chemicals, but there are currently no good
80 evidence-based studies to answer the question.

We would like to think that organic food is grown locally, put in a wheelbarrow and brought directly to our homes. However, much of it comes from countries where regulations might not be as
85 tightly enforced as in the U.S., and labeling of the foods might be misleading. And just because food is labeled organic doesn't mean it is completely free of pesticides. Contamination can occur from soil and ground water containing previously used chemicals,
90 or during transport, processing and storage. Organochlorine insecticides were recently found in organically grown root crops and tomatoes even though these pesticides haven't been used for 20 years.
95 Given what we know, the best diet advice we can give families is to eat a wide variety of produce and whole grains. Whether they want to buy organic is up to them.

12

The author's main purpose in Passage 1 appears to be to

A) discuss the implications of new research into the health effects of organic foods.

B) persuade readers that eating organic food has potential health benefits.

C) critique research which claims to show that there are no health benefits from eating organic food.

D) argue that more funding is required to perform better research about organic food.

13

The first passage most strongly suggests that

A) study results conflict on some points, but agree that it is healthiest to eat an all-organic diet.

B) organic diets have unique health benefits, despite some incomplete studies that claim the contrary.

C) all studies conducted on humans show that organic diets are essential to health.

D) studies are inconclusive regarding the benefits of an organic diet, except when it comes to the diets of children.

14

Which choice provides the best evidence for the answer to the previous question?

A) Lines 2-5 ("Robust scientific ... humans")

B) Lines 13-17 ("That study ... urine")

C) Lines 25-29 ("And many ... health")

D) Lines 34-39 ("Left out ... produce")

15

The attitude of the author of Passage 2 towards health claims about organic foods would best be described as

A) derisive.

B) skeptical.

C) enthusiastic.

D) quizzical.

16

As used in line 48, "definitive" most nearly means

A) conclusive.

B) consummate.

C) accepted.

D) specific.

17

As used in line 77, "adverse" most nearly means

A) harmful.

B) antagonistic.

C) unlucky.

D) contrary.

18

The author's purpose in lines 81-83 ("We would … homes") is most likely to

A) provide a detailed description of the process that most people believe is implied by organic labeling.

B) characterize the organic food industry as inefficient and unsophisticated.

C) caricature misconceptions about organic food to help create a stark contrast with reality.

D) offer a vision for how organic agriculture could operate if the author's recommendations are adopted.

CONTINUE

19

Passage 1 differs from Passage 2 in that

A) Passage 1 argues that only organic foods should be eaten, while Passage 2 argues that only non-organic foods should be.

B) Passage 1 argues that people should consume more organic foods, while Passage 2 states that it is more important to focus on eating a less processed diet.

C) Passage 1 argues that organic foods are important for health, while Passage 2 argues they are harmful.

D) Passage 1 argues that organic foods are overemphasized in the media, while Passage 2 argues they are not emphasized enough.

20

The authors of both passages would most likely agree with which of the following statements?

A) It is reasonable to conclude that long-term exposure to even low levels of pesticides has a negative effect on human health.

B) Scientific studies on organic foods cannot be trusted, as they often conflict with one another.

C) Food labels are highly variable and all but useless, and it is better to select foods based on their freshness.

D) There is enough information available about the health impacts of various foods to enable informed decisions about diet.

21

Based on the two passages, which best describes the relationship between organic food and health risks?

A) Organic foods offer nutritional benefits which more than offset their health risks.

B) Organic foods clearly protect against a variety of known health risks.

C) Organic foods have a reputation for being healthy, but actually increase certain risks.

D) Organic foods may reduce exposure to possible but unconfirmed health risks.

22

Which choice provides the best evidence for the answer to the previous question?

A) Lines 52-54 ("Therefore, our ... not")

B) Lines 71-77 ("While it's ... outcomes")

C) Lines 81-83 ("We would ... homes")

D) Lines 91-94 ("Organochlorine insecticides ... years")

CONTINUE

Questions 23-32 are based on the following passage.

This passage is adapted from Lynne Peeples "Moths Use Sonar-Jamming Defense to Fend Off Hunting Bats." © 2009 by Scientific American.

An insect with paper-thin wings may carry much the same defense technology as some of the military's heavy-duty warships. The finding that a
Line species of tiger moth can jam the sonar of
5 echolocating bats to avoid being eaten seems to be the "first conclusive evidence of sonar jamming in nature," says Aaron Corcoran, a biology PhD student at Wake Forest University and the lead author of the paper reporting the discovery. "It
10 demonstrates a new level of escalation in the bat-moth evolutionary arms race."

Before Corcoran's study, scientists were puzzled by why certain species of tiger moths made sound. Some speculated that the moths use it to startle bats.
15 A few pointed to its potential interference with their echolocation. General consensus, however, fell with a third hypothesis: clicks function to warn a predator not to eat the clicking prey because it is toxic, or at least pretending to be.
20 To test these hypotheses, Corcoran and his team pitted the tiger moth *Bertholdia trigona* against the big brown bat *Eptesicus fuscus*, a battle frequently fought after sundown from Central America to Colorado. High-speed infrared cameras and an
25 ultrasonic microphone recorded the action over nine consecutive nights. The process of elimination began. If moth clicks served to startle, previous studies suggested the bats should become tolerant of the sound within two or three days. "But that's not
30 what we found," says Corcoran, explaining the lack of success bats had in capturing their clicking prey even through the last nights of the study.

How about the toxic warning theory? If this were the case, according to Corcoran, bats would not find
35 the moths palatable or, if they were indeed tasty, they would quickly learn they'd been tricked. Either way, bats should start to ignore the moth's unique ultrasonic clicks. Also, bats partook readily when

offered *B. trigona* that lacked the ability to click, and
40 they kept coming back for more. This attraction also held true for clicking *B. trigona*: the predators persisted after their prey despite only reaching them about 20 percent of the time. Bats actually launched four times as many successful attacks against a
45 control group of silent moths. These findings are "only consistent with the jamming hypothesis," Corcoran notes. "But the most distinctive evidence was in the echolocation sequences of the bats."

Normally, a bat attack starts with relatively
50 intermittent sounds. They then increase in frequency—up to 200 cries per second—as the bat gets closer to the moth "so it knows where the moth is at that critical moment," Corcoran explains. But his research showed that just as bats were increasing
55 their click frequency, moths "turn on sound production full blast," clicking at a rate of up to 4,500 times a second. This furious clicking by the moths reversed the bats' pattern—the frequency of bat sonar decreased, rather than increased, as it
60 approached its prey, suggesting that it lost its target.

The biological mechanism behind the moth's defense strategy is still unclear to researchers. "Most likely, moth clicks are disrupting the bat's neural processing of when echoes return," Corcoran says.
65 Bats judge how far away a moth is based on the time delay between making the cry and its audible return. This "blurring" of the bat's vision, he explains, "may be just enough to keep the moth safe."

CONTINUE

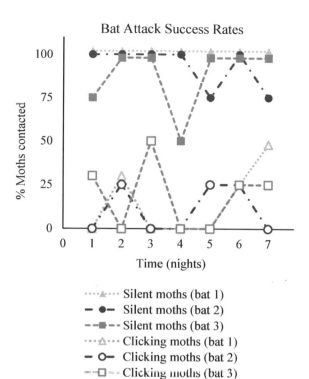

Bat Attack Success Rates

·····▲···· Silent moths (bat 1)
— ●— Silent moths (bat 2)
—■—· Silent moths (bat 3)
····△···· Clicking moths (bat 1)
— ○— Clicking moths (bat 2)
··□·· Clicking moths (bat 3)

23

The passage is primarily concerned with

A) the ways *Eptesicus fuscus* bats capture moths.

B) the discovery that tiger moths can jam bats' sonar.

C) how the tiger moths' clicking defense works.

D) why tiger moths developed defenses against bats.

24

The author describes alternate hypotheses of the moths' clicking defense in order to

A) support her claim that researchers need more evidence before they can draw any conclusions.

B) show how the researchers' experiment disproved all but one of these hypotheses.

C) signal to the reader that the researchers' data shows only one side of the debate.

D) explain the multiple reasons that this defense is effective for the moths.

25

According to Aaron Corcoran's research, which of the following represents the tiger moths' most effective defensive countermeasure?

A) Poisonous bodies

B) Defensive maneuvering

C) Clicking ultrasonically

D) Hearing ability

26

Which choice provides the best evidence for the answer to the previous question?

A) Lines 3-9 ("The finding ... discovery")

B) Lines 16-19 ("General consensus ... be")

C) Lines 27-29 ("If moth ... days")

D) Lines 43-45 ("Bats actually ... moths")

CONTINUE

27

According to the passage, the bats would not attack some tiger moths because

A) they lost "sight" of the moths via sonar when pursuing them.

B) they realized the moths were toxic after a few nights.

C) they preferred to focus their attention on easier prey.

D) the moths' ultrasonic clicks startled them, frightening them away.

28

Which choice provides the best evidence for the answer to the previous question?

A) Line 14 ("Some speculated … bats")

B) Lines 33-36 ("If this … tricked")

C) Lines 57-60 ("This furious … target")

D) Lines 65-66 ("Bats judge … return")

29

As used in line 38, "partook readily" most nearly means

A) consumed without difficulty.

B) ate without hesitation.

C) shared happily.

D) participated promptly.

30

As used in line 50, "intermittent" most nearly means

A) random.

B) sporadic.

C) alternating.

D) scattered.

31

The passage discusses all of the following EXCEPT

A) the moths' effectiveness in warding off attacks from their predators.

B) whether these particular species would encounter one another in nature.

C) the lessons that can be learned by engineers from the moth's natural sonar jamming.

D) the bats' responses to moths that lacked the ability to click.

32

Information from the graph best supports which of the following statements?

A) Bats were more effective at hunting silent moths at the end of the study than they were at the start.

B) Bats devoured half as many clicking moths as they did silent moths.

C) Bats became increasingly effective at hunting clicking moths with each subsequent night.

D) Silent moths were consistently more likely to be captured than clicking moths.

CONTINUE

Questions 33-42 are based on the following passage.

The following passage is adapted from the story "The Godchildren," by Tessa Hadley, first published in The New Yorker in 2009.

The three heirs, in three separate taxis, converged on 33 Everdene Walk on a fine afternoon in late May. They were in their early fifties, and had not
Line met since they were sixteen or seventeen. Amanda,
5 who had been officious even as a teenager, had organized the meeting by e-mail, via the solicitors: "If we're all going to the house, why don't we go at the same time? Wouldn't it be fun to meet up?"
Now each was regretting having agreed to this.
10 Chris, who was a lecturer at a new university, was certain that he had spotted Amanda at the station, ahead of him in the queue for taxis; he had been too embarrassed to make himself known to her, even though they could have shared the fare. She
15 surely hadn't had all that red hair thirty-five years ago, and she hadn't seemed so tall then, or so loosely put together: the woman in the queue wasn't large, exactly, but physically complicated, with a bright-colored striped wrap tossed over one shoulder
20 which made him think of beachwear. Perhaps she lived in a hot country. He'd recognized her only when she threw her unguarded, emphatic glance at everyone behind her in the queue—boldly but blindly. Quailing, Chris was suddenly his anguished
25 seventeen-year-old self again, stripped of his disguise as someone experienced and distinguished.
His memories of Mandy, young, were dim but had an ominous intensity. He wished he hadn't come. He knew already that he wouldn't want
30 anything, anyway, from the horrible old house. At least he wouldn't be alone with Amanda; although when he tried to recover his memories of Susan, the other godchild, he couldn't find anything at all, only a neatly labeled vacancy.
35 The three taxis bore them, just a few minutes apart, out of the city center, then, swooping decorously downhill between traffic lights, through a species of suburb that seemed more remote from

their present lives than anywhere they ever went on
40 holiday.
By the time these three had come, as children, to visit their godmother here, their more fashionable parents had already decided that the suburbs were dreary: places to joke about, not to aspire to. Their
45 parents were doing up, in those days, spindly dilapidated eighteenth-century houses, bought cheap, in the city center. Susan's mother still lived in one of these, now worth a great deal, and Susan had spent the previous night in her childhood bed. In her
50 taxi, she was hardly thinking of the meeting ahead—except to wish that she weren't going to it. She was obsessing over jagged old irritations, roused by a conversation with her mother that morning.
Chris's and Susan's taxis pulled up outside 33
55 Everdene Walk at the same moment; Amanda had got there before them, and the front door stood open to what seemed, to their foreboding, a seething blackness, in contrast to the glare outside. Who knew what state the house would be in? Susan was
60 quicker, paying her taxi off; Chris was always afraid that he would tip too little or too much. She looked away while he probed in his change purse, then they politely pretended to recognize each other. He tried to dig back in his mind to their old acquaintance:
65 how hadn't he seen that the invisible, unremembered Susan might grow into this slim, long-faced, long-legged dark woman, somewhat ravaged but contained and elegant?
Meanwhile, Amanda, watching from a window
70 she had just opened upstairs, saw thirty-five years of change heaped in one awful moment on both their heads. They looked broken-down to her, appalling. On her way to the house, she had bullied her resisting taxi-driver into two consecutive U-turns
75 between the lime trees: visited by a premonition of just this disappointment, and then recovering, repressing her dread, willing herself to hope. Amanda remembered the old days more vividly than either of the others, cherished the idea of their
80 shared past—strangely, because at the time she had seemed the one most ready to trample it underfoot,

CONTINUE

on her way to better things. Now she revolted at
Chris's untidy gray-white locks, windswept
without wind, around his bald patch: why did men
85 yield so readily to their disintegration? At least
Susan had the decency to keep her hair brown and
well cut. Chris was stooping and bobbing at
Susan, smiling lopsidedly, self-deprecatory.
        She whistled from the window, piercing the
90 Walk's tranquility.
        "Come on up!" she shouted. "Prepare for the
Chamber of Horrors!"

33

Amanda, Susan, and Chris are meeting up because

A) their father died and they need to discuss his
   will.

B) they wanted to have a reunion after thirty-five
   years, since they had once been great friends.

C) they are going to an open house that is in a
   desirable neighborhood.

D) their godmother passed away and they need to
   sort through her belongings.

34

Based on the information in the passage, Chris's
memories of the other two godchildren

A) perfectly matched his impressions of them
   later on.

B) were colored negatively by his subsequent
   interactions with them.

C) were almost non-existent, as he had forgotten
   all about them over the years.

D) seemed inadequate and incomplete when
   confronted with the women in-person.

35

In the passage, Amanda, Chris, and Susan all
experience the greatest sense of foreboding about

A) seeing one another again after all these years.

B) entering the dilapidated, potentially unsafe
   house.

C) confronting the memories of their dead
   godparent.

D) whether they'll receive the fair portion of their
   inheritance.

36

Which choice provides the best evidence for the
answer to the previous question?

A) Lines 3-4 ("They were ... seventeen")

B) Line 9 ("Now each ... this")

C) Lines 29-30 ("He knew ... house")

D) Lines 91-92 ("Prepare for ... Horrors")

37

The passage hints that Chris

A) has an unresolved history with Amanda.

B) used to be in love with Susan.

C) is a reformed rebel.

D) was always their godparent's favorite.

38

Which choice provides the best evidence for the
answer to the previous question?

A) Lines 21-24 ("He'd recognized ... blindly")

B) Lines 27-28 ("His memories ... intensity")

C) Lines 63-68 ("He tried ... elegant")

D) Lines 82-85 ("Now she ... disintegration")

CONTINUE

39

As used in line 5, "officious" most nearly means

A) presumptuous.

B) busy.

C) pushy.

D) informal.

40

The rhetorical effect of the phrase "a neatly labeled vacancy" (line 34) is to suggest that

A) Chris had intentionally suppressed painful memories about Susan.

B) Chris often had difficulties in recalling his childhood.

C) Chris had no strong memories of one of his fellow godchildren.

D) Susan had been so dull in her youth that few people remembered her.

41

As used in line 52, "roused" most nearly means

A) provoked.

B) stimulated.

C) excited.

D) galvanized.

42

How does Amanda's assessment of her two old acquaintances compare with Chris's assessment?

A) Chris was delighted to see the other two, while Amanda was annoyed.

B) Chris was surprised at the changes in his acquaintances, while Amanda was disappointed in them.

C) Chris thought the two women looked overdressed, while Amanda thought the others should have put more effort into their appearance.

D) Chris thought the other two looked old, while Amanda thought they looked surprisingly good for their age.

CONTINUE

Questions 43-52 are based on the following passage.

This passage is adapted from a speech given by President Richard Nixon when he resigned his office on August 9, 1974. His decision followed the revelation that five men connected to the Nixon administration were caught breaking into the headquarters of the opposing political party. At the time of Nixon's resignation, proceedings had already begun in Congress to impeach him and seemed likely to succeed.

Good evening. This is the 37th time I have spoken to you from this office, where so many decisions have been made that shaped the history of
Line this Nation. Each time I have done so to discuss with
5 you some matter that I believe affected the national interest. Throughout the long and difficult period of Watergate, I have felt it was my duty to persevere— to make every possible effort to complete the term of office to which you elected me. In the past few days,
10 however, it has become evident to me that I no longer have a strong enough political base in the Congress to justify continuing that effort. As long as there was such a base, I felt strongly that it was necessary to see the constitutional process through to
15 its conclusion; that to do otherwise would be unfaithful to the spirit of that deliberately difficult process, and a dangerously destabilizing precedent for the future. But with the disappearance of that base, I now believe that the constitutional purpose
20 has been served. And there is no longer a need for the process to be prolonged.

I would have preferred to carry through to the finish, whatever the personal agony it would have involved, and my family unanimously urged me to
25 do so. But the interests of the nation must always come before any personal considerations. From the discussions I have had with Congressional and other leaders I have concluded that because of the Watergate matter I might not have the support of the
30 Congress that I would consider necessary to back the very difficult decisions and carry out the duties of this office in the way the interests of the nation will require.

I have never been a quitter. To leave office
35 before my term is completed is abhorrent to every instinct in my body. But as President, I must put the interests of America first. America needs a full-time President and a full-time Congress, particularly at this time with problems we face at home and abroad.
40 To continue to fight through the months ahead for my personal vindication would almost totally absorb the time and attention of both the President and the Congress in a period when our entire focus should be on the great issues of peace abroad and prosperity
45 without inflation at home. Therefore, I shall resign the Presidency effective at noon tomorrow. Vice President Ford will be sworn in as President at that hour in this office.

By taking this action, I hope that I will have
50 hastened the start of that process of healing which is so desperately needed in America. I regret deeply any injuries that may have been done in the course of the events that led to this decision. I would say only that if some of my Judgments were wrong, and
55 some were wrong, they were made in what I believed at the time to be the best interest of the Nation.

As I recall the high hopes for America with which we began this second term, I feel a great
60 sadness that I will not be here in this office working on your behalf to achieve those hopes in the next two and a half years. But in turning over direction of the Government to Vice President Ford, I know, as I told the nation when I nominated him for that office
65 ten months ago, that the leadership of America would be in good hands.

So let us all now join together in affirming that common commitment and in helping our new President succeed for the benefit of all Americans. I
70 shall leave this office with regret at not completing my term but with gratitude for the privilege of serving as your President for the past five and a half years. These years have been a momentous time in the history of our nation and the world. They have
75 been a time of achievement in which we can all be proud, achievements that represent the shared efforts

CONTINUE

of the administration, the Congress and the people. But the challenges ahead are equally great. And they, too, will require the support and
80   the efforts of the Congress and the people, working in cooperation with the new Administration.

May God's grace be with you in all the days ahead.

43

Nixon's primary purpose in delivering this speech was most likely to

A) ask the American public for their forgiveness for his mistakes.

B) announce his resignation and offer an explanation to the public.

C) condemn the press for trying him in the court of public opinion before all the facts were available.

D) express his full confidence in Vice President Ford.

44

Which choice provides the best evidence for the answer to the previous question?

A) Lines 6-9 ("Throughout the ... me")

B) Lines 36-37 ("But as ... first")

C) Lines 40-45 ("To continue ... home")

D) Lines 46-48 ("Vice President ... office")

45

Nixon's tone in the passage can best be described as

A) regretful.

B) hopeful.

C) livid.

D) uncertain.

46

Which of the following is NOT a reason Nixon gives for resigning the presidency?

A) He no longer feels he has enough congressional support.

B) He can't fulfill his obligations as President while also fighting for his personal vindication in the Watergate scandal.

C) Vice President Ford stated he was ready to take on the duties of the presidency.

D) The United States faces great challenges in the coming years and requires a cooperative government to face them.

47

The passage implies that Nixon

A) wanted to continue in his office, but felt obligated to resign.

B) was in fact relieved to step aside.

C) resigned in order to spend more time with his family.

D) was blackmailed into resigning by Congress.

CONTINUE

48

Which choice provides the best evidence for the answer to the previous question?

A) Lines 1-4 ("This is ... Nation")

B) Lines 25-26 ("But the ... considerations")

C) Lines 62-66 ("But in ... hands")

D) Lines 69-73 ("I shall ... years")

49

Nixon's use of the phrase "dangerously destabilizing precedent for the future" (lines 17-18) is primarily meant to refer to

A) forcing congress to initiate impeachment proceedings.

B) permitting the president's party to get away with crimes.

C) resigning too easily while he still had political support.

D) finishing out his term in the face of serious accusations.

50

Which of the following is an issue that Nixon states Americans must address in the coming years?

A) A potential economic collapse

B) An overly powerful Congress

C) A trial of those involved in Watergate

D) A struggle for peace

51

As used in line 35, "abhorrent" most nearly means

A) pitiful.

B) shocking.

C) disgusting.

D) repugnant.

52

As used in line 67, "affirming" most nearly means

A) stating.

B) defending.

C) upholding.

D) swearing.

STOP

If you complete this section before the end of your allotted time, check your work on this section only. Do NOT use the time to work on another section.

Section 2

Writing and Language Test

35 MINUTES, 44 QUESTIONS

Turn to Section 2 of your answer sheet to answer the questions in this section.

DIRECTIONS

Every passage comes with a set of questions. Some questions will ask you to consider how the writer might revise the passage to improve the expression of ideas. Other questions will ask you to consider correcting potential errors in sentence structure, usage, or punctuation. There may be one or more graphics that you will need to consult as you revise and edit the passage.

Some questions will refer to a portion of the passage that has been underlined. Other questions will refer to a particular spot in a passage or ask that you consider the passage in full.

After you read the passage, select the answers to questions that most effectively improve the passage's writing quality or that adjust the passage to follow the conventions of standard written English. Many questions give you the option to select "NO CHANGE." Select that option in cases where you think the relevant part of the passage should remain as it currently is.

Questions 1-11 are based on the following passage.

A Marine Biologist's Day in Maine

Lucy is up by eight in the morning. **1** By nine, she's out the door. She'll be on the beach by nine thirty, but Lucy isn't headed out to tan; Lucy is a marine biologist. She got her PhD last year, and she's now doing post-doctorate research on the coast of Maine.

1

(A) NO CHANGE

B) Lucy goes out the door after that.

C) Then she just walks out the door.

D) It's 9:00 o'clock when she leaves.

CONTINUE

[1] She meets the other researchers out by the tide pools. [2] They're focused this month on the effects of an **2** intrusive green crab population that has been harming the balance of the coastal ecosystem. [3] This loss of clams affects other species as well as the economy: the Maine clam industry typically makes $17 million annually, and the lost profits will affect fishermen, distributors, and consumers. [4] **3** The crabs eat soft-shell clams and as a result the clam population is plummeting, and clams are invertebrates. [5] Today, the research team will gather samples of both crabs and clams. **4**

2

A) NO CHANGE

B) encroaching

C) invasive

D) infringing

3

Which choice best improves or maintains the focus of the paragraph?

A) NO CHANGE

B) The crabs eat soft-shell clams and as a result the clam population is plummeting.

C) The crabs eat soft-shell clams, and clams are invertebrates.

D) Soft-shell clams are invertebrates, and their population is plummeting as they are eaten by crabs.

4

To make this paragraph most logical, sentence 3 should be placed

A) where it is now.

B) before sentence 1.

C) after sentence 4.

D) after sentence 5.

CONTINUE

Arriving at the work [5] cite, Lucy feels a misty spray on her arms as breakers crash on the rocks. The air is chilly; it's early June but it still feels more like spring than summer. Lucy hears another researcher say, "I love everything about this job except having freezing fingers first thing in the morning." Plunging her hands into a tide pool, she can't help but disagree. [6] The cold is a welcome shock to the system, instantly making Lucy feel more alert and invigorated.

5

A) NO CHANGE
B) sight
C) sleight
D) site

6

The writer is considering deleting the underlined sentence. Should the sentence be kept or deleted?

A) Kept, because it helps to maintain a clear chronology of events in the story.

B) Kept, because it helps to explain why Lucy disagrees with the other researcher.

C) Deleted, because Lucy's opinions about cold water are not statements of fact.

D) Deleted, because it doesn't provide relevant information about the qualifications necessary to become a marine biologist.

CONTINUE

They spend the morning collecting specimens. Crabs scuttle around, and clams lie still in their respective buckets. The day gets warmer, and Lucy works up a sweat. Compared to sitting at a desk, **7** the animals are lively. By noon, Lucy and her colleagues are gathering up their specimens and equipment to head indoors. **8**

Lucy spends the afternoon entering and analyzing data on a computer, tagging crabs in preparation for an experiment the following day, and monitoring the results of an ongoing experiment that focuses on the birthrate of phytoplankton, which are the primary component of the soft-shell clam's diet. **9** After dinner and a phone call, the phone call being from her sister, she puts in some hours on a research paper. Tomorrow will again start with a trip to the field station, as they continue to examine the changing ecosystem's challenges.

7

A) NO CHANGE

B) working with the animals is a lively activity.

C) the biologists are livelier.

D) the animal is lively.

8

The writer wants to insert another sentence here to wrap up the events of this paragraph, and provide an effective transition to the next. Which of the following choices best accomplishes these goals?

A) Lucy is sad to leave the shore, because working on the shore is her favorite part of the day.

B) After depositing their specimens in holding tanks, they have a quick break for lunch and then get to work in the lab.

C) They work quickly, because it's almost time for lunch and everyone has worked up an appetite collecting specimens.

D) The equipment will be stored for later use, and the specimens will be placed in holding tanks.

9

A) NO CHANGE

B) After dinner, and also after a phone call from her sister, she works on putting in some hours on a research paper.

C) After dinner and a phone call from her sister, she works on a research paper.

D) After eating dinner and then speaking on the phone with her sister, she then works on doing some work for a research paper.

CONTINUE

10 <u>When we hear about problems in the ocean, it's easy for us to think that we don't affect us.</u> However, changes in ocean populations affect populations on land, as well as the economy. **11** <u>Nobody are at the forefront</u> of addressing these oceanic environmental concerns like marine biologists.

10

A) NO CHANGE

B) When we hear about problems in the ocean, it's easy for them to think that they don't affect them.

C) When we hear about problems in the ocean, it's easy for us to think that they don't affect us.

D) When you hear about problems in the ocean, it's easy for us to think that they don't affect us.

11

A) NO CHANGE

B) Nobody at the forefront

C) Somebody are at the forefront

D) Nobody is at the forefront

CONTINUE

Questions 12-22 are based on the following passage.

Comets, Briefly Brightening our Skies

[12] Blazing through the sky for short periods of time before disappearing into the galaxy, humans have long been fascinated by comets. Comets are balls of dust and ice, comprised of leftover materials that did not become planets during the formation of our solar system.

12

A) NO CHANGE

B) Before disappearing into the galaxy, humans have long been fascinated by comets, blazing through the sky for brief periods of time.

C) Comets, blazing through the sky for brief periods of time before disappearing into the galaxy, have long fascinated humans.

D) For brief periods of time, humans have long been fascinated by comets, blazing through the sky before disappearing into the galaxy.

CONTINUE

Comets travel around the sun in a highly elliptical orbit. When far from the sun, a comet consists of only its nucleus, which is a few kilometers wide. As the nucleus gets closer to the sun (about as close as Jupiter), some of its ice sublimates, or turns directly into gas without melting into liquid first. The coma, a cloud of gas created by the process of sublimation, is very large compared to the initial size of the nucleus. **13** Solar winds disrupt **14** rock particles dust, and gas, creating distinct tails of particles streaming out from the coma.

13

The writer wants to insert a sentence here which will provide additional support for the preceding sentence. Which choice best accomplishes this goal?

A) On the surface of Mars, frozen CO_2 sublimates in warmer months.

B) Comas vary in size, depending on the initial size of the nucleus and environmental factors.

C) The coma can reach up to 10,000 kilometers in diameter, which is close to the size of the planet Earth.

D) At least one comet's tail was longer than 320 million kilometers.

14

A) NO CHANGE

B) rock particles, dust, and gas,

C) rock particles dust and gas

D) rock particles, dust, and, gas

CONTINUE

These tails can exceed 150 million kilometers in **15** length are visible from Earth. **16** Because tails are caused by solar winds, they are always moving away from the sun. Thus, surprisingly, if a comet is moving away from the sun then it is following **17** it's tail. Comets that are sublimating and have a tail are among the fastest objects in our solar system, reaching speeds up to 160,000 kilometers per hour.

15

A) NO CHANGE

B) length, are

C) length and are

D) length, further are

16

Which choice most clearly explains why comet tails move away from the sun?

A) NO CHANGE

B) Tails, because of their cause, solar winds, are always moving away from the sun.

C) They are being caused by solar winds, and tails are always moving away from the sun.

D) Tails are always moving away from the sun, being caused by solar winds.

17

A) NO CHANGE

B) it

C) its'

D) its

CONTINUE

The sun is near the center of Earth's orbit. However, a comet travels differently: the sun is at one of the far sides of its elliptical orbit. As the comet approaches the sun its velocity [18] increases, and as it moves farther away from the sun its velocity increases. Some comets [19] do an orbit around the sun in a few years, while others take thousands of years to do so.

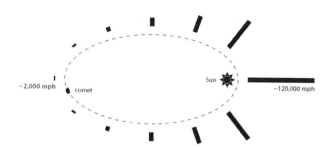

18

Which choice completes the sentence with accurate information based on the graphic?

A) NO CHANGE

B) increases as the length of its tail increases, which decreases as it moves away from the sun.

C) increases, and as it moves farther away from the sun its velocity decreases.

D) decreases, and as it moves closer to the sun the length of its tail decreases.

19

A) NO CHANGE

B) make an orbit of

C) orbit

D) complete a whole entire orbit around

CONTINUE

Although it is a rare occurrence, sometimes [20] comets collide with another celestial body. A popular theory is that a comet first brought water to Earth. The last known collision on Earth was 65 million years ago, when a comet or an asteroid hit the Earth just south of the Yucatan peninsula, creating a massive crater. The impact caused a global dust cloud to rise which blocked the sun and cooled the entire planet.

[21] When Halley's Comet last neared the Earth in 1986, scientists determined that it is made up of carbon, hydrogen, oxygen, and nitrogen in proportions similar to those of the human body. As distant and as different as comets may seem from us as they trail across the sky, we are [22] composed of the same elements.

20

A) NO CHANGE

B) comets collides with another celestial body.

C) a comet collides with other celestial bodies.

D) comets collide with other celestial bodies.

21

The writer is considering dividing the underlined sentence into two sentences. Should the underlined sentence be divided into two sentences?

A) Yes, because it is a run-on sentence.

B) Yes, because the sentence mixes unrelated pieces of information without explanation.

C) No, because the conjunction "and" effectively links the various ideas expressed in the sentence.

D) No, because the several pieces of information in the sentence serve to express a single complete thought.

22

A) NO CHANGE

B) constituted with

C) arranged among

D) produced through

CONTINUE

Questions 23-33 are based on the following passage.

Hamilton's Essential Contributions to the United States' Economy

[23] Of all the Founding Fathers, Alexander Hamilton's contributions to the establishment of the United States' economy were unparalleled. A trusted advisor of George Washington during the Revolutionary War, Hamilton spent a lot of time thinking about what kind of government the new country needed. He studied European economies and governments, and maintained that strong federal power was necessary for the nation's survival. [24] You may not know that when delegates convened in 1787 to create a Constitution for the new country, Hamilton was active at the Convention and instrumental in the Constitution's ratification. He convinced states to approve it through speeches and the influential Federalist Papers which he co-authored.

23

A) NO CHANGE

B) Even among those of all of the Founding Fathers, Alexander Hamilton's contributions to the establishment of the United States' economy

C) Alexander Hamilton's were the greatest, the contributions of all of the Founding Fathers

D) Alexander Hamilton, more than any other contributions to the establishment of the United States' economy,

24

A) NO CHANGE

B) I have heard that when delegates convened

C) When delegates convened

D) Posterity remembers that when delegates convened

CONTINUE

[1] **25** President Washington decided on the choice of Hamilton as the first Secretary of the Treasury. [2] Washington and his cabinet had no example to follow: they set the **26** preceding for how the executive branch of the government would operate. [3] Thus, Hamilton was largely responsible for establishing the United States' early economic policies. [4] Thomas Jefferson was influential as Secretary of State as well. [5] Without sound economic policies, the country might not have survived. **27** .

25

A) NO CHANGE

B) President Washington made the choice to have Hamilton be the first Secretary

C) President Washington chose Hamilton to be the first Secretary

D) President Washington made his choice and decided on Hamilton as first Secretary

26

A) NO CHANGE

B) precedent

C) proceeding

D) president

27

Which sentence should be removed in order to improve the focus of this paragraph?

A) Sentence 1

B) Sentence 2

C) Sentence 3

D) Sentence 4

[28] Hamilton knew the United States needed to have strong businesses and industries, which could not form without a strong national economy. The country was still deep in debt from the war and needed additional revenue to initiate national projects. Although taxes were [29] unpopular—a major cause of the Revolutionary War was American resentment toward British taxes, Hamilton argued for their necessity. Without capital, how could the government accomplish anything?

28

A) NO CHANGE
B) Hamilton knew; the United States
C) Hamilton knew, the United States
D) Hamilton, knew the United States,

29

A) NO CHANGE
B) unpopular, a major cause of the Revolutionary War was American resentment toward British taxes; Hamilton
C) unpopular, a major cause of the Revolutionary War was American resentment toward British taxes—Hamilton
D) unpopular—a major cause of the Revolutionary War was American resentment toward British taxes—Hamilton

CONTINUE

30 Hamilton's "Report on Credit" stated that the government needed to repay its war bonds, take on the war debts of the states, and place a tax on imported goods. Many **31** members of Congress thought covering states' war debts expanded the central government's power too much, but Hamilton pointed out the difficulties of each state doing so independently. Virginia was strongly opposed to Hamilton's proposal, so Hamilton met secretly with Virginia Congressman James Madison. They agreed that Virginia would support the measure if the nation's new capital would be just outside Virginia, rather than in New York. With Virginia's support, the measures of the "Report on Credit" passed.

Another of Hamilton's ideas that met **32** obstacles was a national bank. Again, many states thought a federal bank would place too much power in the hands of the central **33** government and so for the sake of efficiency, and to establish credit for the federal government, the nation needed a centralized bank. In 1790, the idea was approved.

30

Which choice most effectively establishes the main topic of the paragraph?

A) Virginians and New Yorkers wanted the nation's capital to be in their respective states.

B) On January 14, 1790, Hamilton presented Congress with a plan of action for jumpstarting the economy.

C) President Washington relied on Hamilton.

D) Hamilton threw himself into his work, becoming increasingly obsessive as he developed his plans.

31

A) NO CHANGE

B) members' of Congress thought covering states war debts

C) members of Congress thought covering state's war debts

D) members of Congress thought covering states war debts

32

A) NO CHANGE

B) resistance

C) problems

D) hardships

33

A) NO CHANGE

B) government. However,

C) government and however,

D) government. Thus,

CONTINUE

Questions 34-44 are based on the following passage.

Artistic Game Changer: Marcel Duchamp

The twentieth century saw a major expansion of the definition of "art." Though visual art developed and flourished in practically every culture worldwide for millennia before the twentieth century, most schools of art had emphasized formal elements and aesthetics. The modern art movement, which began in the second half of the nineteenth century, had already **34** lengthened the scope of what the public accepted as art. Rather than aiming to represent their subjects directly, modern artists experimented with color and form to produce striking visual effects. By challenging the public's expectations for visual art, they laid the groundwork for the conceptual **35** art movement. Conceptual artists shifted the focus even further, from visual effects to ideas. They rejected the notion that a piece of art must be beautiful, or that it should demonstrate artistic skill—proclaiming, **36** rather, that as long as it expresses, an artistic concept, it should be considered art. Marcel Duchamp was a pioneer of the Conceptual art movement.

34
A) NO CHANGE
B) expanded
C) built
D) deepened

35
A) NO CHANGE
B) art movement—Conceptual artists
C) art movement, conceptual artists
D) art movement: and conceptual artists

36
A) NO CHANGE
B) rather: that as long as it expresses, an artistic concept, it should
C) rather, that as long as it expresses an artistic concept it should
D) rather that as long as it expresses an artistic concept it should

CONTINUE

[1] Duchamp was born in France in 1887, **37** and by young adulthood it is true that he had spent time creating art in both France and the United States. [2] Many critics claimed that the piece was not legitimate, but he maintained that it was the provocative, innovative nature of his act that made it art. [3] Disenchanted with the commercial art world, he refused to engage in practices generally seen as necessary for financial success and recognition: developing an identifiable aesthetic, frequently showing his work publicly, **38** or creating pieces similar to each other for the sake of profit, and in 1955 he became a U.S. citizen. [4] He developed the notion of a "Readymade," a pre-existing object that an artist finds, chooses, and claims as art, **39** modifying the object only by signing it. [5] Famously, Duchamp's 1917 submission to an art exhibition, Fountain, consisted of a urinal that he rotated ninety degrees and signed with a pseudonym. **40**

37

A) NO CHANGE

B) and had spent time creating, by young adulthood, art

C) and created art, which by young adulthood he had spent time creating

D) and by young adulthood had spent time creating art

38

Which of the following choices most improves the focus of the passage?

A) or creating profits and becoming a citizen.

B) and in 1955 he became a U.S. citizen.

C) or creating pieces similar to each other for the sake of profit.

D) or creating pieces similar to each other for the sake of profit, and he became a U.S. citizen.

39

A) NO CHANGE

B) modifying the object only by signing it by the artist.

C) modifying the object, the piece of art, only by signing it.

D) modifying the object only by applying his or her, the artist's, signature.

40

To make the paragraph most logical, sentence 2 should be placed

A) where it is now

B) before sentence 1

C) before sentence 5

D) after sentence 5

CONTINUE

In an interview in 1955, Duchamp **41** <u>says</u>, "You should wait for fifty . . . or a hundred years for your true public. That is the only public that interests me." **42** <u>Because</u> he did not receive critical acclaim for much of his career, over fifty years later Duchamp is seen as one of the most influential artists of the twentieth century. Duchamp's influence can be seen in the work of later conceptual artists: Andy Warhol, with his pop art images and prints of everyday objects; Jackson Pollock, with his canvases covered in splattered paint; Sol LeWitt, **43** <u>who made</u> cubic steel "structures." Thus, Duchamp achieved the respect of the public he cared **44** <u>about! Duchamp</u> and the conceptual art movement permanently changed ideas about art's definition, its scope, and its possibilities.

41

A) NO CHANGE

B) was saying

C) is saying

D) said

42

A) NO CHANGE

B) Considering that

C) Although

D) However

43

A) NO CHANGE

B) with his

C) in making

D) by making

44

A) NO CHANGE

B) about. Duchamp

C) about—Duchamp

D) about? Duchamp

STOP

If you complete this section before the end of your allotted time, check your work on this section only. Do NOT use the time to work on another section.

Section 3

Math Test – No Calculator

25 MINUTES, 20 QUESTIONS

Turn to Section 3 of your answer sheet to answer the questions in this section.

   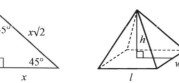

CONTINUE

1

If $42 = 3(x - 4)$, what is the value of x?

A) 4

B) 10

C) 18

D) 20

[handwritten: $42 = 3x - 12$, $3x = 54$, $x =$]

2

For what value of k does $x^2 + kx + 9 = (x + 3)^2$?

A) 0

B) 3

C) 6

D) 9

[handwritten: $(x+3)(x+3)$, $x^2 + 6x + 9$]

3

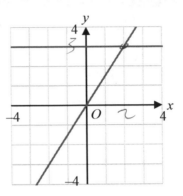

If (x, y) is the solution to the system of equations graphed above, what is the value of x in terms of y?

A) y

B) $\frac{2}{3}y$

C) $\frac{1}{3}y$

D) $-\frac{1}{3}y$

[handwritten: $x = 2$, $y = 3$]

4

A barrel of crude oil is extracted from shale at a cost of $51, and then transported to and from the refinery at a cost of $6 each direction. Oil is processed three times at the refinery plant, at a cost of $9 each time. What is the profit, in dollars per barrel, if one barrel is sold for $93? (Profit is equal to revenue minus expenses.)

A) 1

B) 2

C) 3

D) 4

[handwritten: $51 + 12 + 27$, $63 + 27$, 90]

CONTINUE

5

If $c - 1 = 3$, what is the value of $c^2 - 1$?

A)   3

B)   8

C)   10

D)   15

7

If $2(3a - b) = 4b$ and $b = 6$, what is the value of a?

A)   6

B)   −6

C)   2

D)   5

Handwritten: 6 24 · $6a - 12 = 24$ · $6a = 36$ · $a = 6$

6

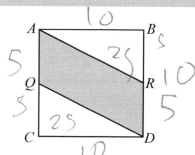

The square above has an area of 100. If Q is the midpoint of $\overline{AC}$ and R is the midpoint of $\overline{BD}$, what is the area of the shaded area?

A)   40

B)   50

C)   60

D)   75

8

$$\frac{2x}{x-1} - \frac{3x}{x+1}$$

Which of the following expressions is equivalent to the expression above?

A) $-\dfrac{x}{x^2 - 1}$

B) $\dfrac{5x - x^2}{x^2 - 1}$

C) $-\dfrac{x}{x - 1}$

D) $-\dfrac{6x}{x^2 - 1}$

Handwritten: $x = 2$ · $\frac{4}{1} - \frac{6}{3}$ · $4 - 2 = 2$

CONTINUE

9

Joel is a years older than Luca. In b years, Joel will be twice as old as Luca. What is Joel's present age, in terms of a and b?

$J = L + a$

A) $-2(a-b)$

B) $-2a-b$

C) $2a-b$

D) $a-b$

10

$$|x-3| \leq 5$$

Which of the following inequalities is equivalent to the absolute value inequality above?

A) $-2 \leq x \leq 8$

B) $-8 \leq x \leq 2$

C) $x \leq -2$ or $x \geq 8$

D) $x \leq -8$ or $x \geq 2$

$|x| \leq 8$

11

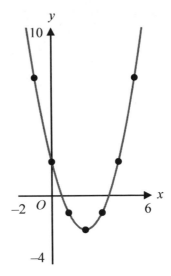

The figure above shows the graph of a quadratic function f with a minimum point at $(2, -2)$. If $f(5) = n$, what is a possible value for n?

A) $f(-2)$

B) $f(-1)$

C) $f(0)$

D) $f(1)$

CONTINUE

12

$$\frac{16^x}{4^a + 4^a + 4^a + 4^a} = \frac{1}{4}$$

Which equation best represents the value of x in terms of a?

A) $\frac{a}{4} = x$

B) $\frac{a}{2} = x$

C) $a = x$

D) $2a = x$

13

The sum of a and b is 132. If a is the square of b and the product of a and b is negative, what is a?

A) -12

B) 11

C) 121

D) 144

14

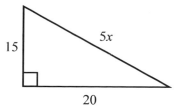

What is the value of x in the triangle above?

A) 5

B) 10

C) 25

D) 31

15

$$y = 5x^2 - 3x - 1$$

$$y + 6 = 7x$$

In the system of equations above, what is the value of y in terms of x?

A) $-x$

B) x

C) $2x$

D) $3x$

CONTINUE

DIRECTIONS

Questions **16-20** ask you to solve a problem and enter your answer in the grid provided on your answer sheet. When completing grid-in questions:

1. You are required to bubble in the circles for your answers. It is recommended, but not required, that you also write your answer in the boxes above the columns of circles. Points will be awarded based only on whether the circles are filled in correctly.

2. Fill in only one circle in a column.

3. You can start your answer in any column as long as you can fit in the whole answer.

4. For questions 16-20, no answers will be negative numbers.

5. **Mixed numbers,** such as $4\frac{2}{5}$, must be gridded as decimals or improper fractions, such as 4.4 or as 22/5. "42/5" will be read as "forty-two over five," not as "four and two-fifths."

6. If your answer is a **decimal** with more digits than will fit on the grid, you may round it or cut it off, but you must fill the entire grid.

7. If there are **multiple correct solutions** to a problem, all of them will be considered correct. Enter only **one** on the grid.

[Grid-in answer examples: 5/11, 8.4, 3/7 (top row); .422, .326, .125 (bottom row)]

CONTINUE

16

A stone is dropped from a height of 9 meters above the ground. If the height function can be modelled by the equation $h(t) = a - t^2$, where t is time in seconds and h is height in meters, how many seconds does it take for the stone to hit the ground?

19

$$\frac{d}{y} = \frac{12}{d}$$

$$y^2 = 6y - 9$$

If d is positive, what is the value of d in the series of equations above?

17

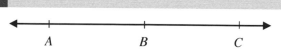

A, B and C lie on a line, as shown above. The length of $\overline{AB}$ is $x - 4$ and the length of $\overline{AC}$ is $x + 6$. What is the length of $\overline{BC}$?

20

The imaginary number i is defined such that $i^2 = -1$. What is the value of $(1 - i\sqrt{5})(1 + i\sqrt{5})$?

18

If $f(x) = 8x + 1$ and $g(x) - 3x - 1$, what is the value of $\dfrac{f(2)}{g(f(0))}$?

STOP

If you complete this section before the end of your allotted time, check your work on this section only. Do NOT use the time to work on another section.

Section 4

Math Test – Calculator

55 MINUTES, 38 QUESTIONS

Turn to Section 4 of your answer sheet to answer the questions in this section.

DIRECTIONS

Questions **1-30** ask you to solve a problem, select the best answer among four choices, and fill in the corresponding circle on your answer sheet. Questions **31-38** ask you to solve a problem and enter your answer in a grid provided on your answer sheet. There are detailed instructions on entering answers into the grid before question 31. You may use your test booklet for scratch work.

NOTES

1. You **may** use a calculator.
2. Variables and expressions represent real numbers unless stated otherwise.
3. Figures are drawn to scale unless stated otherwise.
4. Figures lie in a plane unless stated otherwise.
5. The domain of a function f is defined as the set of all real numbers x for which $f(x)$ is also a real number, unless stated otherwise.

REFERENCE

$$A = \frac{1}{2}bh$$

$$a^2 + b^2 = c^2$$

Special Triangles

$$V = \frac{1}{3}lwh$$

$$V = \frac{1}{3}\pi r^2 h$$

$$A = lw$$

$$V = lwh$$

$$V = \pi r^2 h$$

$$A = \pi r^2$$
$$C = 2\pi r$$

$$V = \frac{4}{3}\pi r^3$$

There are 360° in a circle.

The sum of the angles in a triangle is 180°.

The number of radians of arc in a circle is 2π.

CONTINUE

1

If $y = x - 2$, and $x = 2y + 4$, what is the value of x?

A) 1

B) 0

C) –2

D) –6

2

x	0	2	4	6
$f(x)$	3	4	5	6

Which of the following expressions defines $f(x)$ in the table above?

A) $f(x) = x + 3$

B) $f(x) = \dfrac{1}{2}x + 3$

C) $f(x) = x$

D) $f(x) = 2x$

3

If a farmer in Kansas purchases 8 pigs for every 1.5 acres of land and has 6 acres of land set aside for pigs, how many pigs will she purchase?

A) 20

B) 32

C) 40

D) 48

4

$$\frac{x-1}{3} = \frac{2x-6}{4}$$

What is the value of x that satisfies the equation above?

A) 5

B) 7

C) 8

D) 16

5

If $8x + 4 = 48$, what is $2x + 1$?

A) 9

B) 10

C) 11

D) 12

CONTINUE

6

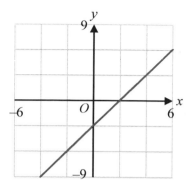

What is the slope of the function in the graph above?

A) 2

B) $\dfrac{3}{2}$

C) $\dfrac{2}{3}$

D) $\dfrac{1}{2}$

7

The population of an invasive species of moth doubles every 5 years. If the initial population is 300, what will be the population after 15 years?

A) 900

B) 1200

C) 2000

D) 2400

8

John fills his bag with five cent candies, v, and ten cent candies, t. If he has a total of 54 candies and his candies are worth \$3.10, which of the following is true?

   I.   \$0.05v + \$0.10t = \$3.10

   II. 54 = v + t

   III. \$0.05 × (54 − v) + \$0.10v = \$3.10

A) I only

B) I and II only

C) I, II, and III

D) None of the above

9

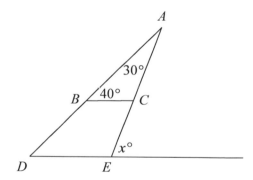

In the figure above, if $\overline{BC} \parallel \overline{DE}$, what is the value of x?

A) 30

B) 40

C) 70

D) 110

CONTINUE

10

Ali buys 10 burgers and 7 chocolate milkshakes for $50.95. If the price of a chocolate milkshake is $0.25 cheaper than the price of a burger, what is the price of a chocolate milkshake?

A) $2.85

B) $3.10

C) $4.05

D) $5.09

11

The acute angles of a right triangle have a ratio of 12 to 3. What is the difference between the two angle measures?

A) 42 degrees

B) 54 degrees

C) 64 degrees

D) 72 degrees

12

A number is a palindrome if it is the same written backwards and forwards (6336 is an example of a palindrome). What number divides into every 4 digit palindrome?

A) 2

B) 3

C) 7

D) 11

13

Day	Number of books
Monday	x
Tuesday	$2x$
Wednesday	$0.5x$
Thursday	x
Friday	$3.5x$

The above table outlines how many books Anthony reads per day in terms of x. What is the average daily number of books that Anthony reads, in terms of x?

A) $\dfrac{5x}{8}$

B) x

C) $\dfrac{8x}{5}$

D) $8x$

14

$$x^2 - 1 < x^3$$

For which of the following values is the above inequality true?

A) $x = -3$

B) $x = -2$

C) $x = -1$

D) $x = 0$

CONTINUE

15

Growth of Bacteria Populations

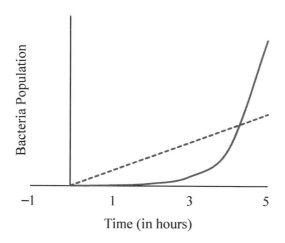

Bacteria *A* is represented by the solid line and Bacteria *B* is represented by the dotted line in the graph shown above. Which of the following statements is TRUE?

A) Bacteria *A* is growing at a linear rate.

B) Bacteria *B* is growing at an exponential rate.

C) Neither Bacteria *A* nor Bacteria *B* is growing at a linear rate.

D) Bacteria *B* is growing linearly, but Bacteria *A* is growing exponentially.

16

Which of the following values of x results in the largest value of y in the equation $y = -(x - 2)^2 + 4$?

A) –2

B) 0

C) 2

D) 4

17

$$x = 12$$
$$3x = 4y^2$$

In the system of equations above, if $y > 0$, what is the value of $x^2 y$?

A) 36

B) 108

C) 432

D) 1296

18

The product of two positive consecutive even numbers is 168. What is the smaller of the two numbers?

A) 24

B) 21

C) 14

D) 12

CONTINUE

19

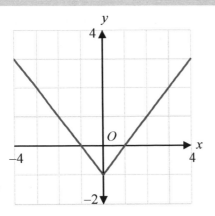

The function $f(x)$ is graphed above. If $g(x) = f(x) - 1$, which of the following statements is true?

A) $g(x)$ is greater than or equal to zero.

B) $g(x)$ is greater than or equal to negative one.

C) $g(x)$ is greater than or equal to negative two.

D) $g(x)$ is greater than negative one, but smaller than five.

20

Three different integers are randomly selected from a group of five unique integers consisting of 1 through 5. What is the probability that these numbers are 1, 2, and 3?

A) One in five

B) One in ten

C) One in twenty

D) One in sixty

21

The ratio of $d:c$ is 3:1. If the sum of d and c is s, what is the value for d, in terms of s?

A) $\dfrac{4}{3}s$

B) $\dfrac{3}{4}s$

C) $s - 3$

D) $s - 4$

CONTINUE

23

Questions 22 and 23 refer to the following information.

A survey on coffee consumption was conducted among a random sample of students at a university. A total of 200 students were surveyed. The table below displays a summary of the results.

Cups of Coffee (Per Day)				
Student Year	0	1	2 or more	Total
Freshman	25	9	16	50
Sophomore	5	19	26	50
Junior	10	6	50	66
Senior	0	2	32	34
Total	40	36	124	200

22

Based on the information in the table, who would be least likely to drink any cups of coffee during the day?

A) a freshman

B) a sophomore

C) a junior

D) a senior

23

Which of the following statements about the students surveyed is not supported by the table above?

A) A higher percentage of juniors than sophomores drink 2 or more cups of coffee per day.

B) A higher percentage of juniors than seniors drink 2 or more cups of coffee per day.

C) 20% of all students surveyed do not drink coffee.

D) 50% of the freshmen do not drink coffee.

CONTINUE

24

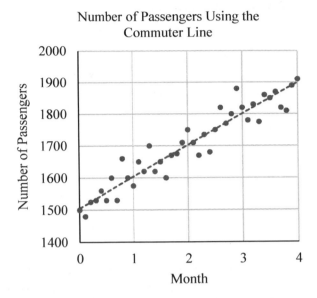

Number of Passengers Using the
Commuter Line

The graph above shows the number of passengers on a train line over 4 months. If m is the number of months, which of the following functions best represents the graph's line of best fit?

A) $f(m) = 200 + 1500m$

B) $f(m) = 150 + 100m$

C) $f(m) = 1500 + 100m$

D) $f(m) = 150m + 1500$

25

Produce at the Farmer's Market	
Fruit	Price
Apples	3 for 2 dollars
Peaches	1 for 1 dollar
Oranges	4 for 3 dollars

The chart above shows the prices for fruit at a farmer's market. Claire spends 4 dollars on apples, 2 dollars on peaches, and 3 dollars on oranges and puts all of her fruits in a brown bag. If she randomly selects a fruit from her bag, what is the probability she grabs an apple?

A) $\dfrac{1}{4}$

B) $\dfrac{1}{3}$

C) $\dfrac{1}{2}$

D) $\dfrac{2}{3}$

26

j is equal to 925 and k is equal to 5,550. A number, n, is added to j, such that the ratio of $j + n$ to k is 1:3. What is the ratio of n to $j + n$, expressed as a percentage of $j + n$?

A) 30%

B) 40%

C) 50%

D) 60%

CONTINUE

27

When Amelia goes cliff diving in Bali, her height above the water can be modelled by the function $f(t) = -2t^2 + 4t + 30$, where t represents time in seconds. How long, in seconds, does it take for Amelia to hit the water?

A) 3

B) 4

C) 5

D) 6

28

The average of 5 positive numbers is 85. If the highest of these numbers is 100, which of the following statements cannot be true?

A) The lowest score is 20.

B) The highest range possible is 75.

C) The median is greater than 25.

D) The mode is 85.

29

Number of Foreign Languages
Offered in a High School Curriculum

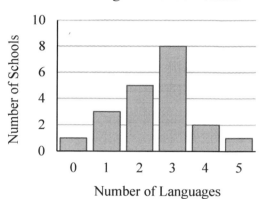

Number of Languages

20 high schools were surveyed on the number of languages offered in their curriculum. The results are shown in the chart above. How many schools offer fewer languages than average across the 20 schools?

A) 9

B) 10

C) 11

D) 17

30

A city wants to replace 10% of its bus fleet with hydrogen-powered buses. Each hydrogen-powered bus costs $200,000. If there are 180 buses in the city, how much money, in dollars, will it cost for the city to meet its goal?

A) 1,800,000

B) 2,000,000

C) 3,600,000

D) 4,000,000

CONTINUE

DIRECTIONS

Questions **31-38** ask you to solve a problem and enter your answer in the grid provided on your answer sheet. When completing grid-in questions:

1. You are required to bubble in the circles for your answers. It is recommended, but not required, that you also write your answer in the boxes above the columns of circles. Points will be awarded based only on whether the circles are filled in correctly.

2. Fill in only one circle in a column.

3. You can start your answer in any column as long as you can fit in the whole answer.

4. For questions 31-38, no answers will be negative numbers.

5. **Mixed numbers,** such as $4\frac{2}{5}$, must be gridded as decimals or improper fractions, such as 4.4 or as 22/5. "42/5" will be read as "forty-two over five," not as "four and two-fifths."

6. If your answer is a **decimal** with more digits than will fit on the grid, you may round it or cut it off, but you must fill the entire grid.

7. If there are **multiple correct solutions** to a problem, all of them will be considered correct. Enter only **one** on the grid.

PRACTICE TEST 1 | Ivy Global

CONTINUE

31

If $2x$ is equal to the sum of 11, 12, and 13, what is the value of x?

32

$$-15(2 + n) = -16(n - 7)$$

What is the value of n in the equation above?

33

If x is 60% of y, and y is 30% of z, x is what percent of z?

34

$$8^{3x-1} = \frac{1}{4^{3x-21}}$$

What is the value of x in the equation above?

35

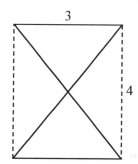

A rectangle has side lengths 3 and 4 as shown in the figure above. What is the total length of the solid lines?

36

What is the radius of the circle with the equation $x^2 + y^2 - 7 = 9$?

CONTINUE

Questions 37 and 38 refer to the following information.

Susan is training for a marathon. To track her progress, she has been keeping a record of her recent practice runs. The table below summarizes her training progress.

Time For Practice Runs		
Week	Distance (in miles)	Time (in minutes)
1	10	100
2	12	108
3	8	68
4	10	87
5	12	105

37

How much faster, in seconds, did Susan run each mile in Week 3 compared to Week 4?

38

Susan would like to run 26 miles in 3 hours and 54 minutes. Currently, she can run 26 miles at a pace of 11 minutes/mile. If she plans on improving her pace by 15 seconds/mile every week, how many weeks will it take Susan to reach her goal?

STOP

If you complete this section before the end of your allotted time, check your work on this section only. Do NOT use the time to work on another section.

Essay

Essay (Optional)

50 MINUTES

Turn to the lined pages of your answer sheet to write your essay.

DIRECTIONS

This essay is optional. It is a chance for you to demonstrate how well you can understand and analyze a written passage. Your essay should show that you have carefully read the passage and should be a concisely written analysis that is both logical and clear.

You must write your entire essay on the lines in your answer booklet. No additional paper will be provided aside from the Planning Page inside your answer booklet. You will be able to write your entire essay in the space provided if you make use of every line, keep tight margins, and write at a suitable size. Don't forget to keep your handwriting legible for the readers evaluating your essay.

You will have 50 minutes to read the passage in this booklet and to write an essay in response to the prompt provided at the end of the passage.

REMINDERS

- What you write in this booklet will not be evaluated. Write your essay in the answer booklet only.

- Essays that are off-topic will not be evaluated.

As you read the passage below, consider how Frank Pasquale uses

- evidence, like examples or facts, to support his arguments.
- logical reasoning to develop his ideas and to connect his claims to his evidence.
- stylistic or persuasive techniques, such as the choice of particular words or appeals to his readers' emotions, to give power to the ideas put forth.

Adapted from Frank Pasquale, "The Dark Market for Personal Data," © 2014 by The New York Times Company. Originally published October 16, 2014.

1   The reputation business is exploding. Having eroded privacy for decades, shady, poorly regulated data miners, brokers and resellers have now taken creepy classification to a whole new level....

2   There are lists of "impulse buyers." Lists of suckers: gullible consumers who have shown that they are susceptible to "vulnerability-based marketing." And lists of those deemed commercially undesirable because they live in or near trailer parks or nursing homes. Not to mention lists of people who have been accused of wrongdoing, even if they were not charged or convicted.

3   Typically sold at a few cents per name, the lists don't have to be particularly reliable to attract eager buyers—mostly marketers, but also, increasingly, financial institutions vetting customers to guard against fraud, and employers screening potential hires.

4   There are three problems with these lists. First, they are often inaccurate. For example, as The Washington Post reported, an Arkansas woman found her credit history and job prospects wrecked after she was mistakenly listed as a methamphetamine dealer. It took her years to clear her name and find a job.

5   Second, even when the information is accurate, many of the lists have no business being in the hands of retailers, bosses or banks. Having a medical condition, or having been a victim of a crime, is simply not relevant to most employment or credit decisions.

6   Third, people aren't told they are on these lists, so they have no opportunity to correct bad information. The Arkansas woman found out about the inaccurate report only when she was denied a job. She was one of the rare ones.

7   "Data-driven" hiring practices are under increasing scrutiny, because the data may be a proxy for race, class or disability. For example, in 2011, CVS settled a charge of disability discrimination after a job applicant challenged a personality test that probed mental health issues. But if an employer were to secretly use lists based on inferences about mental health, it would be nearly impossible for an affected applicant to find out what was going on. Secrecy is discrimination's best friend: Unknown unfairness can never be detected, let alone corrected.

8   These problems can't be solved with existing law. The Federal Trade Commission has strained to understand personal data markets—a $156-billion-a-year industry—and it can't find out where the data brokers get their information, and whom they sell it to. Hiding behind a veil of trade secrecy, most refuse to divulge this vital information…

9   It's unrealistic to expect individuals to inquire, broker by broker, about their files. Instead, we need to require brokers to make targeted disclosures to consumers. Uncovering problems in Big Data (or decision models based on that data) should not be a burden we expect individuals to solve on their own.

10 Privacy protections in other areas of the law can and should be extended to cover consumer data. The Health Insurance Portability and Accountability Act, or Hipaa, obliges doctors and hospitals to give patients access to their records. The Fair Credit Reporting Act gives loan and job applicants, among others, a right to access, correct and annotate files maintained by credit reporting agencies.

11 It is time to modernize these laws by applying them to all companies that peddle sensitive personal information. If the laws cover only a narrow range of entities, they may as well be dead letters. For example, protections in Hipaa don't govern the "health profiles" that are compiled and traded by data brokers, which can learn a great deal about our health even without access to medical records.

12 Congress should require data brokers to register with the Federal Trade Commission, and allow individuals to request immediate notification once they have been placed on lists that contain sensitive data. Reputable data brokers will want to respond to good-faith complaints, to make their lists more accurate. Plaintiffs' lawyers could use defamation law to hold recalcitrant firms accountable.

13 We need regulation to help consumers recognize the perils of the new information landscape without being overwhelmed with data. The right to be notified about the use of one's data and the right to challenge and correct errors is fundamental. Without these protections, we'll continue to be judged by a big-data Star Chamber of unaccountable decision makers using questionable sources.

Write an essay in which you explain how Frank Pasquale builds an argument to persuade his audience that privacy laws should be updated to regulate the modern data industry. In your essay, analyze how Pasquale uses one or more of the features listed in the directions on the previous page (or features of your own choice) to strengthen the logic and persuasiveness of his argument. Be sure that your analysis focuses on the most relevant features of the passage.

Your essay should not explain whether you agree with Pasquale's claims, but rather explain how Pasquale builds an argument to persuade his audience.

PRACTICE TEST 2

SAT

Directions

- Work on just one section at a time.

- If you complete a section before the end of your allotted time, use the extra minutes to check your work on that section only. Do NOT use the time to work on another section.

Using Your Test Booklet

- No credit will be given for anything written in the test booklet. You may use the test booklet for scratch paper.

- You are not allowed to continue answering questions in a section after the allotted time has run out. This includes marking answers on your answer sheet that you previously noted in your test booklet.

- You are not allowed to fold pages, take pages out of the test booklet, or take any pages home.

Answering Questions

- Each answer must be marked in the corresponding row on the answer sheet.

- Each bubble must be filled in completely and darkly within the lines.

Correct ●   Incorrect

- Be careful to bubble in the correct part of the answer sheet.

- Extra marks on your answer sheet may be marked as incorrect answers and lower your score.

- Make sure you use a No. 2 pencil.

Scoring

- You will receive one point for each correct answer.

- Incorrect answers will NOT result in points deducted. Even if you are unsure about an answer, you should make a guess.

**DO NOT BEGIN THIS TEST
UNTIL YOUR PROCTOR TELLS YOU TO DO SO**

Download printable answer sheets, answer keys, and Excel scoring sheets from:

ivyglobal.com/study

Section 1

	A B C D		A B C D		A B C D		A B C D		A B C D
1	○ ○ ○ ○	12	○ ○ ○ ○	23	○ ○ ○ ○	34	○ ○ ○ ○	45	○ ○ ○ ○
2	○ ○ ○ ○	13	○ ○ ○ ○	24	○ ○ ○ ○	35	○ ○ ○ ○	46	○ ○ ○ ○
3	○ ○ ○ ○	14	○ ○ ○ ○	25	○ ○ ○ ○	36	○ ○ ○ ○	47	○ ○ ○ ○
4	○ ○ ○ ○	15	○ ○ ○ ○	26	○ ○ ○ ○	37	○ ○ ○ ○	48	○ ○ ○ ○
5	○ ○ ○ ○	16	○ ○ ○ ○	27	○ ○ ○ ○	38	○ ○ ○ ○	49	○ ○ ○ ○
6	○ ○ ○ ○	17	○ ○ ○ ○	28	○ ○ ○ ○	39	○ ○ ○ ○	50	○ ○ ○ ○
7	○ ○ ○ ○	18	○ ○ ○ ○	29	○ ○ ○ ○	40	○ ○ ○ ○	51	○ ○ ○ ○
8	○ ○ ○ ○	19	○ ○ ○ ○	30	○ ○ ○ ○	41	○ ○ ○ ○	52	○ ○ ○ ○
9	○ ○ ○ ○	20	○ ○ ○ ○	31	○ ○ ○ ○	42	○ ○ ○ ○		
10	○ ○ ○ ○	21	○ ○ ○ ○	32	○ ○ ○ ○	43	○ ○ ○ ○		
11	○ ○ ○ ○	22	○ ○ ○ ○	33	○ ○ ○ ○	44	○ ○ ○ ○		

Section 2

	A B C D		A B C D		A B C D		A B C D		A B C D
1	○ ○ ○ ○	10	○ ○ ○ ○	19	○ ○ ○ ○	28	○ ○ ○ ○	37	○ ○ ○ ○
2	○ ○ ○ ○	11	○ ○ ○ ○	20	○ ○ ○ ○	29	○ ○ ○ ○	38	○ ○ ○ ○
3	○ ○ ○ ○	12	○ ○ ○ ○	21	○ ○ ○ ○	30	○ ○ ○ ○	39	○ ○ ○ ○
4	○ ○ ○ ○	13	○ ○ ○ ○	22	○ ○ ○ ○	31	○ ○ ○ ○	40	○ ○ ○ ○
5	○ ○ ○ ○	14	○ ○ ○ ○	23	○ ○ ○ ○	32	○ ○ ○ ○	41	○ ○ ○ ○
6	○ ○ ○ ○	15	○ ○ ○ ○	24	○ ○ ○ ○	33	○ ○ ○ ○	42	○ ○ ○ ○
7	○ ○ ○ ○	16	○ ○ ○ ○	25	○ ○ ○ ○	34	○ ○ ○ ○	43	○ ○ ○ ○
8	○ ○ ○ ○	17	○ ○ ○ ○	26	○ ○ ○ ○	35	○ ○ ○ ○	44	○ ○ ○ ○
9	○ ○ ○ ○	18	○ ○ ○ ○	27	○ ○ ○ ○	36	○ ○ ○ ○		

Section 3 (No calculator)

1 A B C D   4 A B C D   7 A B C D   10 A B C D   13 A B C D
2 A B C D   5 A B C D   8 A B C D   11 A B C D   14 A B C D
3 A B C D   6 A B C D   9 A B C D   12 A B C D   15 A B C D

Only answers that are gridded will be scored. You will not receive credit for anything written in the boxes.

16   17   18   19   20

Section 4 (Calculator)

1   A B C D   7   A B C D   13 A B C D   19 A B C D   25 A B C D
2   A B C D   8   A B C D   14 A B C D   20 A B C D   26 A B C D
3   A B C D   9   A B C D   15 A B C D   21 A B C D   27 A B C D
4   A B C D   10 A B C D   16 A B C D   22 A B C D   28 A B C D
5   A B C D   11 A B C D   17 A B C D   23 A B C D   29 A B C D
6   A B C D   12 A B C D   18 A B C D   24 A B C D   30 A B C D

Only answers that are gridded will be scored. You will not receive credit for anything written in the boxes.

31 32 33 34 35

Only answers that are gridded will be scored. You will not receive credit for anything written in the boxes.

36 37 38

Section 5 (Optional)

Important: Use a No. 2 pencil. Write inside the borders.

You may use the space below to plan your essay, but be sure to write your essay on the lined pages. Work on this page will not be scored.

Use this space to plan your essay.

_____

_____

_____

_____

_____

_____

_____

_____

_____

_____

_____

_____

_____

_____

_____

_____

_____

_____

_____

_____

_____

_____

_____

_____

_____

Continue on the next page.

Continue on the next page.

Continue on the next page.

_____

_____

_____

_____

_____

_____

_____

_____

_____

_____

_____

_____

_____

_____

_____

_____

_____

_____

_____

_____

_____

_____

_____

_____

_____

STOP.

Section 1

Reading Test

65 MINUTES, 52 QUESTIONS

Turn to Section 1 of your answer sheet to answer the questions in this section.

DIRECTIONS

Every passage or paired set of passages is accompanied by a number of questions. Read the passage or paired set of passages, then use what is said or implied in what you read and in any given graphics to choose the best answer to each question.

Questions 1-10 are based on the following passage.

This passage is adapted from Edith Wharton, The House of Mirth, originally published in 1905.

Selden paused in surprise. In the afternoon rush of the Grand Central Station his eyes had been refreshed by the sight of Miss Lily Bart.

Line
5   It was a Monday in early September, and he was returning to his work from a hurried dip into the country; but what was Miss Bart doing in town at that season? If she had appeared to be catching a train, he might have inferred that he had come on her in the act of transition between one and another of
10   the country-houses which disputed her presence after the close of the Newport season; but her desultory air perplexed him. She stood apart from the crowd, letting it drift by her to the platform or the street, and wearing an air of irresolution which
15   might, as he surmised, be the mask of a very definite purpose. It struck him at once that she was waiting for some one, but he hardly knew why the idea arrested him. There was nothing new about Lily Bart, yet he could never see her without a faint
20   movement of interest: it was characteristic of her that she always roused speculation, that her simplest acts seemed the result of far-reaching intentions.

An impulse of curiosity made him turn out of his direct line to the door, and stroll past her. He knew

25   that if she did not wish to be seen she would contrive to elude him; and it amused him to think of putting her skill to the test.

"Mr. Selden—what good luck!"

She came forward smiling, eager almost, in her
30   resolve to intercept him. One or two persons, in brushing past them, lingered to look; for Miss Bart was a figure to arrest even the suburban traveler rushing to his last train.

Selden had never seen her more radiant. Her
35   vivid head, relieved against the dull tints of the crowd, made her more conspicuous than in a ball-room, and under her dark hat and veil she regained the girlish smoothness, the purity of tint, that she was beginning to lose after eleven years of late hours
40   and indefatigable dancing. Was it really eleven years, Selden found himself wondering, and had she indeed reached the nine-and-twentieth birthday with which her rivals credited her?

"What luck!" she repeated. "How nice of you to
45   come to my rescue!"

He responded joyfully that to do so was his mission in life, and asked what form the rescue was to take.

"Oh, almost any—even to sitting on a bench and
50   talking to me. One sits out a cotillion—why not sit out a train? It isn't a bit hotter here than in Mrs. Van Osburgh's conservatory—and some of the women

CONTINUE

are not a bit uglier." She broke off, laughing, to
explain that she had come up to town from
55 Tuxedo, on her way to the Gus Trenors' at
Bellomont, and had missed the three-fifteen train
to Rhinebeck. "And there isn't another till half-
past five." She consulted the little jeweled watch
among her laces. "Just two hours to wait. And I
60 don't know what to do with myself. My maid
came up this morning to do some shopping for
me, and was to go on to Bellomont at one o'clock,
and my aunt's house is closed, and I don't know a
soul in town." She glanced plaintively about the
65 station. "It is hotter than Mrs. Van Osburgh's,
after all. If you can spare the time, do take me
somewhere for a breath of air."

He declared himself entirely at her disposal:
the adventure struck him as diverting. As a
70 spectator, he had always enjoyed Lily Bart; and
his course lay so far out of her orbit that it amused
him to be drawn for a moment into the sudden
intimacy which her proposal implied.

1

Which of the following provides the most
reasonable summary of the passage?

A) Two close friends meet to spend the day
together.

B) A traveler notices a woman acting
suspiciously.

C) Two acquaintances unexpectedly run into one
another.

D) A couple prepare to board a train for a
romantic getaway.

2

Selden's attitude towards Lily Bart is primarily
one of

A) attraction.

B) fascination.

C) disdain.

D) pity.

3

Which choice provides the best evidence for the
answer to the previous question?

A) Lines 1-3 ("In the … Bart")

B) Lines 7-12 ("If she … him")

C) Lines 18-22 ("There was … intentions")

D) Lines 24-27 ("He knew … test")

4

Over the course of the passage, the main focus of
the narrative shifts from the

A) grim and suspicious attitude of one character
to the gregarious behavior of another.

B) meticulous plans laid by one character to the
carefree adventures enjoyed by another.

C) appreciation of abstract beauty to the
enjoyment of living in the moment.

D) private thoughts of one character about
another to a friendly interaction between the
two.

CONTINUE

5

The passage suggests that Lily thinks it is good luck to run into Selden because

A) she is in grave danger and thinks he can save her.

B) she has been meaning to talk to him for a long time.

C) she likes him better than the person she was planning to see.

D) she has nothing to do until her train arrives.

6

Which choice provides the best evidence for the answer to the previous question?

A) Lines 16-18 ("It struck … him")

B) Lines 46-48 ("He responded … take")

C) Lines 59-60 ("And I … myself")

D) Lines 65-67 ("It is … air")

7

The primary purpose of lines 6-12 ("but what … him") is to

A) establish that Miss Bart does not live in town.

B) suggest that Miss Bart owns many houses in Newport.

C) imply that Selden thinks Miss Bart is untrustworthy.

D) explain why Selden is surprised to see Miss Bart.

8

Selden walks towards Lily because

A) he is curious about why she is at the station.

B) he is hoping she will suggest they spend time together.

C) he wants to see if she remembers him.

D) he has missed her very much.

9

As used in line 32 the word "arrest" most nearly means

A) apprehend.

B) detain.

C) impede.

D) enthrall.

10

In the context of the passage, the author's use of the phrase "eleven years of late hours and indefatigable dancing" (lines 39-40) is primarily meant to convey the idea that Lily

A) is a professional dancer.

B) prefers late parties to daytime activities.

C) has never really been very punctual.

D) has spent much of her youth in lively recreation.

CONTINUE

Questions 11-20 are based on the following passage.

This passage is adapted from a speech given by President Lyndon B. Johnson at the University of Michigan on May 22, 1964, announcing his plan to establish several new governmental social service organizations.

For a century we labored to settle and to subdue a continent. For half a century we called upon unbounded invention and untiring industry to create

Line an order of plenty for all of our people. The
5　challenge of the next half century is whether we have the wisdom to use that wealth to enrich and elevate our national life, and to advance the quality of our American civilization.

Your imagination and your initiative and your
10　indignation will determine whether we build a society where progress is the servant of our needs, or a society where old values and new visions are buried under unbridled growth. For in your time we have the opportunity to move not only toward the
15　rich society and the powerful society, but upward to the Great Society. The Great Society rests on abundance and liberty for all. It demands an end to poverty and racial injustice, to which we are totally committed in our time. But that is just the beginning.

20　The Great Society is a place where every child can find knowledge to enrich his mind and to enlarge his talents. It is a place where leisure is a welcome chance to build and reflect, not a feared cause of boredom and restlessness. It is a place
25　where the city of man serves not only the needs of the body and the demands of commerce but the desire for beauty and the hunger for community. It is a place where man can renew contact with nature. It is a place which honors creation for its own sake and
30　for what it adds to the understanding of the race. It is a place where men are more concerned with the quality of their goals than the quantity of their goods.

But most of all, the Great Society is not a safe
35　harbor, a resting place, a final objective, a finished work. It is a challenge constantly renewed, beckoning us toward a destiny where the meaning of

our lives matches the marvelous products of our labor. Within your lifetime powerful forces, already
40　loosed, will take us toward a way of life beyond the realm of our experience, almost beyond the bounds of our imagination. For better or for worse, your generation has been appointed by history to deal with those problems and to lead America toward a
45　new age. You have the chance never before afforded to any people in any age. You can help build a society where the demands of morality, and the needs of the spirit, can be realized in the life of the Nation.

50　So, will you join in the battle to give every citizen the full equality which God enjoins and the law requires, whatever his belief, or race, or the color of his skin? Will you join in the battle to give every citizen an escape from the crushing weight of
55　poverty? Will you join in the battle to make it possible for all nations to live in enduring peace—as neighbors and not as mortal enemies? Will you join in the battle to build the Great Society, to prove that our material progress is only the foundation on
60　which we will build a richer life of mind and spirit?

There are those timid souls that say this battle cannot be won, that we are condemned to a soulless wealth. I do not agree. We have the power to shape the civilization that we want. But we need your will
65　and your labor and your hearts, if we are to build that kind of society. Those who came to this land sought to build more than just a new country. They sought a new world. So I have come here today to your campus to say that you can make their vision
70　our reality. So let us from this moment begin our work so that in the future men will look back and say: It was then, after a long and weary way, that man turned the exploits of his genius to the full enrichment of his life.

CONTINUE

11

Based on the passage, what is the best description of Johnson's vision of the Great Society?

A) A time when each American has an equal share of the nation's wealth

B) A nation in which citizens continuously seek to improve themselves and society

C) A very exclusive club for the most powerful people in the country

D) An organization dedicated to strengthening public infrastructure

12

Which choice provides the best evidence for the answer to the previous question?

A) Lines 4-8 ("The challenge … civilization")

B) Lines 13-16 ("For in … Society")

C) Lines 36-39 ("It is … labor")

D) Lines 66-68 ("Those who … world")

13

What is the most likely reason Johnson refers to the founding of the United States?

A) To link the Great Society to the original mission of the country

B) To emphasize how morally superior current generations are to previous ones

C) To decry how far Americans have fallen from their former greatness

D) To provide information about the history of the country

14

Which choice provides the best evidence for the answer to the previous question?

A) Lines 9-13 ("Your imagination … growth")

B) Lines 28-30 ("It is … race")

C) Lines 42-45 ("For better … age")

D) Lines 68-70 ("So I … reality")

15

Which of the following would Johnson probably see as a negative symptom of "unbridled growth" (line 13)?

A) A business increases its profits by forcing its employees to work much longer hours.

B) A railroad company expands its tracks across the country in a few months.

C) A higher percentage of a city's children are in school than have been previously.

D) More people purchase at least ten books in a year than ever before.

16

How does Johnson characterize the relationship between the Great Society and "abundance and liberty for all" (line 17)?

A) The Great Society will make abundance and liberty for all possible.

B) Abundance and liberty for all are the ultimate goals of the Great Society.

C) The Great Society and abundance and liberty for all are mutually exclusive.

D) Abundance and liberty for all are the first requirements of the Great Society.

CONTINUE

17

As used in line 19, "committed" most nearly means

A) consigned.

B) entrusted.

C) assigned.

D) dedicated.

18

Which best describes lines 20-33? ("The Great … goods")

A) A list of ways in which the Great Society is already a reality

B) A description of the hardships preventing Americans from realizing the Great Society

C) An explanation of how Johnson came up with the vision for the Great Society

D) A description of different aspects of Johnson's vision for the Great Society

19

As used in line 40, "loosed" most nearly means

A) unleashed.

B) relaxed.

C) extricated.

D) slackened.

20

Johnson most likely repeats the phrase "will you" (lines 50-60) in order to

A) demonstrate that his audience has many options before them.

B) inspire his listeners to join him in achieving his goal.

C) scold younger generations for neglecting his plans so far.

D) repeat key information to ensure that listeners can understand what he is saying.

CONTINUE

Questions 21-31 are based on the following passage.

This passage is adapted from Cindi May, "The Surprising Problem of Too Much Talent." ©2014 by Scientific American.

Whether you're the owner of the Dallas Cowboys or captain of the playground dodge ball team, the goal in picking players is the same: Get the top
Line talent. Hearts have been broken, allegiances tested,
5 and budgets busted as teams contend for the best athletes. The motivation for recruiting peak performers is obvious—exceptional players are the key to team success—and this belief is shared not only by coaches and sports fans, but also by
10 corporations, investors, and even whole industries. Everyone wants a team of stars.

While there is no denying that exceptional players can put points on the board and enhance team success, new research by Roderick Swaab and
15 colleagues suggests there is a limit to the benefit top talents bring to a team. Swaab and colleagues compared the amount of individual talent on teams with the teams' success, and they found striking examples of more talent hurting the team.

20 The researchers looked at three sports: basketball, soccer, and baseball. In each sport, they calculated both the percentage of top talent on each team and the teams' success over several years. For example, they identified top NBA talent using each
25 player's Estimated Wins Added (EWA), a statistic commonly employed to capture a player's overall contribution to his team, along with selection for the All-Star tournament. Once the researchers determined who the elite players were, they
30 calculated top-talent percentage at the team level by dividing the number of star players on the team by the total number of players on that team. Finally, team performance was measured by the team's win-loss record over 10 years. For both basketball and
35 soccer, they found that top talent did in fact predict team success, but only up to a point. Furthermore, there was not simply a point of diminishing returns with respect to top talent; there was in fact a cost.

Basketball and soccer teams with the greatest
40 proportion of elite athletes performed worse than those with more moderate proportions of top level players.

Why is too much talent a bad thing? Think teamwork. In many endeavors, success requires
45 collaborative, cooperative work towards a goal that is beyond the capability of any one individual. When a team roster is flooded with individual talent, pursuit of personal star status may prevent the attainment of team goals. The basketball player
50 chasing a point record, for example, may cost the team by taking risky shots instead of passing to a teammate who is open and ready to score.

Two related findings by Swaab and colleagues indicate that there is in fact tradeoff between top
55 talent and teamwork. First, Swaab and colleagues found that the percentage of top talent on a team affects intrateam coordination. For the basketball study, teams with the highest levels of top performers had fewer assists and defensive
60 rebounds, and lower field-goal percentages. These failures in strategic, collaborative play undermined the team's effectiveness. The second revealing finding is that extreme levels of top talent did not have the same negative effect in baseball, which
65 experts have argued involves much less interdependent play. In the baseball study, increasing numbers of stars on a team never hindered overall performance. Together these findings suggest that high levels of top talent will be
70 harmful in arenas that require coordinated, strategic efforts, as the quest for the spotlight may trump the teamwork needed to get the job done.

The lessons here extend beyond the ball field to any group or endeavor that must balance competitive
75 and collaborative efforts, including corporate teams, financial research groups, and brainstorming exercises. Indeed, the impact of too much talent is even evident in other animals: When hen colonies have too many dominant, high-producing chickens,
80 conflict and hen mortality rise while egg production drops. So before breaking the bank to recruit

CONTINUE

superstars, team owners and industry experts might want to consider whether the goal they are trying to achieve relies on individual talent alone, or a cooperative synergy from the team. If the latter, it would be wise to reign in the talent and focus on teamwork.

85

Coordination as a Function of Top Talent

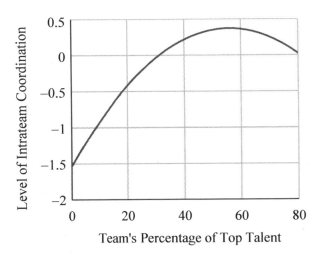

21

Which of the following best describes the structure of the passage as a whole?

A) A collection of anecdotes about sports

B) A description of a study and its potential implications

C) A set of pieces of advice for managers in sports and business

D) A series of arguments in favor of changing recruitment methods

22

Based on information in the passage, it can be inferred that the researchers' results

A) contradict most people's beliefs about team success.

B) confirm the conventional wisdom of sports recruitment.

C) provide information only about performance in a laboratory setting.

D) can be used to explain team results in all sports, as well as some other settings.

23

Which choice provides the best evidence for the answer to the previous question?

A) Lines 12-16 ("While there … team")

B) Lines 39-42 ("Basketball and … players")

C) Lines 44-46 ("In many … individual")

D) Lines 66-68 ("In the … performance")

24

Which of the following best summarizes the passage's interpretation of the researchers' findings?

A) Teamwork is the most important quality for sports teams.

B) Individual talent is the most important quality for sports teams.

C) Individual talent matters, but teamwork can be a decisive factor in some sports.

D) Although individual talent is more important, very strong teamwork can make up for weak talent.

CONTINUE

25

Which choice provides the best evidence for the answer to the previous question?

A) Lines 6-10 ("The motivation … industries")

B) Lines 34-36 ("For both … point")

C) Lines 46-49 ("When a … goals")

D) Lines 68-72 ("Together these … done")

26

The primary purpose of the first paragraph (lines 1-11) is to

A) explain why a high level of talent is so important.

B) explore possible reasons for the success of various teams.

C) endorse a particular recruitment strategy for sports management.

D) establish the conventional wisdom about talent and success.

27

As used in line 26, "employed" most nearly means

A) occupied.

B) used.

C) appointed.

D) hired.

28

As used in line 70, "coordinated" most nearly means

A) negotiated.

B) synchronized.

C) communicated.

D) light-footed.

29

The passage suggests that a study of the effect of top talent in baseball produced different results than the basketball study because

A) top baseball players are better at cooperative play than top basketball players.

B) there tend to be fewer elite athletes on baseball teams than on basketball teams.

C) there are fewer team members on the court at once in basketball than are on the field at once in baseball.

D) the sport of baseball requires less cooperative play than the sport of basketball.

CONTINUE

30

Based on lines 81-87 ("So before … teamwork"), in which of the following situations should decision makers "reign in the talent and focus on teamwork"?

A) A professor deciding which student papers to select as examples for future classes

B) A conductor auditioning singers for a choir to perform at a competition

C) A gymnastics coach helping his team members with their solo routines

D) A newspaper editor hiring journalists to cover local crime stories

31

Which of the following claims is best supported by information in the passage and graph?

A) A basketball team with no top talent will generally perform slightly better than an all-star team.

B) Basketball teams should aim to have top talent for about half of the team.

C) A struggling basketball team should replace its best players instead of its worst ones.

D) Around half of the players on an average basketball team tend to be considered top talent.

CONTINUE

Questions 32-41 are based on the following passage.

This passage is adapted from David Noonan, "Meet the Two Scientists Who Implanted a False Memory Into a Mouse." ©2014 by Smithsonian Magazine.

Steve Ramirez, a 24-year-old doctoral student at the time, placed the mouse in a small metal box with a black plastic floor. Instead of curiously sniffing
Line around, though, the animal instantly froze in terror,
5 recalling the experience of receiving a foot shock in that same box. It was a textbook fear response, and if anything, the mouse's posture was more rigid than Ramirez had expected. Its memory of the trauma must have been quite vivid. Which was amazing,
10 because the memory was bogus: The mouse had never received an electric shock in that box. Rather, it was reacting to a false memory that Ramirez and his MIT colleague Xu Liu had planted in its brain.

The observation culminated more than two years
15 of a long-shot research effort and supported an extraordinary hypothesis: Not only was it possible to identify brain cells involved in the encoding of a single memory, but those specific cells could be manipulated to create a whole new "memory" of an
20 event that never happened. What Ramirez and Liu have been able to see and control are the flickering clusters of neurons, known as engrams, where individual memories are stored. Joining forces in late 2010, the two men devised an elaborate new
25 method for exploring living brains in action, a system that combines classic molecular biology and the emerging field of optogenetics, in which lasers are deployed to stimulate cells genetically engineered to be sensitive to light.

30 In the first study, published in Nature in March 2012, Ramirez and Liu identified, labeled and then reactivated a small cluster of cells encoding a mouse's fear memory, in this case a memory of an environment where the mouse had received a foot
35 shock. The feat provides strong evidence for the long-held theory that memories are encoded in engrams. Ramirez and Liu assembled a customized set of techniques to render mouse brain cells in their target area, the dentate gyrus, sensitive to light.
40 Working with a specialized breed of genetically engineered lab mice, the team injected the dentate gyrus with a biochemical cocktail that included a gene for a light-sensitive protein, channelrhodopsin-2. Dentate gyrus cells participating in memory
45 formation would produce the protein, thus becoming light-sensitive themselves. The idea was that after the memory had been encoded, it could be reactivated by zapping those cells with a laser.

To do that, Ramirez and Liu surgically implanted
50 thin filaments from the laser through the skulls of the mice and into the dentate gyrus. Reactivating the memory—and its associated fear response—was the only way to prove they had actually identified and labeled an engram. The researchers examined the
55 brain tissues under a microscope to confirm the existence of the engrams; cells involved in a specific memory glowed green after treatment with chemicals that reacted with channelrhodopsin-2. When Ramirez and Liu looked at the treated neurons
60 through the microscope, "it was like a starry night," says Liu, "where you can see individual stars." Though these active cells were just one part of a widely distributed foot shock engram, reactivating them was enough to trigger a fear response.

65 The next step was to manipulate a specific engram to create a false memory, an elegant experiment detailed in Ramirez and Liu's second paper, published in Science in July 2013. They prepared the mouse, injecting the biochemical
70 cocktail into the dentate gyrus. Next, they put the mouse in a box without shocking it. As the animal explored, a memory of this benign experience was encoded as an engram. The following day, the mouse was placed in a different box, where its
75 memory of the first (safe) box was triggered by shooting the laser into the dentate gyrus. At that exact moment, the mouse received a foot shock. On the third day, the mouse was returned to the safe box—and immediately froze in fear. It had never
80 received a foot shock there, but its false memory, created by the researchers in another box, caused

CONTINUE

it to behave as if it had.

Reactivating a Memory

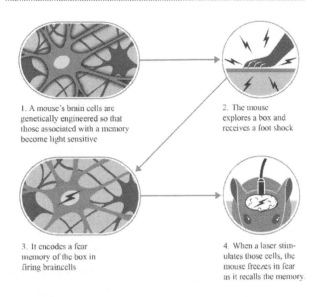

1. A mouse's brain cells are genetically engineered so that those associated with a memory become light sensitive

2. The mouse explores a box and receives a foot shock

3. It encodes a fear memory of the box in firing braincells

4. When a laser stimulates those cells, the mouse freezes in fear as it recalls the memory.

32

The author's attitude towards Ramirez and Liu's innovation is best described as that of

A) a zealous proponent.

B) an interested observer.

C) a wary critic.

D) a skeptical colleague.

33

Based on the passage, what is the primary significance of the research described?

A) It suggests new technologies might prevent memory loss.

B) It proves that memories cannot be tampered with.

C) It shows how specific interventions can alter memories.

D) It clarifies the purpose of the dentate gyrus.

34

Which choice provides the best evidence for the answer to the previous question?

A) Lines 16-20 ("Not only … happened")

B) Lines 37-39 ("Ramirez and … light")

C) Lines 46-48 ("The idea … laser")

D) Lines 62-64 ("Though these … response")

35

In relation to the other events described in the passage, when did the events described in the first paragraph most likely take place?

A) Before the first study

B) During the first study

C) During the second study

D) After the conclusion of the second study

36

Based on the passage, which choice best describes the relationship between neurons and memories?

A) Multiple neurons may work together to store one memory.

B) Each neuron stores exactly one memory.

C) Neurons are involved in making memories but do not store them.

D) Multiple memories are stored in each neuron.

37

As used in line 38, "render" most nearly means

A) provide.

B) make.

C) depict.

D) express.

CONTINUE

38

The goal of Ramirez and Liu's first study was to

A) implant a false memory engram in a mouse.

B) study the development of fear responses in mice.

C) identify an engram storing a particular memory.

D) discover whether they could make mice more sensitive to light.

39

Which choice provides the best evidence for the answer to the previous question?

A) Lines 30-35 ("In the … shock")

B) Lines 44-46 ("Dentate gyrus … themselves")

C) Lines 51-54 ("Reactivating the … engram")

D) Lines 59-61 ("When Ramirez … stars")

40

As used in line 65, "manipulate" most nearly means

A) handle.

B) palpate.

C) engineer.

D) exploit.

41

Based on the passage and the graphic, the purpose of making certain cells light-sensitive is to

A) allow the researchers to reactivate a memory with a laser.

B) ensure that memories are encoded in engrams.

C) prevent the mouse from recalling the memory in a new location.

D) heighten the fear reaction in response to a foot shock.

CONTINUE

Questions 42-52 are based on the following passages.

Passage 1 is adapted from Andrew Steele, "Your phone screen just won the Nobel Prize in physics." © Andrew Steele, 2014. Passage 2 is adapted from Sarah Zielinski, "The Potential Dark Side of Nobel-Winning LEDs: Pest Problems." © Smithsonian Magazine, 2014.

Passage 1

Blue LEDs are important for two reasons: First, the blue light has specific applications of its own and second, because it's a vital component of the white
Line light which makes white LEDs, and therefore LED
5 computer and phone screens, possible. Blue light has a short wavelength, which allows the pits on a Blu-ray disc to be smaller and closer together than on a DVD, which is read with red light. This means we can pack over five times as much data onto a disk
10 the same size as a DVD.

Their biggest impact, however, is surely in giving us the ability to produce white LEDs. White light is actually a mixture of all the colors of the rainbow, as you can see if you split it up with a prism, or indeed
15 if you catch a multicolored reflection in the surface of a Blu-ray disc, DVD or CD. However, the human eye has just three types of color receptor inside it: red, green and blue.

We can therefore make something which looks
20 like white light using only these three colors. Combining red and green LEDs with blue ones allows us to create highly efficient white lighting, providing around 20 times as much light as an equivalent incandescent bulb. White LEDs are
25 slowly making their way onto ceilings of homes, shops and factories around the world, but their real ubiquity today is as the back-light for computer and phone screens.

Unlock your phone or turn on a recent flat-screen
30 monitor, and red, green and blue LEDs shining through a layer of liquid crystal allows you to browse the web and watch movies. The result is a technology which is all around us in the developed world, and making headway into the developing
35 world too.

Passage 2

The Nobel Prize in Physics was recently awarded to three scientists who invented blue light-emitting diodes. The work was crucial for producing bright white LED lighting, which is more energy-efficient
40 than traditional incandescent bulbs. But there's a possible downside to widespread use of LEDs: They could make light pollution worse. For decades streetlights have generally used yellow, high-pressure sodium vapor lamps, which light up by
45 sending an arc of electricity through vaporized sodium metal. Now, white LEDs are quickly replacing the sodium lamps, but a study published in Ecological Applications shows why that might be an environmental problem.

50 "The main driver of the ecological impacts that result from a shift to white LED lighting will be the increase in emissions of short wavelength 'blue' light," says Stephen Pawson, an entomologist at the New Zealand research institute Scion. "The behavior
55 of many animals is influenced by light in the blue portion of the spectrum. For example, insects have specific photoreceptors for blue light. Thus large-scale adoption of 'white' lighting is likely to increase the impacts of nighttime lighting on all
60 species sensitive to 'blue' light."

In the study, Pawson and his Scion colleague Martin Bader looked at the effects of industrial white LEDs versus sodium lamps on insects. They set out the lamps in a field at night, placing sheets of
65 a sticky material next to the lights to catch any insects that came near. On average, the white LEDs attracted 48 percent more flying invertebrates than the sodium lamps. The researchers hypothesized that certain white LEDs might be less attractive to
70 invertebrates than others. Unfortunately, that wasn't the case.

If installed as currently designed, white LEDs could exacerbate pest problems, Pawson and Bader note in their study. Midge swarms, for instance, are
75 already known to be more attracted to white lighting.

CONTINUE

42

Passage 1 presents blue LEDs primarily as

A) a fascinating demonstration of little-understood physical principles.

B) a scientific curiosity of interest to select groups of people.

C) a major technological breakthrough that has already proven important.

D) a promising prototype that may become highly significant.

43

Which choice provides the best evidence for the answer to the previous question?

A) Lines 8-10 ("This means ... DVD")

B) Lines 12-16 ("White light ... CD")

C) Lines 21-24 ("Combining red ... bulb")

D) Lines 32-35 ("The result ... too")

44

As used in line 3, "vital" most nearly means

A) lively.

B) vigorous.

C) essential.

D) compelling.

45

According to Passage 1, blue light is important for creating white LEDs because

A) blue LEDs are cheaper to manufacture than white LEDs.

B) blue is one of the colors for which human eyes have receptors.

C) all colors must be present for humans to perceive white light.

D) blue light is the easiest to produce artificially.

46

Passage 2 primarily focuses on

A) different kinds of evidence that suggest white LEDs are harmful.

B) what makes white LEDs different from sodium lights.

C) the author's opinion that we use too many white LEDs.

D) a study demonstrating a specific effect of white LEDs.

47

The researchers in Passage 2 are primarily concerned that white LEDs will

A) result in significant losses of native insects.

B) disrupt the habitats of nocturnal animals.

C) cause an increase in invertebrate populations.

D) attract more pests than sodium lamps do.

CONTINUE

48

Which choice provides the best evidence for the answer to the previous question?

A) Lines 42-46 ("For decades … metal")

B) Lines 61-63 ("In the … insects")

C) Lines 66-68 ("On average … lamps")

D) Lines 74-75 ("Midge swarms … lighting")

49

As used in line 40, "traditional" most nearly means

A) standard.

B) time-honored.

C) habitual.

D) conservative.

50

Which of the following is the best example of one of the "impacts of nighttime lighting" mentioned in line 59?

A) Insects can be caught in sheets of sticky material placed near lights.

B) White LEDs are likely to emit more blue light than sodium lamps.

C) Light sources often attract unwanted pests, such as midge swarms.

D) Insects are drawn to things they have not seen before.

51

Which of the following best describes the relationship between the two passages?

A) Passage 2 describes a new application of the technology explained in Passage 1.

B) Passage 2 highlights a potential downside of the innovation described in Passage 1.

C) Passage 2 details an experiment performed to test the tools discussed in Passage 1.

D) Passage 2 criticizes the researchers profiled in Passage 1.

52

The authors of both passages would probably agree that

A) the most significant use of blue LEDs is in making white LEDs.

B) blue LEDs could be dangerous and should be used with caution.

C) the primary harm blue LEDs might cause would be to humans.

D) blue LEDs are too difficult to manufacture to be used widely.

STOP

If you complete this section before the end of your allotted time, check your work on this section only. Do NOT use the time to work on another section.

Section 2

Writing and Language Test

35 MINUTES, 44 QUESTIONS

Turn to Section 2 of your answer sheet to answer the questions in this section.

DIRECTIONS

Every passage comes with a set of questions. Some questions will ask you to consider how the writer might revise the passage to improve the expression of ideas. Other questions will ask you to consider correcting potential errors in sentence structure, usage, or punctuation. There may be one or more graphics that you will need to consult as you revise and edit the passage.

Some questions will refer to a portion of the passage that has been underlined. Other questions will refer to a particular spot in a passage or ask that you consider the passage in full.

After you read the passage, select the answers to questions that most effectively improve the passage's writing quality or that adjust the passage to follow the conventions of standard written English. Many questions give you the option to select "NO CHANGE." Select that option in cases where you think the relevant part of the passage should remain as it currently is.

Questions 1-11 are based on the following passage.

The Adaptive Arms Race

Every environment on Earth, from placid lakes to sun-scorched deserts, **1** is full of living beings engaged in life-and-death struggles. Predators constantly try to capture and eat prey, while **2** escaping predators is what prey tries to do. Over the course of many generations, predators tend to evolve to be better at spotting and catching their next meal, while prey animals evolve adaptations for evading and fighting off predators. Many prey animals have thus evolved fascinating defenses against being eaten.

1

A) NO CHANGE
B) has been full
C) was full
D) being full

2

A) NO CHANGE
B) escaping predators is prey's goal
C) prey is trying to escape predators
D) prey tries to escape predators

CONTINUE

3 The porcupine, for instance, is covered in barbed quills that can lodge painfully in the paws or skin of predators unwise enough to attack it. More intimidating still is the Texas horned lizard, which can fire a jet of foul-tasting blood from its eyes at a range of up to five feet. **4** <u>That's way too gross for most predators to handle.</u> Predators faced with noxious or dangerous defenses like these often choose to seek out easier prey.

Other prey animals avoid being eaten by blending in with their environment or imitating inedible objects. Many insects use this strategy, including stick insects and leaf insects, which have body shapes and colors that resemble parts of plants. Their **5** <u>mockery</u> is so convincing that even people can have a hard time picking them out from surrounding vegetation. **6** <u>Even so,</u> such camouflage is very effective, since a prey animal that cannot be found cannot be eaten.

3

The writer would like to insert a sentence here to help establish the main topic of the following paragraph. Which choice most effectively conveys the main topic of this paragraph?

A) Some prey animals have evolved defensive weapons to ward off predators.

B) Evolution rarely results in the simplest solution to a problem, so many prey adaptations are quite elaborate.

C) Although prey animals defend themselves when threatened, most animals prefer to avoid a fight whenever possible.

D) For many prey animals, simply running away from predators is the best solution.

4

A) NO CHANGE

B) This disgusts and deters most predators.

C) Most predators say, "no thanks!" to the horned lizard after that.

D) This convinces most predators that the horned lizard is way too gross to eat

5

A) NO CHANGE

B) duplication

C) mimicry

D) deceit

6

A) NO CHANGE

B) Nevertheless,

C) Naturally,

D) And then,

CONTINUE

[1] Why, then, are some prey animals brightly colored instead? [2] Surely such animals would be spotted and **7** quickly devoured right away, leaving them unable to pass on their genes. [3] As it turns out, bright colors are usually part of another anti-predation strategy called *aposematism*. [4] The visually distinctive patterns on animals using aposematism warn predators that their potential prey tastes bad, is poisonous, or wields a dangerous defense. [5] These warning patterns are often quite beautiful. [6] For example, the striking orange and black coloration on the wings of monarch butterflies **8** indicate that their bodies are loaded with foul-tasting poison. [7] Any bird that tries to eat a monarch butterfly quickly learns to make its next meal out of a more drab insect. **9**

Aposematism works so well that some animals have even evolved to display such warnings despite actually being harmless, a strategy called *Batesian mimicry*. Batesian mimics include the drone fly, which bears the black and yellow colors of the honey bee but lacks **10** its ability to sting. Thanks to this trickery, predators that have experienced the pain of a real bee's sting will not risk running afoul of **11** it.

7

A) NO CHANGE
B) quickly eaten up immediately
C) immediately
D) devoured immediately

8

A) NO CHANGE
B) indicates
C) will indicate
D) indicated

9

Which of the following changes would most improve the focus of the passage?

A) Move sentence 2 so that it follows sentence 3.
B) Move sentence 5 so that it follows sentence 6.
C) Delete sentence 5.
D) Delete sentence 4.

10

A) NO CHANGE
B) it's
C) their
D) they're

11

A) NO CHANGE
B) them
C) these
D) the drone fly

CONTINUE

Questions 12-22 are based on the following passage.

Life and Legacy of Alexander III

    When Alexander III inherited the throne of Macedon in the year 336 BC, he could hardly have come to power under better circumstances. He had the best education money could buy, having been tutored by the famed scholar Aristotle, and his power over all of Greece was already **12** secure. Thanks to decades of war and diplomacy overseen by his father, Philip II. Alexander was well-positioned to continue his father's military expansion and earn the title "Alexander the Great."

    Alexander began his conquest by invading the mighty Persian Empire. Thanks to his brilliant strategy and **13** how experienced his troops were, he quickly defeated the armies of Persia and took control of what is now the Middle East and Iran. **14** This early success encouraged him. He decided to continue pushing east despite his army's exhaustion. Threatening to mutiny, **15** he was eventually forced by his troops to turn back and end his campaign. Even so, by the time he turned thirty in 326 BC, Alexander was the ruler of the largest empire the world had yet **16** seen; it stretched from Egypt in the west all the way to India in the east.

12

A) NO CHANGE
B) secure: thanks
C) secure; thanks
D) secure, thanks

13

A) NO CHANGE
B) experienced troops
C) how much experience his troops had
D) his troops being very experienced

14

Which choice most effectively combines the two sentences at the underlined portion?

A) While this early success encouraged him, he
B) He, encouraged by his earlier success, then
C) Encouraged by this early success, he
D) Encouragement coming from this success, he

15

A) NO CHANGE
B) he eventually was forced by his troops
C) his troops eventually forced him
D) he and his troops were eventually forced

16

A) NO CHANGE
B) seen, it
C) seen; it,
D) seen it

CONTINUE

Alexander had a grand vision for his new empire. He hoped to mix the cultures of Asia and Europe by transferring settlers among different regions of the empire. However, many Greek and Macedonian nobles disliked Alexander's adoption of **17** the customs that the Persians had; his decision to proclaim himself a god, as the Persian emperor had, was particularly unpopular. **18** Nevertheless, Alexander failed to unite his native Greek culture with the cultures of the peoples he had conquered.

[1] In 323 BC, Alexander died of a sudden illness. [2] Many historians, ancient and modern, have suggested that he was poisoned by a political rival. **19** [3] The reading of Alexander's will showed that his death had cut short many grandiose plans. [4] He had hoped to invade Arabia and even circumnavigate Africa. [5] His plans went unrealized as his empire quickly crumbled. [6] Without Alexander's leadership, his generals quickly turned to fighting among themselves to carve out their own kingdoms. **20**

17

A) NO CHANGE

B) Persia

C) the customs of the Persians

D) Persian customs

18

A) NO CHANGE

B) As a result,

C) In addition,

D) In spite of this,

19

Which choice, inserted here, most effectively adds support for the claim in sentence 2?

A) Poisons may be derived from toxic plants or animal venom, but some minerals are also toxic.

B) Macedonian nobles often poisoned their opponents to remove them from power.

C) Alexander had taken many wounds in battle, leading to an overall decline in his health.

D) Alexander's unhealthy diet and lifestyle had taken a toll on his body.

20

To make this paragraph most logical, sentence 4 should be placed

A) where it is now.

B) after sentence 1.

C) after sentence 2.

D) after sentence 6.

CONTINUE

21 His conquests spread Greek culture across much of the Old World, influencing art as far away as India and establishing Greek as the language of international communication for centuries afterward. The Romans, who would later conquer much of Alexander's former territory, adopted Greek philosophy and made many **22** illusions to Greek literature in their own writings, ensuring that Greek culture would survive to influence Western thought for millennia.

Which choice, inserted here, most effectively conveys the main topic of this paragraph?

A) As a result, Alexander's work was entirely undone soon after his death.

B) Although his empire was short-lived, Alexander's conquest had an enormous impact on history.

C) Despite his early successes as a conqueror, Alexander had failed to achieve his objectives as a ruler.

D) Alexander was remembered long after his death as a fair and just ruler.

22

A) NO CHANGE

B) elusions

C) elisions

D) allusions

CONTINUE

Questions 23-33 are based on the following passage.

The Pressing Need for Clinical Psychologists

Clinical psychologists study, diagnose, and treat mental illnesses. Their work is vital given the high rates of mental illness among adolescents and adults. More psychologists are needed to contribute to research on the causes of and treatments for mental illness and give therapy to patients.

Mental illness is quite common in the United States. In 2012, the National Institutes of Mental Health estimated that almost 20% of adults in the US were diagnosed with a mental illness. Anxiety disorders, which involve excessive **23** <u>stressing out about stuff,</u> were the most common. Other relatively common illnesses were attention-deficit hyperactivity disorder (ADHD), which involves difficulties focusing, and major depression, which saps the mood and energy of its sufferers.

23

A) NO CHANGE

B) worry and stress

C) worrying all the time

D) difficulty taking it easy

CONTINUE

[1] Adolescents between the ages of 13 and 18 are particularly vulnerable to these disorders; NIMH estimates indicate that **24** about 25% of them likely suffer from at least one anxiety disorder. [2] That figure is just below 10% for ADHD and depression. [3] Another disorder that has drawn the attention of psychologists and the general public is autism spectrum disorder (ASD). [4] People with ASD often show symptoms from a very early age; **25** his or her symptoms can include difficulties with motor coordination and delayed literacy acquisition. [5] ASD is becoming increasingly common; **26** 1 in 150 children born in 2000 had ASD, while by 2010 the rate had increased to 1 in 68. **27**

Surveillance Year	Birth Year	Number of Sites Reporting	Prevalence per 1,000 Children	This is about 1 in X children
2000	1992	6	6.7	1 in 150
2002	1994	14	6.6	1 in 150
2004	1996	8	8.0	1 in 125
2006	1998	11	9.0	1 in 110
2008	2000	14	11.3	1 in 88
2010	2002	11	14.7	1 in 68

24

A) NO CHANGE

B) about 25% of them likely suffer from at least one anxiety disorder as well

C) about 25% of adolescents likely suffer from at least one anxiety disorder and teens as well

D) about 25% of adolescent and teenage youth likely suffer from at least one anxiety disorder

25

A) NO CHANGE

B) their

C) one's

D) his

26

Which choice completes the sentence with accurate data based on the table?

A) NO CHANGE

B) 1 in 150 children born in 1992 had ASD, while by 2002 the rate had increased to 1 in 68.

C) 6.7% of children born in 2000 had ASD, while by 2010 the rate had increased to 14.7%.

D) 6.7% of children born in 1992 had ASD, while by 2002 the rate had increased to 14.7%.

27

To make this paragraph most logical, sentence 2 should be placed

A) where it is now.

B) before sentence 1.

C) after sentence 4.

D) after sentence 5.

CONTINUE

If more students became **28** a psychologist, they could perform research to address many questions relating to mental illness. For instance, many researchers are currently unsure if mental illness is truly becoming more common or if clinical psychologists are simply more likely to spot it than in the past. Broad studies of the population are needed to address the issue. **29** Without a doubt, the root causes and biological underpinnings of many disorders are not known. More studies of the **30** gene's and brain's of people with mental illness are needed to develop fuller understandings of these disorders.

28

A) NO CHANGE
B) psychologists
C) psychologist
D) the psychologist

29

A) NO CHANGE
B) However,
C) Conversely,
D) Consequently,

30

A) NO CHANGE
B) gene's and brains
C) genes and brain's
D) genes and brains

CONTINUE

31 Some mental illnesses can be treated with medications, such as antidepressants for depression and stimulants for ADHD, but there are patients for whom **32** it does not work perfectly. Therapy is a vital part of recovery for these people. Even for patients who respond well to medication, regular therapy can also help them develop coping skills and avoid relapse. The availability of psychologists who can meet with patients to deliver therapies **33** are vital to addressing the serious public health challenge of mental illness.

31

The writer would like to insert a sentence here to help establish the main idea of the paragraph. Which choice most effectively conveys the main topic of this paragraph?

A) Though the causes of mental illnesses are not well understood, psychologists have found that many are at least partially heritable.

B) The Internet has helped people with mental illnesses form communities to support one another.

C) More psychologists are also needed to provide treatment for mental illnesses.

D) Unfortunately, mental illness is sometimes stigmatized in American society.

32

A) NO CHANGE

B) they do

C) which does

D) they does

A) NO CHANGE

B) can be

C) is

D) was

CONTINUE

Questions 34-44 are based on the following passage.

Several French Existentialists

In the years following World War II, France responded to its liberation from Nazi occupation with a remarkable flourishing of culture and intellectualism. One of the foremost movements to emerge during this time was the philosophical school of existentialism. Authors and thinkers **34** affiliated to this movement produced a formidable yet accessible body of literature that is still read by many today.

A) NO CHANGE
B) affiliated in
C) affiliated by
D) affiliated with

CONTINUE

One of the pioneers of existentialism was the author Jean-Paul Sartre, whose book *Existentialism is a Humanism* [35] concluded the philosophical principles of the movement. Sartre argued that human beings as individuals must define the meaning and purpose of their [36] own lives, by developing their own values and acting in accordance with them. His worldview thus emphasized the importance of individual responsibility [37] and also freedom of choice as well. Sartre's literary works explored these ideas, often by focusing on the thoughts and actions of irresponsible and immoral characters. [38]

35

A) NO CHANGE
B) contrived
C) expounded
D) insinuated

36

A) NO CHANGE
B) own lives by developing
C) own lives. By developing
D) own lives: by developing

37

A) NO CHANGE
B) and also freedom of choice
C) and freedom of choice
D) and freedom of choice as well

38

Which choice, inserted here, most effectively provides support for the claim in the preceding sentence?

A) For example, his short story *The Wall* depicts a captured soldier who refuses to give up his comrade's location.
B) In fact, despite being offered the Nobel Prize in 1964, he actually declined it.
C) For instance, his play *No Exit* portrays three people condemned to Hell and forced to reflect on their misdeeds.
D) For example, the main character of his novel *Nausea* becomes consumed by anxiety and disgust with life.

CONTINUE

[39] Though he did not consider himself an existentialist, author Albert Camus also addressed existentialist themes in his writings. Camus often wrote about characters struggling to find meaning in a seemingly meaningless and absurd world. In one of his best-known works, *The Stranger*, the protagonist Meursault drifts apathetically through his life and, after being sentenced to death for murder, tries to come to terms with the apparent indifference of the universe itself. Camus' masterpiece, *The Plague*, depicts a group of citizens in the Algerian city of Oran as it is devastated by an outbreak of disease. [40] Camus was actually a *pied-noir*, a child of French colonists born and raised in Algeria. This setting allows Camus to explore the existentialist themes of [41] moral responsibility and the search for meaning in suffering and the importance of social ties.

39

A) NO CHANGE

B) He did not consider himself an existentialist, though author Albert Camus

C) Author Albert Camus did not consider himself an existentialist. He

D) Not considering himself an existentialist, author Albert Camus

40

The writer is considering deleting the underlined sentence. Should it be kept or deleted?

A) Kept, because it provides an interesting piece of information about the subject.

B) Kept, because the sentence contributes to the logical progression of the passage.

C) Deleted, because the information is not relevant and diminishes the focus of the paragraph.

D) Deleted, because the information in the sentence contradicts information provided earlier in the passage.

41

A) NO CHANGE

B) moral responsibility, and the search for meaning in suffering and the importance of social ties

C) moral responsibility, the search for meaning in suffering, and the importance of social ties

D) moral responsibility and the search for meaning in suffering, and the importance of social ties

CONTINUE ➤

Author 42 Simone de Beauvoir who maintained a lifelong romantic relationship with Sartre, united existentialist ideas with feminist convictions to write about the unique challenges that women faced in the mid-20th century. Her treatise *The Second Sex* examined how social roles and expectations 43 constrain women's choices, shape their identities, and deny them the opportunity to find their own sources of meaning. In her novel *Les Belles Images*, her character Laurence struggles with feelings of dissatisfaction and constraint despite her seemingly ideal married life. Many critics praised de Beauvoir's frank depictions of women and felt that her female characters were more realistic and 44 relatable than Sartre. It is hardly surprising that de Beauvoir's works, like those of the other existentialists, are widely read to this day.

42

A) NO CHANGE

B) Simone de Beauvoir that maintained

C) Simone de Beauvoir—who maintained

D) Simone de Beauvoir, who maintained

43

A) NO CHANGE

B) bind

C) contain

D) oblige

44

A) NO CHANGE

B) relatable than was Sartre

C) relatable than Sartre's

D) relatable than did Sartre

STOP

If you complete this section before the end of your allotted time, check your work on this section only. Do NOT use the time to work on another section.

Section 3

Math Test – No Calculator

25 MINUTES, 20 QUESTIONS

Turn to Section 3 of your answer sheet to answer the questions in this section.

DIRECTIONS

Questions **1-15** ask you to solve a problem, select the best answer among four choices, and fill in the corresponding circle on your answer sheet. Questions **16-20** ask you to solve a problem and enter your answer in a grid provided on your answer sheet. There are detailed instructions on entering answers into the grid before question 16. You may use your test booklet for scratch work.

NOTES

1. You **may not** use a calculator.
2. Variables and expressions represent real numbers unless stated otherwise.
3. Figures are drawn to scale unless stated otherwise.
4. Figures lie in a plane unless stated otherwise.
5. The domain of a function f is defined as the set of all real numbers x for which $f(x)$ is also a real number, unless stated otherwise.

REFERENCE

   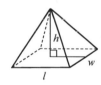

$A = \frac{1}{2}bh$　　$a^2 + b^2 = c^2$　　Special Triangles　　$V = \frac{1}{3}lwh$　　$V = \frac{1}{3}\pi r^2 h$

$A = lw$　　$V = lwh$　　$V = \pi r^2 h$　　$A = \pi r^2$　　$V = \frac{4}{3}\pi r^3$
　　　　　　　　　　　　　　　　　　　$C = 2\pi r$

There are 360° in a circle.

The sum of the angles in a triangle is 180°.

The number of radians of arc in a circle is 2π.

CONTINUE

1

$$x + 6 + 2x = 5x$$

What is the value of x in the above equation?

A) 2

B) 3

C) 4

D) 5

2

If $a^2 + 3a + 1 = c$ and $-4a + 5 = d$, which of the following is equal to $c + d$?

A) $a^2 + a + 6$

B) $a^2 - a + 6$

C) $a^2 + 7a - 4$

D) 6

3

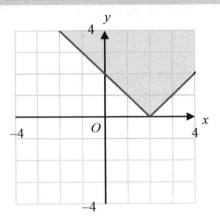

Which inequality is represented by the graph above?

A) $y \geq |x - 2|$

B) $y \geq |x + 2|$

C) $y \leq |x - 2|$

D) $y \leq |x + 2|$

4

Sophie and Jazmin have the same amount of money to invest in the stock market. If Sophie lends $15,000 to Jazmin, Jazmin has twice as much money as Sophie. How much money did Jazmin have originally?

A) $10,000

B) $30,000

C) $45,000

D) $60,000

CONTINUE

5

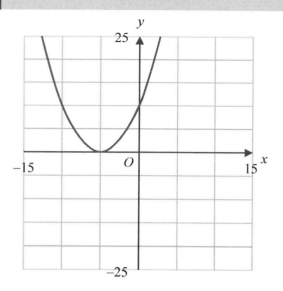

Which function best represents the parabola above?

A) $y = \frac{2}{5}(x-5)^2$

B) $y = \frac{2}{5}(x+5)^2$

C) $y = \frac{2}{5}x + 5$

D) $y = \frac{2}{5}x - 5$

6

Luca pays $1195 per month for rent plus 10 cents per kilowatt hour (kWh) used for electricity. If Luca used x kWh in one month, which expression best represents the amount of money in dollars Luca needs to pay for his apartment?

A) $1195 + 0.1x$

B) $(1195 + 0.1)x$

C) $1195 + 10x$

D) $(1195 + 1)x$

7

Which of the following equations has the same slope as $2y + 6x = 5$?

A) $x + 3y = 1$ $3y = -x + 1$

B) $3x = -y + 5$ $y = -3x + 5$

C) $y - 3x = 4$ $y = 3x + 4$

D) $6y = 2x - 1$ $6y = 2x - 1$

$2y = -6x + 5$

CONTINUE

8

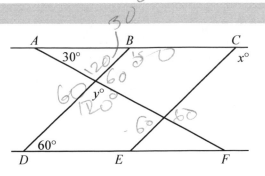

Note: figure is not drawn to scale.

In the figure above, $\overline{AC}\|\overline{DF}$ and $\overline{BD}\|\overline{CE}$. What is the value of $x - y$?

A) 30

B) 60

C) 90

D) 12

9

$$8x + y = 36 = 2y + 4x$$

In the above equation, what is the value of $x + y$?

A) 3

B) 10

C) 12

D) 15

10

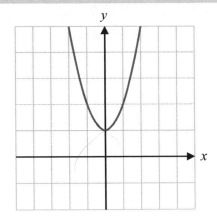

The graph above is a parabola whose equation is $y = ax^2 + b$. If $y = -ax^2 + b$ were drawn on the same graph, how many x-intercepts would the resulting graph have?

A) 0

B) 1

C) 2

D) Need more information

11

$$\frac{(x^2 - 1)(x - 1)}{x + 1}$$

Which of the following is equivalent to the expression above?

A) $x^2 - 1$

B) $(x - 1)^2$

C) $(x + 1)^2$

D) $x^2 + 1$

CONTINUE

12

Grace kicks a soccer ball into the air, where the height of the ball follows the function $h(t) = 8t - t^2$. After how many seconds does the ball return to the ground?

A) 0
B) 4
C) 6
D) 8

handwritten: $8t - t^2 = 0$

13

What is the solution for x in the quadratic equation $y = x^2 - 4x + 6$?

A) $x = 2 \pm \sqrt{2}$
B) $x = -2 \pm \sqrt{2}$
C) $x = 2 \pm 2\sqrt{2}$
D) No real solution

handwritten: $\frac{-b \pm \sqrt{b^2 - 4ac}}{2a}$
$\frac{4 \pm \sqrt{(-4)^2 - 4(1)(6)}}{2(1)}$
$4 \pm \sqrt{16 - 24}$

14

The square of a negative number is decreased by 14. The resulting number is 5 times the original number. What is the reciprocal of the original number?

A) $-\frac{1}{2}$
B) $-\frac{1}{4}$
C) $-\frac{1}{5}$
D) $-\frac{1}{7}$

handwritten: $-x^2 - 14 = 5x$
$-5x$
$-x^2 - 5x - 14$
$-1(x^2 + 5x + 14)$
$(x+7)(x-2)$
$x = 2$

15

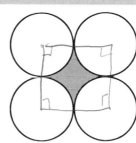

A landscape architect is creating four identical circular gardens so that each circular garden is touching two other gardens, as shown in the figure above. If each circular garden has an area of π, what is the area of the shaded region between the gardens?

A) $64 - \pi$
B) $4 - \pi$
C) π
D) $2 + \pi$

handwritten: $\frac{a}{360}$, πr^2, $r = 2$, $A = 16$, $\frac{4\pi}{360}$

CONTINUE

DIRECTIONS

Questions **16-20** ask you to solve a problem and enter your answer in the grid provided on your answer sheet. When completing grid-in questions:

1. You are required to bubble in the circles for your answers. It is recommended, but not required, that you also write your answer in the boxes above the columns of circles. Points will be awarded based only on whether the circles are filled in correctly.
2. Fill in only one circle in a column.
3. You can start your answer in any column as long as you can fit in the whole answer.
4. For questions 16-20, no answers will be negative numbers.
5. **Mixed numbers,** such as $4\frac{2}{5}$, must be gridded as decimals or improper fractions, such as 4.4 or as 22/5. "42/5" will be read as "forty-two over five," not as "four and two-fifths."
6. If your answer is a **decimal** with more digits than will fit on the grid, you may round it or cut it off, but you must fill the entire grid.
7. If there are **multiple correct solutions** to a problem, all of them will be considered correct. Enter only **one** on the grid.

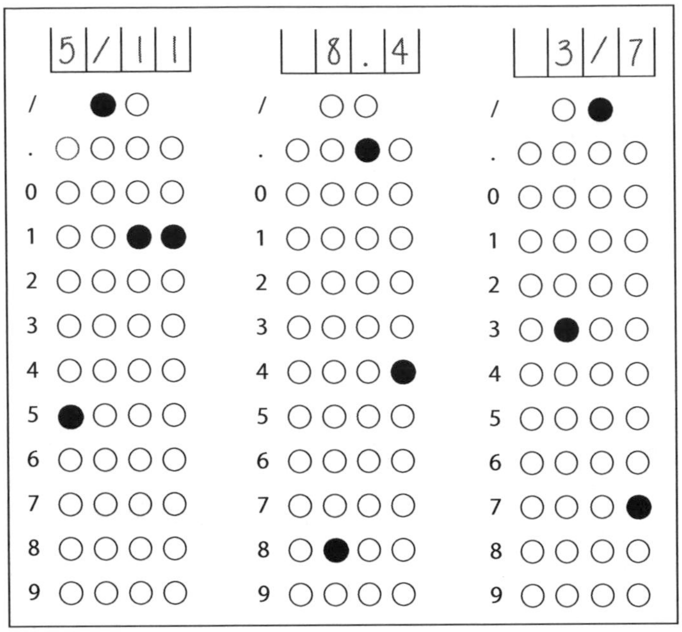

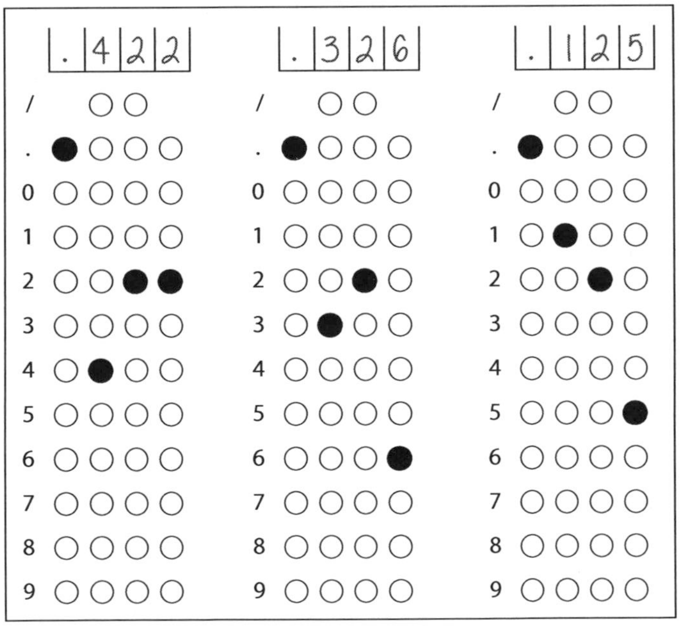

CONTINUE

16

What is the value of $(\sqrt{3} - \sqrt{2})(\sqrt{3} + \sqrt{2})$?

$3 + 3\sqrt{2} - \sqrt{6} - 2$

$\boxed{1 + 3\sqrt{2} - \sqrt{6}}$

17

If $\left|3x - 1\right| \leq 2x$, where $x > 0$, what is a possible value of x?

$|x| \leq 1$

18

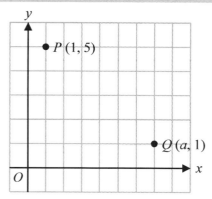

The slope of PQ is $-\dfrac{2}{3}$. What is the value of a?

$y = -\dfrac{2}{3}x + b$

$\quad\quad y = -\dfrac{2}{3}x + \dfrac{17}{3}$

$5 = -\dfrac{2}{3} + b$

$5\dfrac{2}{3} = b \quad\quad 1 = -\dfrac{2}{3}x + \dfrac{17}{3}$

19

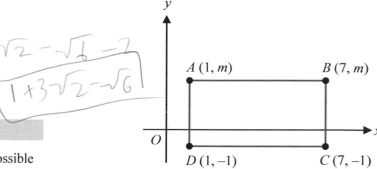

The rectangle $ABCD$ is placed on top of a coordinate grid as shown in the figure above. If the area of the rectangle is 24, what is the value of m?

20

If $x + \dfrac{9}{x} = -6$, what is the value of $x^2 + \dfrac{81}{x^2}$?

STOP

If you complete this section before the end of your allotted time, check your work on this section only. Do NOT use the time to work on another section.

Section 4

Math Test – Calculator

55 MINUTES, 38 QUESTIONS

Turn to Section 4 of your answer sheet to answer the questions in this section.

DIRECTIONS

Questions **1-30** ask you to solve a problem, select the best answer among four choices, and fill in the corresponding circle on your answer sheet. Questions **31-38** ask you to solve a problem and enter your answer in a grid provided on your answer sheet. There are detailed instructions on entering answers into the grid before question 31. You may use your test booklet for scratch work.

NOTES

1. You **may** use a calculator.
2. Variables and expressions represent real numbers unless stated otherwise.
3. Figures are drawn to scale unless stated otherwise.
4. Figures lie in a plane unless stated otherwise.
5. The domain of a function f is defined as the set of all real numbers x for which $f(x)$ is also a real number, unless stated otherwise.

REFERENCE

$A = \dfrac{1}{2} bh$

$a^2 + b^2 = c^2$

Special Triangles

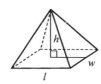

$V = \dfrac{1}{3} lwh$

$V = \dfrac{1}{3} \pi r^2 h$

$A = lw$

$V = lwh$

$V = \pi r^2 h$

$A = \pi r^2$

$C = 2\pi r$

$V = \dfrac{4}{3} \pi r^3$

There are 360° in a circle.

The sum of the angles in a triangle is 180°.

The number of radians of arc in a circle is 2π.

CONTINUE

1

If $a + 4 = 12$, what is $4a$?

A) 8

B) 32

C) 48

D) 64

2

Package	Price
1-hr session	$100
2-hr session	$190
Five 1-hr sessions	$450
Five 2-hr sessions	$850

The table above shows various packages offered by a tutoring company. How much cheaper is it, in dollars per hour, to buy a 2-hr session than a 1-hr session?

A) 5

B) 10

C) 20

D) 90

3

If $f(x) = 2x$ and $g(x) = 5x + 1$, what is $g(f(c))$?

A) $2c$

B) $10c + 1$

C) $10c + 2$

D) $20c + 2$

4

U is 75% of T. If V is 5% of U, what percentage of T is V?

A)   1%

B)   3.75%

C) 10%

D) 75%

CONTINUE

5

Activities over 24 Hours

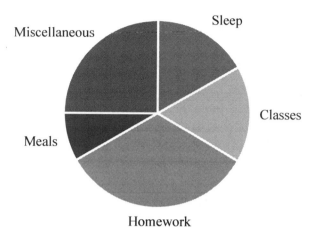

The pie chart above shows how a student spends his time in a 24-hour period. According to this chart, what fraction of his day does he spend sleeping and going to classes?

A) $\dfrac{1}{4}$

B) $\dfrac{1}{3}$

C) $\dfrac{1}{2}$

D) $\dfrac{2}{3}$

6

If $f(x) = 2x + 2$ is a linear function, which of the following is true for $4f(x)$?

A) The slope is four times steeper than $f(x)$.

B) The slope is four times less steep than $f(x)$.

C) All values of x are four times greater than $f(x)$ for the same values of y.

D) The slope changes, but the y-intercept remains the same as $f(x)$.

7

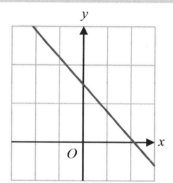

What is a possible equation for the linear function above?

A) $y = -\dfrac{10}{7x} - 3$

B) $y = -\dfrac{10}{7x} + 3$

C) $y = \dfrac{10}{7x} - 3$

D) $y = \dfrac{10}{7x} + 3$

CONTINUE

8

An object measures 3 cm by 9 cm by 4 cm and weighs 54 grams. If another object made from the same material measures 6 cm by 2 cm by 3 cm, what would be the weight of the second object in terms of the first object?

A) 3 times heavier

B) 2 times heavier

C) The same weight

D) 3 times lighter

9

A set of five integers includes 30, 45, 75, 75, and 100. When a sixth integer is added, the mean of the integers does not change. Which of the following is the sixth integer?

A) 45

B) 50

C) 65

D) 75

10

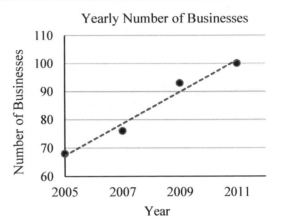

Yearly Number of Businesses

City planners in Beaufort, South Carolina want to estimate the number of businesses in 2015 from data collected from 2005 to 2011. The number of businesses in the city during this period is graphed above. Using the line of best fit, what is the best estimate for the number of businesses in Beaufort operating in 2015?

A) 120

B) 125

C) 130

D) 140

11

If $x = a + 2b$, $y = 2a - b$ and $z = -2b$, what is $x - y + 2z$?

A) $-a - b$

B) $a - b$

C) $-a + b$

D) $-a - 3b$

CONTINUE

12

Dungess crab and Horseshoe crab populations are observed and compared by marine researchers. Researchers notice that the Dungess population increases by 10% each year, and the Horseshoe population increases by 100 each year. If the Dungess crab population is represented by the solid line, and the Horseshoe crab population is represented by the dotted line, which of the following graphs best represents Dungess crab and Horseshoe crab populations?

A)
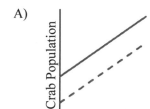

B)
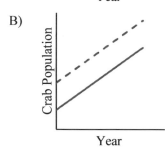

C)
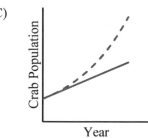

D)
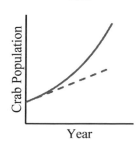

13

Isabella and Tom drive from the same location at 9:46 AM. Isabella drives north with a constant speed of 65 km/h, and Tom drives south with a constant speed of 77 km/h. At what time will Isabella and Tom be 639 km apart?

A) 1:16 PM

B) 2:16 PM

C) 3:30 PM

D) 4:30 PM

14

If $L + 11 = A$ and $L + A = 93$, what is product of L and A?

A) 1230

B) 2132

C) 2150

D) 3276

CONTINUE

15

x	0	1	2	3
$f(x)$	−3	−4	−7	−12

The table above gives values of the quadratic function f for selected values of x. Which of the following expressions defines $f(x)$?

A) $-x^2 - 3$

B) $x^2 - 3$

C) $2x^2 - 3$

D) $x^2 - 2x - 3$

16

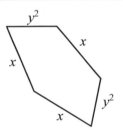

Note: figure is not drawn to scale.

The perimeter of the figure above is 333. If $x = 15$, what is the value of y?

A)   12

B)   30

C)   144

D)   159

17

p	$N(p)$
0	1250
1	2500
2	5000
3	10000
4	20000

A number, $N(p)$, increases according to a defined period, p, as shown in the chart above. What equation best represents the relationship between the number and the period?

A) $N(p) = 1250 \times (2)^p$

B) $N(p) = 1250 + 2p$

C) $N(p) = 1250 + 2p^2$

D) $N(p) = 1250p^2$

18

A company wants to create a solution of pure ethanol and distilled water. The density of ethanol is 0.789 g/cm^3 and the density of the water is 1 g/cm^3. If the company combines 8 cm^3 of ethanol with 4 cm^3 of water, what is the resulting density of the solution, to the nearest one thousandth of a gram? (Density is mass divided by volume.)

A) 0.789 g/cm^3

B) 0.842 g/cm^3

C) 0.859 g/cm^3

D) 0.895 g/cm^3

CONTINUE

19

If $\dfrac{x+1}{x+5} = \dfrac{1}{x-1}$, what are the values of x?

A) 1 and –5

B) 2 and –3

C) 3 and –2

D) –1 and 2

20

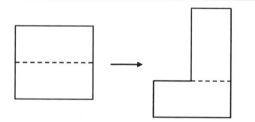

A square with an area of A is cut in half, and arranged as in the diagram above. What is the perimeter of the resulting figure, in terms of A?

A) $\dfrac{5}{2}A$

B) $4A^2$

C) $4\sqrt{A}$

D) $5\sqrt{A}$

21

If $(3^x)(9^y) = 2187$, what is the value of $x + 2y$?

A) 5

B) 6

C) 7

D) 8

22

Number
72
90
87
84
x

Four known numbers and one unknown number are shown in the table above. If the median number of the five numbers is 85, which of the following statements is NOT true?

A) The value for x is equal to the median of the five numbers.

B) The mean of the five numbers is greater than the median.

C) The value for x is greater than the mean of the five numbers.

D) In order to calculate the median, the numbers must be arranged in order.

CONTINUE

23

A group of 11 people are travelling together. Two people are from France, seven are from England, and two are from China. Unfortunately, their travel agent only booked 9 tickets, and two people have to leave the group. The group decides to pick two people at random by drawing lots. If the first person chosen is from England, what is the percent probability that the second person will also be from England?

A) 30

B) 40

C) 50

D) 60

Questions 24, 25 and 26 refer to the following information.

The graph below shows student enrollment for a psychology class and biology class in the years 2000-2004.

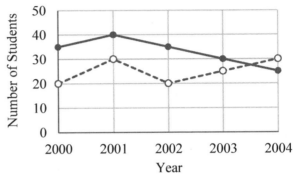

24

What is the total number of students who enrolled in psychology class during the period from 2000 to 2002?

A) 110

B) 130

C) 140

D) 170

CONTINUE

25

Which of the following statements is NOT true for the period from 2000-2004?

A) The median is equal to the mean for the number of students enrolled in biology.

B) Both the median and the mean number of students is greater in psychology than in biology.

C) There are approximately 32% more students enrolled in psychology than in biology on average.

D) The mean is greater than the median for the number of students enrolled in psychology.

26

Which of the following statements is supported by the graph?

A) In 2001, there were twice as many students in the biology class than the psychology class.

B) During the years 2001-2004, enrollment in the psychology class on average decreased by 5 students per year.

C) During the years 2002-2004, enrollment in the biology class on average increased by 10 students per year.

D) In 2003, there were more students in the biology class than in the psychology class.

27

If $x \leq 9$ and $x \geq 1$, which of the following statements are true?

   I. $-1 \leq x \leq 9$
   II. $1 \leq x \leq 9$
   III. $\left| x - 5 \right| \leq 4$

A) I only

B) II and III

C) I and II

D) I, II and III

28

Expression	Value
$A + B$	2.50
$A + C$	2.62
$B + C$	2.12

The table above displays the values of different expressions. What is the value of $A + B + C$?

A) 3.42

B) 3.62

C) 4.62

D) 7.24

CONTINUE

29

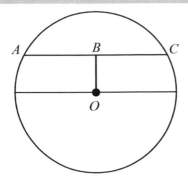

The figure above shows a circle with center O and a diameter of 10. If the chord $\overline{AC}$ is equal to 8, what is the value of $\overline{BO}$?

A) 1

B) 2

C) 3

D) 4

30

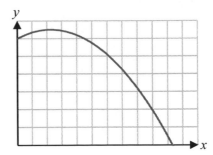

A class of physics students at Seaton high school tests how long it will take a ball to reach a height of ten meters when thrown off the top of a very tall building. Their result is graphed above. The class calculates that the ball follows the function $h(t) = -2t^2 + 10t + 100$, where h is the function of the height of the ball in meters, and t is the time in seconds. How long does it take, in seconds, for the ball to reach the ground?

A) 10

B) 11

C) 12

D) 13

DIRECTIONS

Questions **31-38** ask you to solve a problem and enter your answer in the grid provided on your answer sheet. When completing grid-in questions:

1. You are required to bubble in the circles for your answers. It is recommended, but not required, that you also write your answer in the boxes above the columns of circles. Points will be awarded based only on whether the circles are filled in correctly.

2. Fill in only one circle in a column.

3. You can start your answer in any column as long as you can fit in the whole answer.

4. For questions 31-38, no answers will be negative numbers.

5. **Mixed numbers,** such as $4\frac{2}{5}$, must be gridded as decimals or improper fractions, such as 4.4 or as 22/5. "42/5" will be read as "forty-two over five," not as "four and two-fifths."

6. If your answer is a **decimal** with more digits than will fit on the grid, you may round it or cut it off, but you must fill the entire grid.

7. If there are **multiple correct solutions** to a problem, all of them will be considered correct. Enter only **one** on the grid.

CONTINUE

31

What is the difference between $2x + 7$ and $2x - 1$?

32

$$3(x - 4) - 2(8 - x) = 4(x + 1)$$

What is the value of x in the equation above?

33

Four times b is equal to ten. If b is reduced by 20 percent, what is the value of three times b?

34

$$\sqrt{2x + 10} = x + 5$$

What is the product of the solutions for x in the equation above?

35

Career Preference	Number of Students
Healthcare	🎓 🎓 🎓 🎓 🎓
Education	🎓 🎓 🎓 ◀
Finance	🎓 🎓 🎓
Retail	🎓 🎓 ◀
Unsure	🎓

🎓 = 2 students

The chart above shows career preferences for students in a class. If two different students are randomly chosen, what is the probability they both want to enter finance?

36

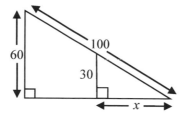

What is the value of *x* in the figure above?

Questions 37 and 38 refer to the following information.

A student is conducting a series of experiments to study the effects of a drug on mouse behavior. For the duration of the experiments, she keeps the mice in cages. One cage can house up to five mice. Each cage costs a flat rate of $1.25 per day to maintain.

37

For her first experiment, the student has six cages of mice at maximum capacity. If there are twice as many female mice as male mice, how many male mice does she have?

38

The animal supplies company offers the student a deal that will reduce the cost of maintaining each cage by half. Taking this opportunity, the student decides to conduct a multi-day experiment. If she wants to test 102 mice and has a budget of 225 dollars for cage maintenance, what is the maximum number of days she can conduct her experiment? (Round your answer to the nearest day.)

STOP

If you complete this section before the end of your allotted time, check your work on this section only. Do NOT use the time to work on another section.

Essay

Essay (Optional)

50 MINUTES

Turn to the lined pages of your answer sheet to write your essay.

DIRECTIONS

This essay is optional. It is a chance for you to demonstrate how well you can understand and analyze a written passage. Your essay should show that you have carefully read the passage and should be a concisely written analysis that is both logical and clear.

You must write your entire essay on the lines in your answer booklet. No additional paper will be provided aside from the Planning Page inside your answer booklet. You will be able to write your entire essay in the space provided if you make use of every line, keep tight margins, and write at a suitable size. Don't forget to keep your handwriting legible for the readers evaluating your essay.

You will have 50 minutes to read the passage in this booklet and to write an essay in response to the prompt provided at the end of the passage.

REMINDERS

- What you write in this booklet will not be evaluated. Write your essay in the answer booklet only.
- Essays that are off-topic will not be evaluated.

As you read the following passage, consider Theresa Brown uses

- evidence, like examples or facts, to support her arguments.
- logical reasoning to develop her ideas and to connect her claims to her evidence.
- stylistic or persuasive techniques, such as the choice of particular words or appeals to her readers' emotions, to give power to the ideas put forth.

Adapted from Theresa Brown, "Hospitals Aren't Hotels," © 2012 by the New York Times Company. Originally published March 14, 2012.

1   "You should never do this procedure without pain medicine," the senior surgeon told a resident. "This is one of the most painful things we do."

2   She wasn't scolding, just firm, and she was telling the truth. The patient needed pleurodesis, a treatment that involves abrading the lining of the lungs in an attempt to stop fluid from collecting there.

3   I have watched patients go through pleurodesis, and even with pain medication, they suffer. We injure them in this controlled, short-term way to prevent long-term recurrence of a much more serious problem: fluid around the lungs makes it very hard to breathe.

4   A lot of what we do in medicine, and especially in modern hospital care, adheres to this same formulation. We hurt people because it's the only way we know to make them better. This is the nature of our work, which is why the growing focus on measuring "patient satisfaction" as a way to judge the quality of a hospital's care is worrisomely off the mark.

5   For several years now, hospitals around the country have been independently collecting data in different categories of patient satisfaction. More recently, the Centers for Medicare and Medicaid Services developed the Hospital Consumer Assessment of Healthcare Providers and Systems survey and announced that by October 2012, Medicare reimbursements and bonuses were going to be linked in part to scores on the survey.

6   The survey evaluates behaviors that are integral to high-quality care: How good was the communication in the hospital? Were patients educated about all new medications? On discharge, were the instructions the patient received clear?

7   These are important questions. But implied in the proposal is a troubling misapprehension of how unpleasant a lot of actual health care is. The survey measures the "patient experience of care" to generate information important to "consumers." Put colloquially, it evaluates hospital patients' level of satisfaction.

8   The problem with this metric is that a lot of hospital care is, like pleurodesis, invasive, painful and even dehumanizing. Surgery leaves incisional pain as well as internal hurts from the removal of a gallbladder or tumor, or the repair of a broken bone. Chemotherapy weakens the immune system. We might like to say it shouldn't be, but physical pain, and its concomitant emotional suffering, tend to be inseparable from standard care.

9   What's more, recent research suggests that judging care in terms of desirable customer experiences could be expensive and may even be dangerous. A new paper by Joshua Fenton, an assistant professor at the University of California, Davis, and colleagues found that higher satisfaction scores correlated with greater use of hospital services (driving up costs), but also with increased mortality.

10   The paper examined patient satisfaction only with physicians, rather than hospitals, and the link between satisfaction and death is obviously uncertain. Still, the results suggest that focusing on what patients want—a certain test, a specific drug—may mean they get less of what they actually need.

11   In other words, evaluating hospital care in terms of its ability to offer positive experiences could easily put pressure on the system to do things it can't, at the expense of what it should.

12   To evaluate the patient experience in a way that can be meaningfully translated to the public, we need to ask deeper questions, about whether our procedures accomplished what they were supposed to and whether patients did get better despite the suffering imposed by our care.

13   Hospitals are not hotels, and although hospital patients may in some ways be informed consumers, they're predominantly sick, needy people, depending on us, the nurses and doctors, to get them through a very tough physical time. They do not come to us for vacation, but because they need the specialized, often painful help that only we can provide. Sadly, sometimes we cannot give them the kind of help they need.

14   If the Centers for Medicare and Medicaid Services is to evaluate the patient experience and link the results to reimbursement, it needs to incorporate questions that address the complete and expected hospital experience. It's fair and even valuable to compare hospitals on the basis of how well they maintain standards of patient engagement. But a survey focused on "satisfaction" elides the true nature of the work that hospitals do. In order to heal, we must first hurt.

Write an essay in which you explain how Theresa Brown builds an argument to persuade her audience that patient satisfaction should not be a major factor in evaluating hospital quality. In your essay, analyze how Brown uses one or more of the features listed in the directions above (or features of your own choice) to strengthen the logic and persuasiveness of her argument. Be sure that your analysis focuses on the most relevant features of the passage.

Your essay should not explain whether you agree with Brown's claims, but rather explain how Brown builds an argument to persuade her audience.

PRACTICE TEST 3

SAT

Directions

- Work on just one section at a time.

- If you complete a section before the end of your allotted time, use the extra minutes to check your work on that section only. Do NOT use the time to work on another section.

Using Your Test Booklet

- No credit will be given for anything written in the test booklet. You may use the test booklet for scratch paper.

- You are not allowed to continue answering questions in a section after the allotted time has run out. This includes marking answers on your answer sheet that you previously noted in your test booklet.

- You are not allowed to fold pages, take pages out of the test booklet, or take any pages home.

Answering Questions

- Each answer must be marked in the corresponding row on the answer sheet.

- Each bubble must be filled in completely and darkly within the lines.

  Correct ●   Incorrect ◯ ⊗ ⦸ ◕ ✸ ◯ ⬒ ◉

- Be careful to bubble in the correct part of the answer sheet.

- Extra marks on your answer sheet may be marked as incorrect answers and lower your score.

- Make sure you use a No. 2 pencil.

Scoring

- You will receive one point for each correct answer.

- Incorrect answers will NOT result in points deducted. Even if you are unsure about an answer, you should make a guess.

**DO NOT BEGIN THIS TEST
UNTIL YOUR PROCTOR TELLS YOU TO DO SO**

Download printable answer sheets, answer keys, and Excel scoring sheets from:

ivyglobal.com/study

Section 1

	A B C D		A B C D		A B C D		A B C D		A B C D
1	○ ○ ○ ○	12	○ ○ ○ ○	23	○ ○ ○ ○	34	○ ○ ○ ○	45	○ ○ ○ ○
2	○ ○ ○ ○	13	○ ○ ○ ○	24	○ ○ ○ ○	35	○ ○ ○ ○	46	○ ○ ○ ○
3	○ ○ ○ ○	14	○ ○ ○ ○	25	○ ○ ○ ○	36	○ ○ ○ ○	47	○ ○ ○ ○
4	○ ○ ○ ○	15	○ ○ ○ ○	26	○ ○ ○ ○	37	○ ○ ○ ○	48	○ ○ ○ ○
5	○ ○ ○ ○	16	○ ○ ○ ○	27	○ ○ ○ ○	38	○ ○ ○ ○	49	○ ○ ○ ○
6	○ ○ ○ ○	17	○ ○ ○ ○	28	○ ○ ○ ○	39	○ ○ ○ ○	50	○ ○ ○ ○
7	○ ○ ○ ○	18	○ ○ ○ ○	29	○ ○ ○ ○	40	○ ○ ○ ○	51	○ ○ ○ ○
8	○ ○ ○ ○	19	○ ○ ○ ○	30	○ ○ ○ ○	41	○ ○ ○ ○	52	○ ○ ○ ○
9	○ ○ ○ ○	20	○ ○ ○ ○	31	○ ○ ○ ○	42	○ ○ ○ ○		
10	○ ○ ○ ○	21	○ ○ ○ ○	32	○ ○ ○ ○	43	○ ○ ○ ○		
11	○ ○ ○ ○	22	○ ○ ○ ○	33	○ ○ ○ ○	44	○ ○ ○ ○		

Section 2

	A B C D		A B C D		A B C D		A B C D		A B C D
1	○ ○ ○ ○	10	○ ○ ○ ○	19	○ ○ ○ ○	28	○ ○ ○ ○	37	○ ○ ○ ○
2	○ ○ ○ ○	11	○ ○ ○ ○	20	○ ○ ○ ○	29	○ ○ ○ ○	38	○ ○ ○ ○
3	○ ○ ○ ○	12	○ ○ ○ ○	21	○ ○ ○ ○	30	○ ○ ○ ○	39	○ ○ ○ ○
4	○ ○ ○ ○	13	○ ○ ○ ○	22	○ ○ ○ ○	31	○ ○ ○ ○	40	○ ○ ○ ○
5	○ ○ ○ ○	14	○ ○ ○ ○	23	○ ○ ○ ○	32	○ ○ ○ ○	41	○ ○ ○ ○
6	○ ○ ○ ○	15	○ ○ ○ ○	24	○ ○ ○ ○	33	○ ○ ○ ○	42	○ ○ ○ ○
7	○ ○ ○ ○	16	○ ○ ○ ○	25	○ ○ ○ ○	34	○ ○ ○ ○	43	○ ○ ○ ○
8	○ ○ ○ ○	17	○ ○ ○ ○	26	○ ○ ○ ○	35	○ ○ ○ ○	44	○ ○ ○ ○
9	○ ○ ○ ○	18	○ ○ ○ ○	27	○ ○ ○ ○	36	○ ○ ○ ○		

Section 3 (No calculator)

1. A B C D 4. A B C D 7. A B C D 10. A B C D 13. A B C D

2. A B C D 5. A B C D 8. A B C D 11. A B C D 14. A B C D

3. A B C D 6. A B C D 9. A B C D 12. A B C D 15. A B C D

Only answers that are gridded will be scored. You will not receive credit for anything written in the boxes.

16. 17. 18. 19. 20.

(gridded response grids for 16–20, digits 0–9 with / and . options)

Section 4 (Calculator)

1. A B C D 7. A B C D 13. A B C D 19. A B C D 25. A B C D

2. A B C D 8. A B C D 14. A B C D 20. A B C D 26. A B C D

3. A B C D 9. A B C D 15. A B C D 21. A B C D 27. A B C D

4. A B C D 10. A B C D 16. A B C D 22. A B C D 28. A B C D

5. A B C D 11. A B C D 17. A B C D 23. A B C D 29. A B C D

6. A B C D 12. A B C D 18. A B C D 24. A B C D 30. A B C D

Only answers that are gridded will be scored. You will not receive credit for anything written in the boxes.

31 32 33 34 35

Only answers that are gridded will be scored. You will not receive credit for anything written in the boxes.

36 37 38

Important: Use a No. 2 pencil. Write inside the borders.

You may use the space below to plan your essay, but be sure to write your essay on the lined pages. Work on this page will not be scored.

Use this space to plan your essay.

START YOUR ESSAY HERE.

Continue on the next page.

Continue on the next page.

_____

_____

_____

_____

_____

_____

_____

_____

_____

_____

_____

_____

_____

_____

_____

_____

_____

_____

_____

_____

_____

_____

_____

_____

_____

_____

_____

_____

Continue on the next page.

STOP.

Section 1

Reading Test

65 MINUTES, 52 QUESTIONS

Turn to Section 1 of your answer sheet to answer the questions in this section.

DIRECTIONS

Every passage or paired set of passages is accompanied by a number of questions. Read the passage or paired set of passages, then use what is said or implied in what you read and in any given graphics to choose the best answer to each question.

Questions 1-10 are based on the following passage.

This passage is adapted from Alice Dunbar-Nelson, "Titee," originally published in 1895.

It was cold that day; the great sharp north wind swept out Elysian Fields Street in blasts that made men shiver, and bent everything in its track. The
Line skies hung lowering and gloomy; the usually quiet
5 street was more than deserted, it was dismal.

Titee leaned against one of the brown freight cars for protection against the shrill norther, and warmed his little chapped hands at a blaze of chips and dry grass. "Maybe it'll snow," he muttered, casting a
10 glance at the sky that would have done credit to a practiced seaman. "Then won't I have fun! Ugh, but the wind blows!"

It was Saturday, or Titee would have been in school—the big yellow school on Marigny Street,
15 where he went every day when its bell boomed nine o'clock. Went with a run and a joyous whoop, presumably to imbibe knowledge, ostensibly to make his teacher's life a burden.

Idle, lazy, dirty, troublesome boy, she called him,
20 to herself, as day by day wore on, and Titee improved not, but let his whole class pass him on its way to a higher grade. A practical joke he relished infinitely more than a practical problem, and a good game at pin-sticking was far more entertaining than

25 a language lesson. Moreover, he was always hungry, and would eat in school before the half-past ten intermission, thereby losing much good play-time for his voracious appetite.

But there was nothing in natural history that Titee
30 didn't know. He could dissect a butterfly or a mosquito-hawk and describe their parts as accurately as a spectacled student with a scalpel and microscope could talk about a cadaver. The entire Third District, with its swamps and canals and
35 commons and railroad sections, and its wondrous, crooked, tortuous streets was as an open book to Titee. He knew just exactly when it was time for crawfish to be plentiful down in the Claiborne and Marigny canals; just when a poor, breadless fellow
40 might get a job in the big bone-yard and fertilizing factory out on the railroad track. All these things, and more, could Titee tell of.

Titee shivered as the wind swept round the freight cars. There isn't much warmth in a bit of a
45 jersey coat.

"Wish 'twas summer," he murmured, casting another sailor's glance at the sky. "Don't believe I like snow, it's too wet and cold." And, with a last parting caress at the little fire he had built for a
50 minute's warmth, he plunged his hands in his pockets, shut his teeth, and started manfully on his mission out the railroad track towards the swamps.

CONTINUE

It was late when Titee came home, to such a home as it was, and he had but illy performed his
55 errand, so his mother sent him to bed supperless. Long walks in the teeth of a biting wind create a keen appetite. But if Titee cried himself to sleep that night, he was up bright and early next morning, and had been to early mass, devoutly kneeling on the
60 cold floor, blowing his fingers to keep them warm, and was home almost before the rest of the family was awake.

There was evidently some great matter of business in this young man's mind, for he scarcely
65 ate his breakfast, and had left the table, eagerly cramming the remainder of his meal in his pockets.

"I wonder what he's up to now?" mused his mother as she watched his little form sturdily trudging the track in the face of the wind, his head,
70 with the rimless cap thrust close on the shock of black hair, bent low, his hands thrust deep in the bulging pockets.

"A new snake, perhaps," ventured the father; "he's a strange child."
75 But the next day Titee was late for school. It was something unusual, for he was always the first on hand to fix some plan or mechanism to make the teacher miserable. She looked reprovingly at him this morning, when he came in during the arithmetic
80 class, his hair all wind-blown, cheeks rosy from a hard fight with the sharp blasts. But he made up for his tardiness by his extreme goodness all day; just think, Titee didn't even eat in school. A something unparalleled in the entire history of his school-life.

1

Which of the following best describes the structure of the passage as a whole?

A) A teacher's philosophy is outlined, and her students are briefly named.

B) A character is introduced, and hints are given that he is doing something unusual.

C) A family's history is recounted, and speculations about the youngest member are made.

D) A child is described, and his school routine is outlined in some detail.

2

What main effect does the description of the setting in lines 1-5 have on the mood of the passage?

A) It creates a cheerful mood, emphasizing the invigorating briskness of the wind.

B) It creates a frightful mood, implying that something sinister is lurking nearby.

C) It creates an ominous mood, highlighting the harshness of the surroundings.

D) It creates a tragic mood, focusing on the hardships faced by members of the neighborhood.

3

As used in line 2, "blasts" most nearly means

A) gusts.

B) explosions.

C) wails.

D) shockwaves.

CONTINUE

4

Which best summarizes lines 19-28?

A) Titee works very hard in school but struggles to make good grades.

B) Titee's teacher wishes she had chosen some other profession instead.

C) Titee does well in science but has difficulty in math class.

D) Titee's teacher is frustrated with his behavior in the classroom.

5

The primary purpose of lines 29-42 is to

A) imply that Titee is on his way to becoming a real troublemaker.

B) show that although Titee has problems at school, his teacher cares about him.

C) demonstrate how concerned Titee's parents are for his well-being.

D) suggest that while Titee is not a great student, he is still intelligent.

6

It can be reasonably inferred that one cause of Titee's bad mood is

A) the weather.

B) his teacher.

C) his parents.

D) the neighborhood.

7

Which choice provides the best evidence for the answer to the previous question?

A) Lines 13-16 ("It … nine o'clock")

B) Lines 46-47 ("Wish … the sky")

C) Lines 73-74 ("A new … child")

D) Lines 78-81 ("She looked … blasts")

8

Titee's parents assume he's up to something they don't know about because he

A) speaks little during breakfast.

B) is late for school.

C) forgets his books at home.

D) doesn't eat much that morning.

9

Which choice provides the best evidence for the answer to the previous question?

A) Lines 48-52 ("And … swamps")

B) Lines 53-55 ("It was … supperless")

C) Lines 63-66 ("There was … pockets")

D) Line 75 ("But the … school")

10

As used in line 77, "mechanism" most nearly means

A) machinery.

B) operation.

C) device.

D) channel.

CONTINUE

Questions 11-21 are based on the following passages.

The first passage is adapted from Carl Zimmer, "Reverse Engineering Birds' Beaks Into Dinosaur Bones." © 2015 by The New York Times Company. The second passage is adapted from John Noble Wilford, "Fossil with Signs of Feathers is Cited as Bird-Dinosaur Link." © 2001 by The New York Times Company.

Passage 1

Birds evolved from dinosaurs 150 million years ago. Some researchers are now trying to pinpoint the genetic changes that turned ground-running
Line dinosaurs into modern birds through experiments on
5 chicken embryos. One group, led by Bhart-Anjan Bhullar of Yale University and Arhat Abzhanov of Harvard University, reports that they have found a way to turn the beaks of chicken embryos back into dinosaur-like snouts.

10 The beak evolved fairly late in bird evolution. It originated from a pair of small, separate plates of bone sitting at the front of the upper jaw, called premaxillae. In the evolution of early birds, the premaxillae stretched out and fused together to form
15 a strong, lightweight beak.

Dr. Bhullar and Dr. Abzhanov set out to find some of the genetic changes that turned the dinosaur premaxillae into a beak. To find clues, they looked at earlier experiments on chicken embryos. The
20 scientists were struck by the fact that even before the embryo has a developed, recognizable face, a large patch of cells in the middle of what will become the bird's face makes a protein called Fgf8. Later, the region produces different proteins, called Lef1.

25 Like the embryos of chickens, those of emus produce the proteins in a single patch of cells, the scientists learned. But in animals other than birds— such as turtles, lizards and crocodiles—the proteins are usually made in a pair of small cell patches.

30 Was it possible, the scientists wondered, that a key step in the evolution of beaks was a shift from small protein-producing patches to a single large one? That change might have allowed birds to develop big, fused premaxillae—the precursors of

35 beaks. If the hypothesis was correct, the researchers figured, they might be able to turn back the clock on evolution. If they caused a chicken embryo to use Fgf8 and Lef1 the way other animals do, it should turn out to be a bird without a beak.

40 To reverse evolution, the scientists wedged a microscopic bead into the middle of what would become the faces of chicken embryos. The bead released chemicals into the surrounding tissue that interfere with Fgf8 and Lef1. The chicken embryos
45 failed to develop beaks and instead gained a pair of rounded, unfused bones—more like what you might have found on a dinosaur's head.

Dr. Ralph S. Marcucio, a developmental biologist, noted that the scientists used chemicals to
50 block Fgf8 and Lef1 proteins that have toxic side effects and can kill cells. The altered anatomy of the chicken skulls might not be an example of reverse evolution, he said, just dying tissue.

Passage 2

Paleontologists have discovered in China a
55 dinosaur fossil with what are reported to be clear traces of feathers from head to tail, the most persuasive evidence so far, scientists say, that feathers predated the origin of birds and that modern birds are descendants of dinosaurs. Other dinosaur
60 remains with what appear to be featherlike traces have been unearthed in recent years, but nothing as complete as this specimen, paleontologists said. Etched in the rock like a filigree decoration surrounding the skeleton are imprints of where the
65 down and feathers appear to have been.

The 130-million-year-old fossils were found a year ago by farmers in Liaoning Province in northeastern China. After an analysis by Chinese and American researchers, the fossil animal was
70 identified as a dromaeosaur, a small, fast-running dinosaur related to velociraptor. The findings are described in the journal *Nature* by the discovery team led by Dr. Ji Qiang, director of the Chinese Academy of Geological Sciences in Beijing, and Dr.
75 Mark A. Norell, chairman of paleontology at the

CONTINUE

American Museum of Natural History in
Manhattan. "This is the specimen we've been
waiting for," Dr. Norell said in a statement. "It
makes it indisputable that a body covering similar
80   to feathers was present in nonavian dinosaurs."
        The specimen's forelimbs were too short to
have supported wings, Dr. Norell said in an
interview, and so it was flightless. But some of
the bone structure—notably the furcula, or
85   wishbone, and the three forward-pointing toes—
bears similarities to that of birds. Other recent
discoveries of birdlike dinosaurs and dinosaurlike
birds have encouraged support for the theory of a
dinosaur-bird ancestral link.
90   Not that these particular dinosaurs were
ancestors of birds—but they may be descendants
of the ancestors. Dr. Norell said the feathered
fossil showed that there was "a more general
distribution of feathers than in birds alone."
95   Studying theropods that lived later than the first
birds, he explained, should provide insights into
bird evolution, just as related "chimps and gorillas
and lemurs help us understand human evolution."

11

Which best summarizes lines 10-15?

A) The beak developed into the premaxillae late
   in the evolution of birds.

B) The beak originated from the upper jaw bone
   stretching out and separating.

C) The beak evolved from a couple of small
   plates of bones that fused together.

D) The beak formed from lightweight tissue
   drawn from the mouth and throat of birds.

12

As used in line 20, "struck" most nearly means

A) thumped.

B) ignited.

C) afflicted.

D) impressed.

13

Based on Passage 1, how did Dr. Bhullar and Dr.
Abzhanov try to reverse evolution in the chicken
embryos?

A) They implanted a microscopic bead that would
   increase production of Fgf8 and Lef1.

B) They surgically removed the rounded, unfused
   bones of the developing embryos.

C) They spliced reptilian genes into the genes of
   what would become the faces of chicken
   embryos.

D) They used chemicals to inhibit Fgf8 and Lef1
   in chicken embryos and thus disrupt beak
   development.

14

In Passage 1, Dr. Ralph S. Marcucio's attitude
towards Dr. Bhullar and Dr. Abzhanov's research
is best described as

A) cautious.

B) encouraging.

C) envious.

D) sincere.

CONTINUE

15

Which choice provides the best evidence for the answer to the previous question?

A) Lines 16-18 ("Dr. Bhullar … beak")

B) Lines 30-33 ("Was it … one")

C) Lines 44-47 ("The chicken … head")

D) Lines 51-53 ("The altered … tissue")

16

As used in line 55, "clear" most nearly means

A) transparent.

B) vibrant.

C) unblemished.

D) unambiguous.

17

The primary purpose of lines 59-62 is to

A) explain why the finding described in the passage is so significant.

B) offer a counterpoint to the evidence described in the rest of the passage.

C) downplay the discovery made by the researchers.

D) set forth the thesis that will be defended in the remainder of the passage.

18

Passage 2 indicates that birds

A) are direct descendants of dromaeosaurs.

B) coexisted with dromaeosaurs for thousands of years.

C) share some common ancestors with dromaeosaurs.

D) have no relationship to dromaeosaurs.

19

Which choice provides the best evidence for the answer to the previous question?

A) Lines 66-68 ("The … China")

B) Lines 78-80 ("It makes … dinosaurs")

C) Lines 81-83 ("The specimen's … flightless")

D) Lines 90-92 ("Not that … ancestors")

20

Passage 2 differs from Passage 1 in that only Passage 1 describes

A) evidence from experiments on bird development.

B) the relationship between dinosaurs and birds.

C) a discovery that may link dinosaurs with birds.

D) the process of evolution as it relates to birds.

21

One difference between the findings described in the two passages is that, unlike the discovery described in Passage 2, the discovery in Passage 1

A) focused on genetic changes that occurred in the evolution of birds.

B) received widespread acceptance by the scientific community.

C) compared specific bone structures that differed in dinosaurs and birds.

D) suffered from controversy that ultimately tainted its findings.

CONTINUE

Questions 22-31 are based on the following passage.

This passage is adapted from "Recapturing America's Moral Vision," a speech given by Robert F. Kennedy at the University of Kansas in 1968.

There are millions living in the hidden places whose names and faces are completely unknown. But I have seen these other Americans. I have seen
Line children in Mississippi starving, their bodies so
5 crippled from hunger and their minds so destroyed for their whole lives that they will have no future. We haven't developed a policy so we can get enough food so that they can live, so that their lives are not destroyed. I don't think that's acceptable in
10 the United States of America, and I think we need a change.

I think we can do much, much better. And I run for the presidency because of that. I run for the presidency because I have seen proud men in the
15 hills of Appalachia, who wish only to work in dignity, but they cannot, for the mines are closed and their jobs are gone and no one—neither industry, nor labor, nor government—has cared enough to help. I think we here in this country, with the unselfish
20 spirit that exists in the United States of America, I think we can do better here also.

If we believe that we, as Americans, are bound together by a common concern for each other, then an urgent national priority is upon us. We must
25 begin to end the disgrace of this other America. And this is one of the great tasks of leadership for us, as individuals and citizens this year.

But even if we act to erase material poverty, there is another greater task: it is to confront the poverty
30 of satisfaction, purpose, and dignity that afflicts us all. Too much and for too long, we seemed to have surrendered personal excellence and community values in the mere accumulation of material things.

Our Gross National Product now is over 800
35 billion dollars a year. But that Gross National Product—if we judge the United States of America by that—that Gross National Product counts air pollution and cigarette advertising and ambulances to clear our highways of carnage. It counts special
40 locks for our doors and the jails for the people who break them. It counts the destruction of the redwoods and the loss of our natural wonder in chaotic sprawl. It counts napalm and it counts nuclear warheads and armored cars for the police to
45 fight the riots in our cities. It counts Whitman's rifle and Speck's knife and the television programs which glorify violence in order to sell toys to our children.

Yet the Gross National Product does not allow for the health of our children, the quality of their
50 education, or the joy of their play. It does not include the beauty of our poetry or the strength of our marriages, the intelligence of our public debate or the integrity of our public officials. It measures neither our wit nor our courage, neither our wisdom
55 nor our learning, neither our compassion nor our devotion to our country. It measures everything, in short, except that which makes life worthwhile. And it can tell us everything about America except why we are proud that we are Americans.

22

Kennedy's attitude toward the situation faced by "other Americans" mentioned in the passage is best described as

A) annoyed.

B) resigned.

C) outraged.

D) bemused.

23

Which choice provides the best evidence for the answer to the previous question?

A) Lines 1-2 ("There are … unknown")

B) Lines 9-11 ("I don't … change")

C) Lines 31-33 ("Too much … things")

D) Lines 53-56 ("It measures … country")

CONTINUE

24

The passage most strongly suggests that the Gross National Product

A) is essential to helping Americans escape from a life of poverty and disgrace.

B) measures economic but not personal or moral value.

C) must increase if Americans are to improve their environment, jails, and cities.

D) does not accurately represent the breakdown of industries in the American economy.

25

Which choice provides the best evidence for the answer to the previous question?

A) Lines 18-21 ("I think … also")

B) Lines 24-25 ("We must … America")

C) Lines 34-35 ("Our Gross … year")

D) Lines 56-57 ("It measures … worthwhile")

26

Based on the passage, which best describes the relationship between the "unselfish spirit" Kennedy describes and the problems he sees in the United States?

A) The unselfish spirit exhibited by Americans can be drawn upon to resolve many of the country's problems.

B) The unselfish spirit of the men of the Appalachia must be harnessed to help avoid further problems.

C) Americans can rely on the unselfish spirit of their government to solve any problems.

D) The unselfish spirit demonstrated by industry is the cause of the United States' problems.

27

As used in line 28, "erase" most nearly means

A) eliminate.

B) delete.

C) obliterate.

D) cancel.

28

Kennedy refers to "the poverty of satisfaction, purpose, and dignity" (line 29-30) primarily to

A) urge Americans to act quickly or face economic failure.

B) suggest that Americans face more than just economic challenges.

C) inspire Americans to be more ambitious in their economic goals.

D) warn Americans that unless they fix the economy, their communities will suffer.

29

The rhetorical effect of the repetition in lines 37-47 is to

A) emphasize the various negative portions of the economy that contribute to the Gross National Product.

B) show how many areas of the economy are included in the Gross National Product.

C) reveal how economic analysts must alter their calculation of the Gross National Product.

D) demonstrate the great diversity of the American economy, as seen in the Gross National Product.

CONTINUE

30

As used in line 48-49, "allow for" most nearly means

A) concede.

B) ponder.

C) grant.

D) include.

31

Kennedy states that the Gross National Product does not measure

A) air pollution and environmental destruction.

B) weapons needed to fight riots in cities.

C) the honesty of public servants.

D) advertising for cigarettes and violent toys.

Questions 32-41 are based on the following passage.

This passage is adapted from Scott Armstrong Elias, "First Americans lived on land bridge for thousands of years, genetics study suggests." © 2014 by Scott Armstrong Elias.

The theory that the Americas were populated by humans crossing a land bridge from Siberia to Alaska was first proposed as far back as 1590, and
Line has been generally accepted since the 1930s. But
5 genetic evidence shows there is no direct ancestral link between the people of ancient East Asia and modern Native Americans. A comparison of DNA from 600 modern Native Americans with ancient DNA recovered from a late Stone Age human
10 skeleton from Mal'ta in southern Siberia shows that Native Americans diverged genetically from their Asian ancestors around 25,000 years ago, just as the last ice age was reaching its peak.

Based on archaeological evidence, humans did
15 not survive the last ice age's peak in northeastern Siberia, and yet there is no evidence they had reached Alaska or the rest of the New World, either. There is evidence to suggest northeast Siberia was inhabited during a warm period about 30,000 years
20 ago, before the last ice age peaked. After this, however, the archaeological record goes silent and only returns 15,000 years ago, after the last ice age ended.

So where did the ancestors of the Native
25 Americans go for 15,000 years, after they split from the rest of their Asian relatives? As John Hoffecker, Dennis O'Rourke and I argue, in an article for *Science*, the answer seems to be that they lived on the Bering Land Bridge, the region between Siberia
30 and Alaska that was dry land when sea levels were lower, as much of the world's freshwater was locked up in ice, but which now lies underneath the waters of the Bering and Chukchi Seas. This theory has become increasingly supported by genetic evidence.
35 The Bering Land Bridge, also known as Central Beringia, is thought to have been up to 600 miles wide. Based on evidence from sediment cores drilled into the now-submerged landscape, it seems that

CONTINUE →

here and in some adjacent regions of Alaska and
40 Siberia, the landscape at the height of the last
glaciation 21,000 years ago was shrub tundra—as
found in Arctic Alaska today.

This shrub tundra would have supported elk,
perhaps some bighorn sheep, and small mammals.
45 But it had the one resource people needed most to
keep warm: wood. The wood and bark of dwarf
shrubs would have been used to start fires that
burned large mammal bones. And there is evidence
from archaeological sites that people burned bones
50 as fuel—the charred remains of leg bones have been
found in many ancient hearths. It is the heat from
these fires that kept these intrepid hunter-gatherers
alive through the bitter cold of Arctic winter nights.

The last ice age ended, and the land bridge began
55 to disappear beneath the sea, some 13,000 years ago.
Global sea levels rose as the vast continental ice
sheets melted, liberating billions of gallons of fresh
water. As the land bridge flooded, the entire
Beringian region grew more warm and moist, and
60 the shrub tundra vegetation spread rapidly, out-
competing the steppe-tundra plants that had
dominated the interior lowlands of Beringia.

While this spelled the end of the woolly
mammoths and other large grazing animals, it
65 probably also provided the impetus for human
migration. As retreating glaciers opened new routes
into the continent, humans travelled first into the
Alaskan interior and the Yukon, and ultimately
south out of the Arctic region and toward the
70 temperate regions of the Americas. The first
definitive archaeological evidence we have for the
presence of people beyond Beringia and interior
Alaska comes from this time, about 13,000 years
ago.
75   These people are called Paleoindians by
archaeologists. The genetic evidence records
mutations in mitochondrial DNA passed from
mother to offspring that are present in today's
Native Americans but not in the Mal'ta remains.
80 This indicates a population isolated from the
Siberian mainland for thousands of years, who are

the direct ancestors of nearly all of the Native
American tribes in both North and South America—
the original "first peoples."

Gene Flow in and Out of Beringia		
Time	West to East	East to West
25,000 years ago	Initial peopling of Beringia	
15,000 years ago	Swift peopling of the Americas	
10,000 years ago	Later arrival of hg D2	Back migration of C1a
<10,000 years ago	Spread of D2a	Back migration of A2a

*Note: D2, D2a, C1a, and A2a are all genetic lineages.

32

What is the author's main point about the ancestors
of Native Americans?

A) Contrary to previous theories, they are
unrelated to any populations in the East.

B) They are more closely related to modern
Native Americans than people from the
ancient Near East.

C) They survived on Beringia for thousands of
years before moving on to the Americas.

D) They crossed the Bering Land Bridge 25,000
years ago at the end of the last ice age.

33

Which choice provides the best evidence for the
answer to the previous question?

A) Lines 4-7 ("But genetic … Americans")

B) Lines 18-20 ("There is … peaked")

C) Lines 26-33 ("As John … Seas")

D) Lines 35-37 ("The Bering … wide")

CONTINUE

34

The author mentions the theory about the land bridge in lines 1-4 in order to

A) explain the theory that the rest of the passage supports.

B) establish the authority of the theory that the passage builds upon.

C) mention the theory that is challenged by evidence the passage will present.

D) ridicule the out-of-date theory that will be debunked in the rest of the article.

35

The author indicates which of the following about the Bering Land Bridge?

A) It was inhospitable to human life until about 600 years ago.

B) It allowed early humans to cross from Siberia to Beringia.

C) It used to be a rich, forested area before the end of the ice age.

D) It disappeared once temperatures and sea levels rose.

36

As used in line 43, "supported" most nearly means

A) braced.

B) held.

C) sustained.

D) reinforced.

37

According to the passage, the shrub tundra was hospitable to early humans mainly because it

A) featured a mild, temperate climate at the time.

B) had numerous large animals that humans could hunt.

C) contained wood, an essential resource.

D) was home to a large number of bones that could be used as fuel.

38

Which choice provides the best evidence for the answer to the previous question?

A) Lines 43-44 ("This shrub ... mammals")

B) Lines 45-46 ("But it ... wood")

C) Lines 48-51 ("And there ... hearths")

D) Lines 58-62 ("As the ... Beringia")

39

As used in line 66, "retreating" most nearly means

A) retiring.

B) disappearing.

C) recoiling.

D) falling.

CONTINUE

40

It can reasonably be inferred from the passage and table that

A) the people of Asia and the Americas have no genetic connection.

B) the flow of people through Beringia moved in both directions.

C) the land bridge on Beringia remained isolated for hundreds of years.

D) only recently did any genetic transfer occur between modern humans.

41

Information from the table best supports which of the following statements?

A) Humans spread rapidly through the Americas about 10-15,000 years ago.

B) Human populations moved from the Americas to Asia over the course of about 10,000 years.

C) The initial peopling of Beringia occurred about 2,500 years ago.

D) Migration of humans always flowed in one direction.

Questions 42-52 are based on the following passage.

This passage is adapted from Declan Perry, "Ravens Have Social Abilities Previously Only Seen in Humans." © 2015 by Declan Perry.

A new study shows that ravens are socially savvier than we give them credit for. They are able to work out the social dynamics of other raven *Line* groups, something that previously only humans had
5 shown the ability to do. Jorg Massen and his colleagues of the University of Vienna wanted to find out more about birds' social skills, so in their study, they looked at whether ravens were intelligent enough to understand relationships in their own
10 social groups, as well as if they could figure out social groups that they had never been a part of.

Ravens within a community squabble over their ranking in the group, as higher ranked ravens have better access to food and other resources. Males
15 always outrank females, and confrontations mostly occur between members of the same sex. These confrontations are initiated by high-ranking ravens, who square up to low-ranking birds and emit a specific call to assert their dominance. Normally, the
20 lower-ranking, or submissive, raven typically makes a specific call to recognize the high-ranking raven's social superiority. Through this process, the dominant raven ensures that its social position is maintained. But sometimes, the lower-ranking bird
25 does not respond in a submissive way to a dominance call, and instead responds with a dominance reversal call. These situations often result in confrontations, and can result in changes in the social structure of raven communities.
30 Massen and his team kept a group of captive ravens and made recordings of conflicts. These included normal conflicts (in which the lower-ranking bird responded submissively to a dominance call) and dominance reversal conflicts. The same
35 method was also used to capture the calls from a different group of ravens that were housed separately. Individual ravens were then taken from the group and isolated in a separate enclosure. The

CONTINUE

recordings of different calls were then played,
40 mimicking a situation in nature where a raven
overhears two other ravens in a confrontation.
Massen said, "We monitored their responses to these
calls to see if they reacted differently to normal
dominance calls and dominance reversals. We also
45 used the recordings taken from the foreign group, to
see if our ravens recognized the same behavior in
other communities."

When presented with a dominance reversal
recording taken from their own group, ravens
50 displayed behavior associated with stress, because
they expected a disturbance in the social order.
Ravens showed even higher levels of stress when
they were played a dominance reversal call from
members of the same sex. This makes sense,
55 because ranking disputes only occur between
members of the same sex. A confrontation between
two females, for example, would not have a big
effect on the social status of a male raven—but
would affect any females who were listening.
60 Female ravens in general were more stressed than
males when they were played dominance reversal
recordings. This may be because females are always
lower ranked than males, so changes in community
structure pose more risks to females at the bottom,
65 which have reduced access to food in the first place.

But perhaps the most impressive finding was that
ravens seemed to notice dominance reversals in a
foreign group of ravens, although they exhibited less
stress than when they heard such calls from their
70 own social community. To be sure that the ravens
weren't just recognizing that call because it was an
audibly different call, Massen played calls from a
different community, which weren't dominance
reversal calls, and saw that the captive ravens were
75 not stressed. Massen said: "This shows that ravens
are able to create a mental representation of
relationship dynamics from groups they have never
interacted with before. This ability has not even been
observed in monkeys yet."
80   However, there are limitations to the study. Alex
Thornton of the University of Exeter explained:

"The results in this study are no doubt exciting,
but it should be recognized that captive ravens
were used. Being kept in such close proximity,
85 with only each other, may have influenced the
ravens ability to judge each other's behavior."

In addition to showing that ravens have social
abilities that were previously only seen in
humans, these findings give a clue that raven
90 intelligence may have evolved along with the
development of social communities. "Being
intelligent helps the ravens play the politics of
their social group, and gain dominance," Massen
said.

Stress Response to In-group Stimuli

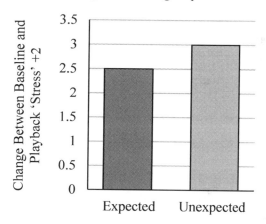

42

The passage primarily focuses on which of the
following?

A) The difficulty of studying natural populations
of ravens in artificial settings

B) The ability of ravens to understand
relationship dynamics within their own and
other social groups

C) The various methods that ravens use in their
battle for dominance within their own social
groups

D) The limitations of a new study on ravens that
fails to take into account the birds' social
natures

CONTINUE

43

Which choice provides the best evidence for the answer to the previous question?

A) Lines 37-38 ("Individual … enclosure")

B) Lines 44-47 ("We also … communities")

C) Lines 66-70 ("But perhaps … community")

D) Lines 82-84 ("The results … used")

44

According to the passage, a dominance reversal call is likely to be used by

A) a lower-ranking raven that decides to not respond submissively to a dominance call.

B) a high-ranking raven that wishes to challenge a lower-ranking raven.

C) a male high-ranking raven that is recognizing the highest-ranking female in a raven social group.

D) a female high-ranking raven that is recognizing the highest-ranked male in a raven social group.

45

Which choice provides the best evidence for the answer to the previous question?

A) Lines 14-16 ("Males always … sex")

B) Lines 19-22 ("Normally … superiority")

C) Lines 24-27 ("But sometimes … call")

D) Lines 30-31 ("Massen … conflicts")

46

As used in line 32, "normal" most nearly means

A) familiar.

B) mainstream.

C) average.

D) typical.

47

In lines 62-65, what is the most likely reason that the author describes why females may be more at risk during changes in community structure?

A) To attempt to explain one of the results seen in the study

B) To suggest a further potential area for research in the field

C) To summarize the ultimate conclusion that the study reached

D) To provide an alternate explanation of a controversial finding

48

As used in line 66, "impressive" most nearly means

A) poignant.

B) significant.

C) rousing.

D) inspirational.

CONTINUE

49

According to the passage, ravens generally experienced more stress when they heard dominance reversals from

A) other communities.

B) their own communities.

C) a juvenile raven.

D) a low-ranking female.

50

It can be most reasonably inferred that Alex Thornton

A) believes the results of the study to be erroneous.

B) feels that the study suffered from a lack of funding.

C) plans to redo the described experiment himself with a larger sample size.

D) is not convinced of the wider applicability of the study's results.

51

The passage indicates that ravens' social development evolved in parallel with their

A) intelligence.

B) politics.

C) dominant personalities.

D) captivity.

52

According to the graph, which statement is true about ravens' response to playback that violated their expectancy of rank relations?

A) Ravens are 50% more likely to express surprise in these situations versus when listening to playback conforming to their expectations of rank relations.

B) Female ravens are 0.5% more likely than male ravens to experience a stress response.

C) Ravens show a greater stress response in these situations versus when listening to playback conforming to their expectations of rank relations.

D) About 60% of ravens exhibit a stress response, while about 40% of ravens do not.

STOP

If you complete this section before the end of your allotted time, check your work on this section only. Do NOT use the time to work on another section.

Section 2

Writing and Language Test

35 MINUTES, 44 QUESTIONS

Turn to Section 2 of your answer sheet to answer the questions in this section.

DIRECTIONS

Every passage comes with a set of questions. Some questions will ask you to consider how the writer might revise the passage to improve the expression of ideas. Other questions will ask you to consider correcting potential errors in sentence structure, usage, or punctuation. There may be one or more graphics that you will need to consult as you revise and edit the passage.

Some questions will refer to a portion of the passage that has been underlined. Other questions will refer to a particular spot in a passage or ask that you consider the passage in full.

After you read the passage, select the answers to questions that most effectively improve the passage's writing quality or that adjust the passage to follow the conventions of standard written English. Many questions give you the option to select "NO CHANGE." Select that option in cases where you think the relevant part of the passage should remain as it currently is.

Questions 1-11 are based on the following passage.

Veterinarians

Many young animal lovers dream of becoming **1** a veterinarian. Those who pursue this profession, which involves diagnosing and treating animal injuries and illnesses, may enter a field that offers intellectual stimulation and opportunities to do good.

1

A) NO CHANGE

B) veterinarian

C) veterinarians

D) the veterinarian

CONTINUE

[1] Veterinarians are medical professionals, but their work differs in many ways from that of doctors who treat human patients. [2] Perhaps most obviously, veterinarians' animal patients, unlike **2** human's, are unable to describe their symptoms. [3] **3** As a result, veterinarians must learn how to identify illnesses based solely on objective medical signs. [4] They rely on careful observations of their patients' bodies and behaviors in order to determine what is wrong. [5] However, some parrots are actually capable of limited speech. [6] Moreover, veterinarians must find ways to deliver treatment to animals that cannot understand why they are being subjected to uncomfortable or frightening procedures. [7] Thus, veterinarians must sometimes deal with animals that actively resist treatment. **4**

2

A) NO CHANGE
B) humans'
C) those of humans
D) humans

3

A) NO CHANGE
B) Additionally,
C) Regardless,
D) It would seem that

4

Which of the following changes would most improve the focus of the passage?

A) Move sentence 5 so that it follows sentence 2.
B) Move sentence 7 so that it follows sentence 4.
C) DELETE sentence 3.
D) DELETE sentence 5.

CONTINUE

Veterinarians work in many different settings. Most people are familiar with small animal veterinarians, who tend to focus on treating animals that people keep as pets, such as cats, dogs, rabbits, and hamsters. Some small animal veterinarians treat many different species of **5** animals. Whereas others work in practices that are, for example, canine-only or feline-only. Veterinarians that focus on treating pets, or "companion animals," are the most common, **6** making up half of all veterinarians. However, there are also a number of veterinarians who work as large animal veterinarians. These specialists might work on farms to keep livestock healthy, treat injured racehorses, or even **7** reassure the health of large zoo animals.

Private Practice Veterinarians by Focus

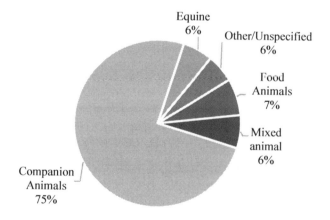

5

A) NO CHANGE

B) animals, whereas others

C) animals: whereas others

D) animals. Whereas, others

6

Based on the graph, which of the following changes would complete the sentence with the most accurate information?

A) NO CHANGE

B) making up 6% of all veterinarians

C) making up 75% of the animals that veterinarians treat

D) making up 75% of private practice veterinarians

7

A) NO CHANGE

B) ensure

C) assuage

D) advocate

CONTINUE

[8] Aspiring veterinarians generally begin their higher education by pursuing a bachelor's degree with a strong emphasis on [9] biology, chemistry, anatomy, and other sciences. Students hoping to enter this profession in the United States also need a four-year doctoral degree in veterinary medicine. The process of applying to veterinary college is very competitive, so [10] you need to work hard in school to build a strong application. In veterinary college, students gain both classroom education and practical experience working with qualified veterinarians.

After graduation, veterinarians must meet some additional licensure requirements. Generally, that means successfully completing an additional examination, and committing to continuing education requirements in order to maintain licensure.

For those compassionate, hard-working individuals with the tenacity to complete the [11] ominous process of becoming a licensed veterinarian, the career offers the rewarding opportunity to promote the health and well-being of animals and provide peace of mind to their owners.

8

Which choice most effectively conveys the main topic of this paragraph?

A) Veterinary medicine is an exceptionally difficult field to enter.

B) Most students with the skills to become veterinarians could also enter other medical professions.

C) Aspiring veterinarians must complete a rigorous course of education and meet other qualifications before beginning their career.

D) Generally speaking, veterinarians must choose to specialize in one of these subfields early in their education.

9

A) NO CHANGE

B) biology, chemistry and anatomy

C) biology; chemistry; anatomy

D) biology: chemistry, and anatomy

10

A) NO CHANGE

B) I think it's important to

C) they probably ought to

D) aspiring veterinarians should

11

A) NO CHANGE

B) daunting

C) forbidding

D) disconcerting

CONTINUE →

Questions 12-22 are based on the following passage.

Impressionism: A General Picture

The mid-1800s were a time of upheaval in France. The country's new emperor, Napoleon III, took power in 1852, launched a massive reconstruction of Paris, and went to war with other European nations. This time of great political and social change also saw an artistic [12] revolution. The Impressionist movement arose to challenge the conventions of art.

Before the arrival of the Impressionists, the conventions of visual art in France were determined by the Académie des Beaux-Arts. The Académie was an institution that set strict rules for the subject matter and techniques that were deemed appropriate in painting. For most of the 19th century, [13] it held that paintings should generally appear realistic, with muted colors and carefully blended brush strokes. [14] As a result, the Académie insisted that paintings generally be about Greek or Roman myths, Biblical tales, or historical allegories. These rules stifled artistic innovation and prevented change.

12

Which choice most effectively combines the sentences at the underlined portion?

A) revolution, and in addition the Impressionist movement also

B) revolution, such as the Impressionist movement that

C) revolution, as the Impressionist movement

D) revolution, but the Impressionist movement

13

A) NO CHANGE

B) he

C) one

D) they

14

A) NO CHANGE

B) Moreover,

C) Suddenly,

D) Even so,

CONTINUE

[1] In the 1860s and 1870s, the Impressionists systematically broke these rules **15** yet produced bold new forms in painting. [2] For instance, Claude Monet, a foundational figure in the movement, created an atmospheric landscape painting depicting a sunrise over the harbor of the city of Le Havre, which he named *Impression, Sunrise*, and from which the movement derived its name. [3] They preferred to paint subjects well outside the established bounds of history and mythology. [4] Many Impressionist paintings sought instead to **16** apprehend the beauty of fleeting moments of everyday life. [5] Camille Pissarro, another well-known Impressionist, produced a number of paintings showing peasants working in fields and city-dwellers walking through streets. [6] Such mundane subject matter would have been unthinkable even a few decades prior. **17**

15

A) NO CHANGE
B) but
C) or
D) and

16

A) NO CHANGE
B) imprison
C) grasp
D) capture

17

To make this paragraph most logical, sentence 2 should be placed

A) where it is now.
B) after sentence 3.
C) after sentence 4.
D) after sentence 6.

CONTINUE

The Impressionists developed new techniques of painting in order to accomplish their goals. They often applied wet paint onto other wet paint in thick layers with short strokes. **18** In my opinion, that created a distinctive style with vivid colors and blurred forms. Impressionist paintings thus did not look realistic on close inspection, but could often **19** invoke the emotional resonance of a scene to great effect. For example, Monet's *Haystacks* series depicts a set of haystacks at different times of day and through changing **20** seasons, his repetition of the same subject matter highlights how effectively his technique could capture changing light and color.

18

A) NO CHANGE

B) Thus, applying wet paint to other wet paint

C) This method

D) That handy trick

19

A) NO CHANGE

B) evoke

C) provoke

D) revoke

20

A) NO CHANGE

B) seasons, his,

C) seasons; his

D) seasons his

[21] Many works by post-Impressionist painters, such as Vincent van Gogh and Georges Seurat, are clearly inspired by Impressionist techniques. Such famous canvasses as van Gogh's *Starry Night* and Seurat's *Sunday Afternoon on the Island of La Grande Jatte* clearly build on [22] their unique methods of painting to capture scenes in imaginative ways and captivate viewers.

21

Which choice, inserted here, would most effectively introduce the main topic of the paragraph?

A) The Impressionist revolution would influence art for years afterward.

B) Contemporary rivals of the Impressionists rejected some aspects of their style.

C) Few critics appreciated the Impressionists.

D) There are still Impressionists painters today.

22

A) NO CHANGE

B) his

C) the Impressionists'

D) the post-Impressionists'

CONTINUE

Questions 23-33 are based on the following passage.

Seeing with Sound

All animals have senses that are finely tuned for dealing with the challenges of their environments. Some organisms have **23** intent eyesight, and use visible light to navigate and hunt. Others have sensitive noses, enabling them to sniff out food and avoid predators by scent. A few species, however, have developed the ability to navigate the world mainly through sound, emitting clicks and listening to their echoes to locate objects. This adaptation, called echolocation, allows animals to operate in low-light environments, or even total darkness.

The best known echolocators are probably **24** the microbats. Named for their small size and small eyes, **25** clicks are emitted by these bats at frequencies far higher than the human ear can hear. The echoes of these clicks allow them to sense obstacles and prey even in the total absence of light. Echolocation thus enables microbats to hunt in the dead of **26** night. This is a time when darkness keeps them safe from predators.

Interestingly, their prey, which are mainly flying insects like moths, **27** has evolved some strategies to counter the bats' echolocation. Some moths fall silent and stop beating their wings when they hear bats draw near; one species can even emit its own clicks to jam its predators' echolocation. Nevertheless, echolocation remains a highly useful ability for these bats.

23
- A) NO CHANGE
- B) fervent
- C) avid
- D) keen

24
- A) NO CHANGE
- B) the echolocating *microbats*
- C) the echolocators known as *microbats*
- D) the *microbats*, a species capable of echolocation

25
- A) NO CHANGE
- B) clicking by these bats occurs
- C) these bats emit clicks
- D) the bats' emissions of clicks are

26
Which choice best combines the sentences at the underlined portion?
- A) night, as
- B) night, being a time when
- C) night, considering that
- D) night, when

27
- A) NO CHANGE
- B) have
- C) had
- D) must have

CONTINUE

[1] The **28** cetaceans, a group of mammals, that includes dolphins and whales can also use echolocation to thrive in unique environments. [2] With it, they are able to sense objects precisely for hundreds of meters around them. [3] Because water scatters and blocks visible light, echolocation is especially useful for these marine creatures. [4] In addition to the high-frequency sounds used for echolocation, whales and dolphins can **29** omit lower-frequency sounds, which travel farther, for long-distance communication. [5] Their clicks and whistles thus allow them not just to navigate and hunt, but also to identify each other and coordinate their activities. **30**

28

A) NO CHANGE

B) cetaceans, a groups of mammals that includes dolphins and whales

C) cetaceans, a group of mammals that includes, dolphins and whales,

D) cetaceans, a group of mammals that includes dolphins and whales,

29

A) NO CHANGE

B) admit

C) emit

D) permit

30

To make this paragraph most logical, sentence 3 should be placed

A) where it is now.

B) after sentence 1.

C) after sentence 4.

D) after sentence 5.

CONTINUE

Humans also use various forms of echolocation. [31] Without a doubt, sonar is essentially mechanical echolocation that enables boats and submarines to navigate more effectively. Medical ultrasound uses bounced sound waves to take detailed images of internal organs and structures, providing previously unavailable diagnostic information. [32]

More surprisingly, some visually impaired people learn to use a kind of echolocation, without the aid of technology, to sense their environments; while [33] there abilities are not as sharp as those of animals that naturally echolocate, they do help them to navigate their environment, avoid hazards, and even play sports.

31

A) NO CHANGE

B) Notwithstanding this,

C) Curiously,

D) For example,

32

Which choice, inserted here, most effectively supports a claim made in the previous sentence?

A) Additionally, MRI technology also lets doctors see inside their patients' bodies.

B) For instance, ultrasound imaging, unlike X-ray photography, does not require exposing the patient to radiation.

C) For example, ultrasound imaging can reveal information about the health and sex of an unborn baby.

D) Unfortunately, ultrasound is mostly blocked by bone.

33

A) NO CHANGE

B) they

C) they're

D) their

CONTINUE

Questions 34-44 are based on the following passage.

Priming and Psychology's Replication Crisis

[1] The existence of a phenomenon called priming is one of the best-known discoveries in psychology. [2] Priming occurs when some stimulus causes unconscious changes in mindset and behavior, often in surprising ways. [3] One priming experiment revealed that research subjects who washed their hands were less judgmental **34** with moral wrongdoing afterward. [4] Another found that students who thought about a professor before taking a test performed better than students who thought about a soccer hooligan instead. **35** [5] Based on results like these, psychologists and reporters alike have claimed that priming studies show our behavior is deeply influenced by factors we don't even notice. **36**

34

A) NO CHANGE
B) for
C) in
D) of

35

Which choice, inserted here, would be the most relevant addition to the paragraph?

A) In another experiment, researchers asked subjects to watch a disgusting scene from a movie.

B) One of the most famous priming studies found that reading words related to old age made subjects walk more slowly.

C) It's not clear what processes in the brain could cause this priming effect.

D) Many people are unnerved by the idea that priming could be used to subtly manipulate our behavior.

36

To make this paragraph most logical, sentence 2 should be placed

A) where it is now.
B) before sentence 1.
C) after sentence 4.
D) after sentence 5.

CONTINUE

Unfortunately, this interpretation has run into trouble as many priming studies have been called into question. The controversy over priming is part of a larger crisis in psychology over replication. Experimental results are not **37** considered or believed to be reliable until they are replicated, or repeated independently. Many results in social psychology have failed to meet this requirement. In a recent effort by social psychologists to replicate many prominent experiments, only one of seven famous priming studies **38** was successfully repeated. These disastrous findings have led some to question whether priming even exists. This "replication crisis" has seriously undermined the credibility of the field, and psychologists must work quickly to **39** understand it. They should address that.

40 For example, academic psychology is a fast-paced field in which researchers must "publish or perish." This pressure can lead psychologists to tweak their statistical methods until their experiments seem to succeed. While not fraudulent, these methods can produce mistaken results. In addition, **41** researcher's samples are sometimes small and biased. Studies conducted on just a couple dozen undergraduates, for example, are likely to give questionable conclusions. The media also contributes to the problem by seizing on and reporting surprising results before they are well-supported. Together, these factors cause unverified experimental results to be taken as fact in the popular imagination.

37

A) NO CHANGE
B) considered to be reliable
C) considered reliable
D) considered

38

A) NO CHANGE
B) is
C) were
D) had been

39

A) NO CHANGE
B) understand it. That's how they can address it.
C) understand it. Subsequently, it needs to be addressed.
D) understand and address it.

40

Which choice most effectively conveys the main topic of the paragraph?

A) Nevertheless, some psychologists fiercely defend the validity of the priming effect.
B) Research psychologists face many challenges.
C) The replication crisis has many causes.
D) Priming is difficult to observe outside of the laboratory.

41

A) NO CHANGE
B) researchers'
C) researchers
D) researchers's

CONTINUE

[42] So what are psychologists supposed to do about it? Perhaps most importantly, the nature of academic publishing must change. As long as "successful" experiments are more likely to be published than negative results or failed replications, the pressure to produce experiment success and the illusion of [43] census that exists around questionable studies will continue. Similarly, there must be more funding available for researchers who wish to perform replications. Too few studies are ever examined and challenged in this way. Finally, the media must also be more cautious in promoting results. Responsible science [44] journalism, that avoids sensationalism will help prevent the spread of misinformation.

42

Which of the following choices is most consistent with the style of the passage as a whole?

A) NO CHANGE

B) What's the best fix for psychology's problem?

C) How can the crisis in psychology be solved?

D) Does anyone have ideas for how to fix this?

43

A) NO CHANGE

B) contention

C) consensus

D) senses

44

A) NO CHANGE

B) journalism: that avoids

C) journalism that avoids,

D) journalism that avoids

STOP

If you complete this section before the end of your allotted time, check your work on this section only. Do NOT use the time to work on another section.

Section 3

Math Test – No Calculator

25 MINUTES, 20 QUESTIONS

Turn to Section 3 of your answer sheet to answer the questions in this section.

DIRECTIONS

Questions **1-15** ask you to solve a problem, select the best answer among four choices, and fill in the corresponding circle on your answer sheet. Questions **16-20** ask you to solve a problem and enter your answer in the grid provided on your answer sheet. There are detailed instructions on entering answers into the grid before question 16. You may use your test booklet for scratch work.

NOTES

1. You **may not** use a calculator.
2. Variables and expressions represent real numbers unless stated otherwise.
3. Figures are drawn to scale unless stated otherwise.
4. Figures lie in a plane unless stated otherwise.
5. The domain of a function f is defined as the set of all real numbers x for which $f(x)$ is also a real number, unless stated otherwise.

REFERENCE

$A = \frac{1}{2}bh$ $\qquad$ $a^2 + b^2 = c^2$ $\qquad$ Special Triangles $\qquad$ $V = \frac{1}{3}lwh$ $\qquad$ $V = \frac{1}{3}\pi r^2 h$

$A = lw$ $\qquad$ $V = lwh$ $\qquad$ $V = \pi r^2 h$ $\qquad$ $A = \pi r^2$ $\qquad$ $V = \frac{4}{3}\pi r^3$

$\qquad\qquad\qquad\qquad\qquad\qquad\qquad\qquad\qquad\qquad\qquad C = 2\pi r$

There are 360° in a circle.

The sum of the angles in a triangle is 180°.

The number of radians of arc in a circle is 2π.

CONTINUE

1

If $3x = 15$ and $2y = 10$, then which of the following values is equal to $6x + 4y$?

A) 35

B) 50

C) 65

D) 70

2

For which value of x is $f(x) = 2x^2 - 8x + 6$ less than 0?

A) −1

B)   0

C)   1

D)   2

3

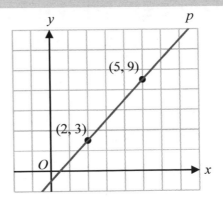

What is the equation that represents the line p in the xy-coordinate plane above?

A) $y = \dfrac{1}{4}x + 1$

B) $y = \dfrac{1}{2}x - 1$

C) $y = x + 1$

D) $y = 2x - 1$

4

A T-shirt printer can produce 40 tank tops with logos in 5 hours. At this rate, how many tank tops with logos can the printer produce in 7 hours?

A) 48

B) 56

C) 64

D) 70

5

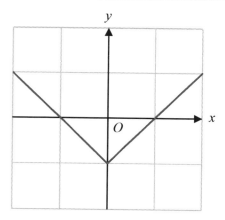

Which equation produces the graph above?

A) $y = |x| - 1$

B) $y = |x - 1|$

C) $y = |x + 1|$

D) $|y| = x + 1$

6

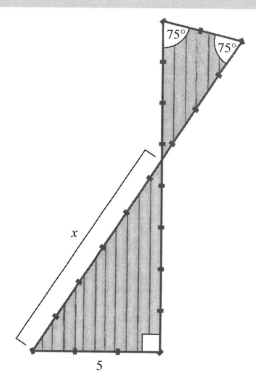

If a landscape architect sketched a plan for two triangular gardens in the diagram above, what is the length x?

A) 8.7

B) 9.6

C) 10

D) 11.2

CONTINUE

7

As the positive integer x increases, which function increases at the greatest rate?

A) $f(x) = 100x$

B) $f(x) = 100^x$

C) $f(x) = x^{-100}$

D) $f(x) = 100 + x$

8

If $f(x) = 3x + 7$, what is the value of $f(-1) + f(3)$?

A) 12

B) 16

C) 20

D) 24

9

The expression $(2i + 3)(i + 4)$ is equivalent to which of the following? (Note: $i = \sqrt{-1}$.)

A) $12i$

B) $9 + 10i$

C) $10 + 11i$

D) $12 + 13i$

10

Which of the following values of x makes the equation $2x + \dfrac{x}{3} = 5x$ true?

A) -3

B) 0

C) 1

D) 2

11

x	y
0	6
1	8
2	14
3	32

Which expression fits the above values?

A) $y = x^3 + 6$

B) $y = 2^x + 6$

C) $y = 3^x + 5$

D) $y = 4x + 4$

CONTINUE

12

Consider the equation $\sqrt{5x-5} = \sqrt{y^2 + 1}$. Which of the following are possible values for the coordinates (x, y)?

A) $(-1, -1)$

B) $(1, 2)$

C) $(3, 3)$

D) $(4, 1)$

13

If $f(x) = x^2 + 2x + 3$ and $g(x) = f(3x)$, what is the value of $g(5) - f(5)$?

A) 220

B) 258

C) 278

D) 296

14

$$2x + y = 10$$
$$x + 2y = 35$$

According to the system of equations above, what is the value of y?

A) 20

B) 25

C) 30

D) 35

15

What is the next value in the sequence 1, 2, 4, 7, 11…?

A) 15

B) 16

C) 17

D) 18

CONTINUE

DIRECTIONS

Questions **16-20** ask you to solve a problem and enter your answer in the grid provided on your answer sheet. When completing grid-in questions:

1. You are required to bubble in the circles for your answers. It is recommended, but not required, that you also write your answer in the boxes above the columns of circles. Points will be awarded based only on whether the circles are filled in correctly.

2. Fill in only one circle in a column.

3. You can start your answer in any column as long as you can fit in the whole answer.

4. For questions 16-20, no answers will be negative numbers.

5. **Mixed numbers,** such as $4\frac{2}{5}$, must be gridded as decimals or improper fractions, such as 4.4 or as 22/5. "42/5" will be read as "forty-two over five," not as "four and two-fifths."

6. If your answer is a **decimal** with more digits than will fit on the grid, you may round it or cut it off, but you must fill the entire grid.

7. If there are **multiple correct solutions** to a problem, all of them will be considered correct. Enter only **one** on the grid.

CONTINUE

16

Jeff and Liz are purchasing 5 chickens for every 1.5 acres of land. If they have 3 acres of land set aside for chickens, how many chickens do they purchase?

17

$$x^2 - y^2 = 20$$
$$x - y = 4$$

What is the value of $x + y$ for the equations above?

18

If $x = 2y + 6$ and $y = -2x - 3$, what is the value of xy?

19

$$F = G\frac{m_1 \times m_2}{d^2}$$

The gravitational force between two stars is inversely proportional to the square of the distance between the two stars, as represented by Newton's Universal Gravitation Equation shown above. G is the universal gravitation constant, d is the distance in light-years, m_1 is the mass of the first star, and m_2 is the mass of the second star. If the force of gravity between two stars that are 4 light-years apart is 64 exanewtons, what is the force, in exanewtons, between the stars if they are 8 light-years apart?

20

What is the perimeter of the triangle bordered by the lines $y = -\frac{4}{3}x + 16$, $x = 0$, and $y = 0$?

STOP

If you complete this section before the end of your allotted time, check your work on this section only. Do NOT use the time to work on another section.

Section 4

Math Test – Calculator

55 MINUTES, 38 QUESTIONS

Turn to Section 4 of your answer sheet to answer the questions in this section.

DIRECTIONS

Questions **1-30** ask you to solve a problem, select the best answer among four choices, and fill in the corresponding circle on your answer sheet. Questions **31-38** ask you to solve a problem and enter your answer in the grid provided on your answer sheet. There are detailed instructions on entering answers into the grid before question 31. You may use your test booklet for scratch work.

NOTES

1. You **may** use a calculator.
2. Variables and expressions represent real numbers unless stated otherwise.
3. Figures are drawn to scale unless stated otherwise.
4. Figures lie in a plane unless stated otherwise.
5. The domain of a function f is defined as the set of all real numbers x for which $f(x)$ is also a real number, unless stated otherwise.

REFERENCE

$$A = \frac{1}{2} bh$$

$$a^2 + b^2 = c^2$$

Special Triangles

$$V = \frac{1}{3} lwh$$

$$V = \frac{1}{3}\pi r^2 h$$

$$A = lw$$

$$V = lwh$$

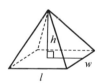
$$V = \pi r^2 h$$

$$A = \pi r^2$$
$$C = 2\pi r$$

$$V = \frac{4}{3}\pi r^3$$

There are 360° in a circle.

The sum of the angles in a triangle is 180°.

The number of radians of arc in a circle is 2π.

CONTINUE

1

A chemist is investigating a new reaction to synthesize barite crystals. She finds that eight grams are synthesized every five minutes. If there are 111 grams of barite after an hour, how many grams of barite did the chemist start with?

A)   0

B)   8

C) 15

D) 71

2

Which of the following graphs could represent the equation $y = 2x^3$?

A)

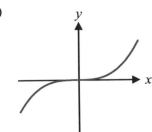

B)

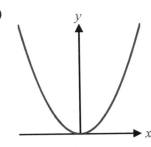

C)

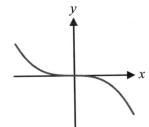

D)

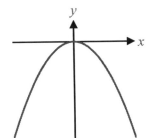

CONTINUE

4

3

A recipe that makes c cupcakes requires e eggs. If Grant wants to make 40 cupcakes, how many eggs will he need, in terms of c and e?

A) $\dfrac{40 \times e}{c}$

B) $\dfrac{40}{e}$

C) $\dfrac{e}{40 \times c}$

D) $\dfrac{1}{40 \times e}$

4

A linear function has two coordinates: $(-2, -5)$ and $(-5, -3)$. What is the slope of this function?

A) $-\dfrac{3}{2}$

B) $-\dfrac{2}{3}$

C) $\dfrac{2}{3}$

D) $\dfrac{3}{2}$

5

A chessboard has 64 squares. If one grain of sand is placed on the first square, two on the second, four on the third, and so on, with the number of grains doubling each time, how many grains of sand will be on the 64th square?

A) 64

B) 64^2

C) 2^{63}

D) 2^{64}

6

In 2014, shoppers spent \$31 billion on gift cards, 13.9% of which were for coffee shops. If 27% of coffee shop gift cards go unused, what is the approximate value of these unused cards?

A) \$1.16 billion

B) \$4.31 billion

C) \$6.55 billion

D) \$8.37 billion

CONTINUE

7

A bakery uses the equation $3b - c = p$ to determine its profits in dollars, p, based on the number of loaves of bread, b, that they produce, and c, their fixed cost. Which of the following correctly explains this equation?

A) The more bread the company produces, the less profit it can expect to make.

B) Fixed cost increases with every loaf of bread that the company produces.

C) Every loaf of bread produced increases the company's profit by three dollars.

D) Profit remains the same regardless of how much bread the company produces.

8

$$\frac{1}{4}x + \frac{1}{3}y = \frac{1}{2}z$$

Which of the following equations is not equal to the equation above?

A) $3x + 4y = 6z$

B) $\frac{1}{2}x + \frac{2}{3}y = z$

C) $x + \frac{4}{3}y = 2z$

D) $x + y = \frac{3}{2}z$

9

Budgets of Highest Selling Films

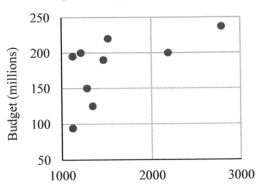

The total sales of films are compared to their total budgets in the graph above. What was the budget of the film with the median total ticket sales?

A) $125 million

B) $190 million

C) $195 million

D) $200 million

10

$$f(z) = \frac{2}{z} + z \times 3$$

According to the equation above, what is the value of $f\left(\frac{2}{3}\right)$?

A) $\frac{2}{3}$

B) 1

C) 5

D) 6

CONTINUE

11

Snails travel at a speed of about 13 mm per second. How many minutes would it take for a snail to climb the 169 m tall Washington Monument?

A)   36

B)   77

C)   130

D)   217

12

Number of Websites on the Internet

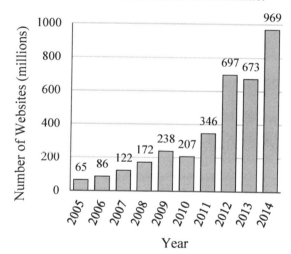

The chart above displays the growth of the number websites on the Internet from 2005 to 2014. Which of the following periods had the greatest percentage growth in number of websites?

A)   2005-2007

B)   2006-2008

C)   2007-2009

D)   2008-2010

13

If the percent increase of the length of a rectangle is L, and the percent increase of the width of the same rectangle is W, which of the following expressions represents the percent increase in the area of the rectangle?

A) $L \times W$

B) $\dfrac{W}{L}$

C) $L(W + 1) + W$

D) $L(W + 1)$

14

$$-5x - 3 + b = 0$$
$$x + 3 + 2b = 0$$

Which of the following is a possible value of b, in terms of x, that satisfies the system of equations above?

A) $b = -\left(\dfrac{x}{2} - \dfrac{3}{2}\right)$

B) $b = -\left(\dfrac{1}{2}\right)(x + 3)$

C) $b = -5x + 3$

D) $b = -6(x - 6)$

CONTINUE

15

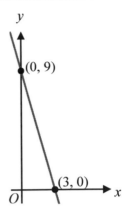

A linear function is graphed above. What is the value of a at the point $(a, 3)$ for this function?

A) 1

B) 2

C) 3

D) 4

16

A function is defined by the expression $f(x) = ax - c$. If $f(-1) = -5$, and $f(1) = -1$, what is the value of a?

A) −2

B) 0

C) 2

D) 3

17

The value a is 40% of b, and is smaller than c. If c is 2 times smaller than d, which of the following is NOT true?

A) $a < d$

B) $a < \dfrac{d}{2}$

C) $\dfrac{a}{b} = \dfrac{2}{5}$

D) $\dfrac{a}{b} = \dfrac{5}{2}$

18

$$b \le 2a - 1$$
$$8 > a - b$$

According to the system of inequalities above, which of the following could be a value for a?

A) −12

B) −8

C) −7

D) −6

CONTINUE

19

If x, y, a, and b are all positive integers, which of the following expressions is NOT equivalent to $(x^a)^b \times (xy)^{ab}$?

A) $(x^2y)^{ab}$

B) $(x^{2a})^b y^{ab}$

C) $x^b x^a x^b x^b y^a$

D) $(x^a)^b (x^b)^a (y^a)^b$

20

Yearly Pollination Rate

The graph above shows the pollination rate of plants in a forested area every two years. Based on the trend line, what is the average annual increase in the pollination rate?

A) 5%

B) 3.8%

C) 2.5%

D) 1.5%

21

If $y = 3x^2 + 10x - 8$, what is one possible value of x when $y = 0$?

A) -4

B) 0

C) 4

D) 8

22

$$y - x = 8$$
$$x^2 - xy = -4$$

According to the system of equations above, what is the value of x?

A) $-\dfrac{17}{2}$

B) $-\dfrac{1}{2}$

C) $\dfrac{1}{2}$

D) $\dfrac{17}{2}$

CONTINUE

Questions 23, 24, and 25 refer to the following information.

The table below shows the number of new apartments that were completed and rented in a 3-month period in 2009. The number, cost, and regional geographic location of each apartment is summarized, according to the U.S. Census Bureau.

Rent for the Year 2009	Number of Apartments Completed and Rented in 3 Months (1000s)				
	U.S.	Northeast	Midwest	South	West
Total Apartments Rented (1000s)	163,000	10,000	17,200	93,300	42,400
Less than $950	57,300	2,700	10,200	35,700	8,800
$950 to $1,049	22,300	400	2,900	15,100	4,000
$1,050 to $1,149	13,300	1,100	1,000	7,300	3,900
$1,150 to $1,249	16,700	800	700	10,200	5,000
$1,250 to $1,349	53,300	5,000	2,500	25,000	20,700
Median Monthly Asking Rent (dollars)	1,063	1,250	857	1,022	1,240

23

Which region of the U.S. had the greatest number of apartments that were rented for less than $950?

A) The Northeast

B) The Midwest

C) The South

D) The West

24

Which of the following statements is true for the year 2009?

A) Since the median rent for newly completed apartments in the U.S. was greater than the median rent in the Midwest, the mean price for these apartments is also greater in the U.S. than in the Midwest.

B) At least 50 percent of the newly completed apartments rented in the South cost less than the U.S. median for newly completed apartments.

C) Apartments that cost between $1,050 and $1,149 make up a greater percentage of newly constructed apartments in the Midwest than they do in the West.

D) With 25,000 thousand newly completed and rented apartments costing between $1,250 and $1,349, the South was the most expensive location to rent new apartments in the U.S.

CONTINUE

25

In 2009, John moved from Georgia to an apartment in the Midwest. In Georgia, John paid a monthly rent of $1,200. If his new apartment in the Midwest had the median monthly rate for that region given in the chart above, how much did John save in annual rental costs?

A) $343

B) $1,686

C) $3,255

D) $4,116

26

A bowl contains a mix of apples and oranges. After 6 oranges are eaten, there are 3 times as many apples as oranges. A short time later, 11 apples are eaten, resulting in a ratio of 4:1 of oranges to apples. How many oranges were originally in the bowl?

A)   4

B)   10

C)   11

D)   12

27

Probability Tree of Genetic Traits

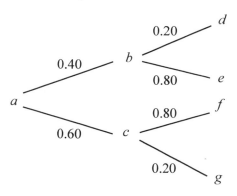

A biologist wants to predict the probability of developing genetic traits in an experiment. The probability tree above represents the probability of outcome of two experiments, the second experiment dependent on the results of the first experiment. As an example, the first experiment, which begins with trait a, has a 40% probability of generating feature b, which in turn has a 80% probability of developing trait e. What is the probability that the biologist's experiment will develop trait g?

A)   12%

B)   20%

C)   48%

D)   60%

CONTINUE

28

$$\frac{3y}{x-2} = 2x + 5$$

$$y = \frac{2x^2 + x - 10}{3}$$

Which of the following is a solution to the system of equations above?

A) No solutions

B) (−2.5, 2)

C) (2, −2.5)

D) Infinitely many solutions

29

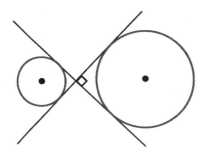

The tangents of two circles intersect at a 90° angle, as shown above. If the radius of the small circle is 1 cm and the radius of the large circle is 3 cm, what is the minimum distance, in cm, between the two circles?

A) $4\sqrt{2}$

B) $3(\sqrt{2} - 1)$

C) $4(\sqrt{2} - 1)$

D) $6(\sqrt{2} - 1)$

30

A city inspector wishes to determine whether a neighborhood of 5,000 residents desires a new sewer system. She surveys 100 residents to see whether they would approve of the new sewers. 70 of the residents agree that the sewers are a good idea. Since she decides to evaluate her results using a 95% confidence level, she determines that her residents' responses represent the neighborhood population, with a confidence interval of 9.7%. Based on this information, she decides to build the sewers, but receives almost 1,700 angry calls from the neighborhood at her call center. What is a possible explanation for these results?

A) A 95% confidence level is not 100% accurate, so the data are not valid.

B) The inspector should have asked fewer people to get clearer results, with a potentially higher percentage of residents approving of the sewers.

C) The confidence interval of 9.7% is too low for the survey to give accurate results about residents' desires.

D) One thousand and seven hundred residents disapproving of the sewers, or 34% of the population, fall within the confidence interval, and is therefore predicted by the survey.

CONTINUE

DIRECTIONS

Questions **31-38** ask you to solve a problem and enter your answer in the grid provided on your answer sheet. When completing grid-in questions:

1. You are required to bubble in the circles for your answers. It is recommended, but not required, that you also write your answer in the boxes above the columns of circles. Points will be awarded based only on whether the circles are filled in correctly.

2. Fill in only one circle in a column.

3. You can start your answer in any column as long as you can fit in the whole answer.

4. For questions 31-38, no answers will be negative numbers.

5. **Mixed numbers,** such as $4\frac{2}{5}$, must be gridded as decimals or improper fractions, such as 4.4 or as 22/5. "42/5" will be read as "forty-two over five," not as "four and two-fifths."

6. If your answer is a **decimal** with more digits than will fit on the grid, you may round it or cut it off, but you must fill the entire grid.

7. If there are **multiple correct solutions** to a problem, all of them will be considered correct. Enter only **one** on the grid.

CONTINUE

31

$$h : j = 6 : 7$$

The ratio of h to j is shown above. If j is 21, what is the value of h?

32

Nanna has two sisters, Laurel and Jennifer. Jennifer is twice as old as Laurel, who is 4 years younger than Nanna. If Nanna is two years younger than Jennifer, what is Nanna's age in years?

33

Rahil notices an invasive species of weed in his yard, which has an area of 243 square feet. The weed initially covers an area of 32 square feet and increases in size by 50% each week. How many weeks will it take the weed to cover the entire yard?

34

When a silo is 40% empty it holds 9 more tons of grain than when it is 40% full. How many tons of grain does the silo hold when it is full?

35

A carrier pigeon flies at an average speed of 75 km per hour, while a Cessna 152 propeller plane travels at an average speed of 180 km per hour. A pigeon and a Cessna set off at the same time from Paris to London, a distance of 500 km. How many minutes earlier will the Cessna arrive in London than the pigeon if both fly the same route? (Round your answer to the nearest minute.)

36

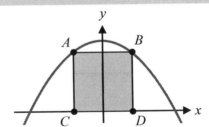

Note: figure is not drawn to scale

The rectangle $ABCD$ has the side CD along the x-axis, and the points A and B touching the function $y = -x^2 + 6$, as shown above. If the point D is at $(1, 0)$, what is the area of the rectangle $ABCD$?

CONTINUE

Questions 37 and 38 refer to the following information.

Zebra and quagga mussels are a major concern, damaging the fresh waterways of the United States and Canada as they spread, destroying ecosystems and infrastructure along the waterways. According to the United States Geological Survey, a fully mature female mussel is capable of producing up to one million eggs per season, and the National Oceanic and Atmospheric Administration (N.O.A.A.) states that as many as 700,000 mussels may be found in one square yard.

Mussel sightings, which began with the discovery of zebra mussels in 1988, have increased dramatically. The map below, which details mussel sightings in 2007, outlines their expansion, from the East to the West of the United States, since their first discovery.

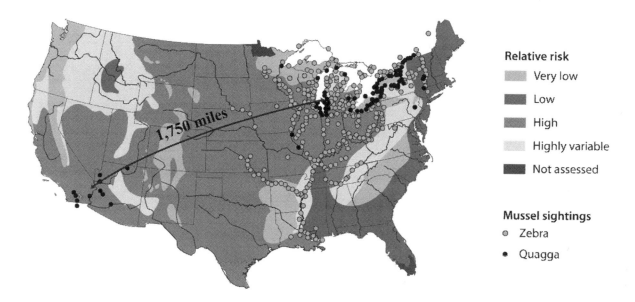

CONTINUE

37

The map on the previous page shows the distance covered by a boat travelling from Lake Michigan to the waterways of California. When it leaves Lake Michigan, the bottom of the boat has 100,000 zebra mussels. If 10% of the original mussel population dies for every 250 miles that the boat travels, how many thousands of mussels will remain when the boat reaches California?

38

The surface area of Lake Michigan is approximately 6.94×10^{10} square yards and Lake Michigan contains 1.75×10^5 mussels per square yard. Statisticians determine that the probability that a boat will spread the mussels to nearby states increases by 1 percent for every quadrillion (10^{15}) mussels in the lake. What is the percent probability that a boat from Lake Michigan will transport mussels to a nearby state's waterways? (Round your answer to the nearest percent.)

STOP

If you complete this section before the end of your allotted time, check your work on this section only. Do NOT use the time to work on another section.

Essay

Essay (Optional)

50 MINUTES

Turn to the lined pages of your answer sheet to write your essay.

DIRECTIONS

This essay is optional. It is a chance for you to demonstrate how well you can understand and analyze a written passage. Your essay should show that you have carefully read the passage and should be a concisely written analysis that is both logical and clear.

You must write your entire essay on the lines in your answer booklet. No additional paper will be provided aside from the Planning Page inside your answer booklet. You will be able to write your entire essay in the space provided if you make use of every line, keep tight margins, and write at a suitable size. Don't forget to keep your handwriting legible for the readers evaluating your essay.

You will have 50 minutes to read the passage in this booklet and to write an essay in response to the prompt provided at the end of the passage.

REMINDERS

- What you write in this booklet will not be evaluated. Write your essay in the answer booklet only.

- Essays that are off-topic will not be evaluated.

As you read the following passage, consider how Stewart Brand uses

- evidence, like examples or facts, to support his arguments.
- logical reasoning to develop his ideas and to connect his claims to his evidence.
- stylistic or persuasive techniques, such as the choice of particular words or appeals to his readers' emotions, to give power to the ideas put forth.

Adapted from Stewart Brand, "Rethinking extinction." © 2015 by Aeon Media Ltd. Originally published April 21, 2015.

1   The way the public hears about conservation issues is nearly always in the mode of "[Beloved Animal] Threatened With Extinction." That makes for electrifying headlines, but it misdirects concern. The loss of whole species is not the leading problem in conservation. The leading problem is the decline in wild animal populations, sometimes to a radical degree, often diminishing the health of whole ecosystems.

2   Viewing every conservation issue through the lens of extinction threat is simplistic and usually irrelevant. Worse, it introduces an emotional charge that makes the problem seem cosmic and overwhelming rather than local and solvable.

3   Most extinctions have occurred on oceanic islands or in restricted freshwater locations, with very few occurring on Earth's continents or in the oceans. The world's greatest conservation problem is not species extinction, but rather the precarious state of thousands of populations that are the remnants of once widespread and productive species.

4   Many new species readily emerge on ocean islands because of the isolation, but there are few other species to co-evolve with and thus they have no defense against invasive competitors and predators. The threat can be total. An endemic species under attack has nowhere to escape to. The island conservationist Josh Donlan estimates that islands, which are just 3 percent of the Earth's surface, have been the site of 95 percent of all bird extinctions since 1600, 90 percent of reptile extinctions, and 60 percent of mammal extinctions. Those are horrifying numbers, but the losses are extremely local. They have no effect on the biodiversity and ecological health of the continents and oceans that make up 97 percent of the Earth.

5   Since the majority of invasive species are relatively benign, they add to an island's overall biodiversity. The ecologist Dov Sax at Brown University in Rhode Island points out that non-native plants have doubled the botanical biodiversity of New Zealand—there are 2,104 native plants in the wild, and 2,065 non-native plants. Ascension Island in the south Atlantic, once a barren rock deplored by Charles Darwin for its "naked hideousness," now has a fully functioning cloud forest made entirely of plants and animals brought by humans in the past 200 years.

6   But the main news from ocean islands is that new methods have been found to protect the vulnerable endemic species from their worst threat, the invasive predators, thus dramatically lowering the extinction rate for the future. New Zealanders are the heroes of this story, beautifully told in *Rat Island: Predators in Paradise and the World's Greatest Wildlife Rescue* (2011) by William Stolzenburg. … In the 1980s, New Zealand conservationists were driven to desperation

by the vulnerability of beloved unique creatures such as a ground-dwelling parrot called the kakapo. They decided to do whatever it took to eliminate every single rat on the kakapo's island refuge. It took many seasons of relentless poisoning and trapping, but when it was done, it was really done.

7   Conservation efforts often appear in the media like a series of defeats and retreats, but as soon as you look up from the crisis-of-the-month, you realize that, in aggregate, conservation is winning. The ecologist Stuart Pimm at Duke University in North Carolina claims that conservationists have already reduced the rate of extinction by 75 percent. Getting the world's extinction rate back down to normal is a reasonable goal for this century.

8   But a perception problem stands in the way.

9   Consider the language of these news headlines: "Fuelling Extinction: Obama Budget Is Killer For Endangered Species" (Huffington Post, February 2015). "'Racing Extinction' Sounds Alarm On Ocean's Endangered Creatures" (NBC News, January 2015). "'Extinction Crisis': 21,000 Of World's Species At Risk Of Disappearing" (Common Dreams, July 2013). "Australian Mammals On Brink Of 'Extinction Calamity'" (BBC, February 2015). … The headlines are not just inaccurate. As they accumulate, they frame our whole relationship with nature as one of unremitting tragedy. The core of tragedy is that it cannot be fixed, and that is a formula for hopelessness and inaction. Lazy romanticism about impending doom becomes the default view.

10   No end of specific wildlife problems remain to be solved, but describing them too often as extinction crises has led to a general panic that nature is extremely fragile or already hopelessly broken. That is not remotely the case. Nature as a whole is exactly as robust as it ever was— maybe more so, with humans around to head off ice ages and killer asteroids. Working with that robustness is how conservation's goals get reached.

Write an essay explaining how Stewart Brand builds his argument to persuade his audience that focusing on extinction harms the goals of the conservation movement. Analyze how Brand utilizes at least one of the features in the box above, or features of your own choosing, to make his argument more logical and persuasive. Your analysis should focus on the most relevant features of the passage.

You should not explain whether you agree with Brand's argument; rather, your essay should explain how Brand builds an argument to persuade his readers.

PRACTICE TEST 4

SAT

Directions

- Work on just one section at a time.
- If you complete a section before the end of your allotted time, use the extra minutes to check your work on that section only. Do NOT use the time to work on another section.

Using Your Test Booklet

- No credit will be given for anything written in the test booklet. You may use the test booklet for scratch paper.
- You are not allowed to continue answering questions in a section after the allotted time has run out. This includes marking answers on your answer sheet that you previously noted in your test booklet.
- You are not allowed to fold pages, take pages out of the test booklet, or take any pages home.

Answering Questions

- Each answer must be marked in the corresponding row on the answer sheet.
- Each bubble must be filled in completely and darkly within the lines.

- Be careful to bubble in the correct part of the answer sheet.
- Extra marks on your answer sheet may be marked as incorrect answers and lower your score.
- Make sure you use a No. 2 pencil.

Scoring

- You will receive one point for each correct answer.
- Incorrect answers will NOT result in points deducted. Even if you are unsure about an answer, you should make a guess.

**DO NOT BEGIN THIS TEST
UNTIL YOUR PROCTOR TELLS YOU TO DO SO**

Download printable answer sheets, answer keys, and Excel scoring sheets from:

ivyglobal.com/study

Section 1

1	A B C D ◯ ◯ ◯ ◯	12	A B C D ◯ ◯ ◯ ◯	23	A B C D ◯ ◯ ◯ ◯	34	A B C D ◯ ◯ ◯ ◯	45	A B C D ◯ ◯ ◯ ◯
2	A B C D ◯ ◯ ◯ ◯	13	A B C D ◯ ◯ ◯ ◯	24	A B C D ◯ ◯ ◯ ◯	35	A B C D ◯ ◯ ◯ ◯	46	A B C D ◯ ◯ ◯ ◯
3	A B C D ◯ ◯ ◯ ◯	14	A B C D ◯ ◯ ◯ ◯	25	A B C D ◯ ◯ ◯ ◯	36	A B C D ◯ ◯ ◯ ◯	47	A B C D ◯ ◯ ◯ ◯
4	A B C D ◯ ◯ ◯ ◯	15	A B C D ◯ ◯ ◯ ◯	26	A B C D ◯ ◯ ◯ ◯	37	A B C D ◯ ◯ ◯ ◯	48	A B C D ◯ ◯ ◯ ◯
5	A B C D ◯ ◯ ◯ ◯	16	A B C D ◯ ◯ ◯ ◯	27	A B C D ◯ ◯ ◯ ◯	38	A B C D ◯ ◯ ◯ ◯	49	A B C D ◯ ◯ ◯ ◯
6	A B C D ◯ ◯ ◯ ◯	17	A B C D ◯ ◯ ◯ ◯	28	A B C D ◯ ◯ ◯ ◯	39	A B C D ◯ ◯ ◯ ◯	50	A B C D ◯ ◯ ◯ ◯
7	A B C D ◯ ◯ ◯ ◯	18	A B C D ◯ ◯ ◯ ◯	29	A B C D ◯ ◯ ◯ ◯	40	A B C D ◯ ◯ ◯ ◯	51	A B C D ◯ ◯ ◯ ◯
8	A B C D ◯ ◯ ◯ ◯	19	A B C D ◯ ◯ ◯ ◯	30	A B C D ◯ ◯ ◯ ◯	41	A B C D ◯ ◯ ◯ ◯	52	A B C D ◯ ◯ ◯ ◯
9	A B C D ◯ ◯ ◯ ◯	20	A B C D ◯ ◯ ◯ ◯	31	A B C D ◯ ◯ ◯ ◯	42	A B C D ◯ ◯ ◯ ◯		
10	A B C D ◯ ◯ ◯ ◯	21	A B C D ◯ ◯ ◯ ◯	32	A B C D ◯ ◯ ◯ ◯	43	A B C D ◯ ◯ ◯ ◯		
11	A B C D ◯ ◯ ◯ ◯	22	A B C D ◯ ◯ ◯ ◯	33	A B C D ◯ ◯ ◯ ◯	44	A B C D ◯ ◯ ◯ ◯		

Section 2

1	A B C D ◯ ◯ ◯ ◯	10	A B C D ◯ ◯ ◯ ◯	19	A B C D ◯ ◯ ◯ ◯	28	A B C D ◯ ◯ ◯ ◯	37	A B C D ◯ ◯ ◯ ◯
2	A B C D ◯ ◯ ◯ ◯	11	A B C D ◯ ◯ ◯ ◯	20	A B C D ◯ ◯ ◯ ◯	29	A B C D ◯ ◯ ◯ ◯	38	A B C D ◯ ◯ ◯ ◯
3	A B C D ◯ ◯ ◯ ◯	12	A B C D ◯ ◯ ◯ ◯	21	A B C D ◯ ◯ ◯ ◯	30	A B C D ◯ ◯ ◯ ◯	39	A B C D ◯ ◯ ◯ ◯
4	A B C D ◯ ◯ ◯ ◯	13	A B C D ◯ ◯ ◯ ◯	22	A B C D ◯ ◯ ◯ ◯	31	A B C D ◯ ◯ ◯ ◯	40	A B C D ◯ ◯ ◯ ◯
5	A B C D ◯ ◯ ◯ ◯	14	A B C D ◯ ◯ ◯ ◯	23	A B C D ◯ ◯ ◯ ◯	32	A B C D ◯ ◯ ◯ ◯	41	A B C D ◯ ◯ ◯ ◯
6	A B C D ◯ ◯ ◯ ◯	15	A B C D ◯ ◯ ◯ ◯	24	A B C D ◯ ◯ ◯ ◯	33	A B C D ◯ ◯ ◯ ◯	42	A B C D ◯ ◯ ◯ ◯
7	A B C D ◯ ◯ ◯ ◯	16	A B C D ◯ ◯ ◯ ◯	25	A B C D ◯ ◯ ◯ ◯	34	A B C D ◯ ◯ ◯ ◯	43	A B C D ◯ ◯ ◯ ◯
8	A B C D ◯ ◯ ◯ ◯	17	A B C D ◯ ◯ ◯ ◯	26	A B C D ◯ ◯ ◯ ◯	35	A B C D ◯ ◯ ◯ ◯	44	A B C D ◯ ◯ ◯ ◯
9	A B C D ◯ ◯ ◯ ◯	18	A B C D ◯ ◯ ◯ ◯	27	A B C D ◯ ◯ ◯ ◯	36	A B C D ◯ ◯ ◯ ◯		

Section 3 (No calculator)

1. A ○ B ○ C ○ D ○   4. A ○ B ○ C ○ D ○   7. A ○ B ○ C ○ D ○   10. A ○ B ○ C ○ D ○   13. A ○ B ○ C ○ D ○
2. A ○ B ○ C ○ D ○   5. A ○ B ○ C ○ D ○   8. A ○ B ○ C ○ D ○   11. A ○ B ○ C ○ D ○   14. A ○ B ○ C ○ D ○
3. A ○ B ○ C ○ D ○   6. A ○ B ○ C ○ D ○   9. A ○ B ○ C ○ D ○   12. A ○ B ○ C ○ D ○   15. A ○ B ○ C ○ D ○

Only answers that are gridded will be scored. You will not receive credit for anything written in the boxes.

16   17   18   19   20

Section 4 (Calculator)

1. A ○ B ○ C ○ D ○   7. A ○ B ○ C ○ D ○   13. A ○ B ○ C ○ D ○   19. A ○ B ○ C ○ D ○   25. A ○ B ○ C ○ D ○
2. A ○ B ○ C ○ D ○   8. A ○ B ○ C ○ D ○   14. A ○ B ○ C ○ D ○   20. A ○ B ○ C ○ D ○   26. A ○ B ○ C ○ D ○
3. A ○ B ○ C ○ D ○   9. A ○ B ○ C ○ D ○   15. A ○ B ○ C ○ D ○   21. A ○ B ○ C ○ D ○   27. A ○ B ○ C ○ D ○
4. A ○ B ○ C ○ D ○   10. A ○ B ○ C ○ D ○   16. A ○ B ○ C ○ D ○   22. A ○ B ○ C ○ D ○   28. A ○ B ○ C ○ D ○
5. A ○ B ○ C ○ D ○   11. A ○ B ○ C ○ D ○   17. A ○ B ○ C ○ D ○   23. A ○ B ○ C ○ D ○   29. A ○ B ○ C ○ D ○
6. A ○ B ○ C ○ D ○   12. A ○ B ○ C ○ D ○   18. A ○ B ○ C ○ D ○   24. A ○ B ○ C ○ D ○   30. A ○ B ○ C ○ D ○

Section 4 (Continued)

Only answers that are gridded will be scored. You will not receive credit for anything written in the boxes.

31 32 33 34 35

Only answers that are gridded will be scored. You will not receive credit for anything written in the boxes.

36 37 38

Important: Use a No. 2 pencil. Write inside the borders.

You may use the space below to plan your essay, but be sure to write your essay on the lined pages. Work on this page will not be scored.

Use this space to plan your essay.

START YOUR ESSAY HERE.

_____

_____

_____

_____

_____

_____

_____

_____

_____

_____

_____

_____

_____

_____

_____

_____

_____

_____

_____

_____

_____

_____

_____

_____

_____

Continue on the next page.

Continue on the next page.

Continue on the next page.

STOP.

Section 1

Reading Test

65 MINUTES, 52 QUESTIONS

Turn to Section 1 of your answer sheet to answer the questions in this section.

DIRECTIONS

Every passage or paired set of passages is accompanied by a number of questions. Read the passage or paired set of passages, then use what is said or implied in what you read and in any given graphics to choose the best answer to each question.

Questions 1-10 are based on the following passage.

This passage is adapted from George Eliot, *Middlemarch*, originally published in 1871-1872.

Will Ladislaw was struck mute for a few moments. He had never been fond of Mr. Casaubon, and if it had not been for the sense of obligation,
Line would have laughed at him as a Bat of erudition. But
5 the idea of this dried-up pedant, this elaborator of small explanations about as important as the surplus stock of false antiquities kept in a vendor's back chamber, having first got this adorable young creature to marry him, stirred him with a sort of
10 comic disgust: he was divided between the impulse to laugh aloud and the equally unseasonable impulse to burst into scornful invective.

For an instant he felt that the struggle was causing a queer contortion of his mobile features,
15 but with a good effort he resolved it into nothing more offensive than a merry smile.

Dorothea wondered; but the smile was irresistible, and shone back from her face too. Dorothea said inquiringly, "Something amuses
20 you?"

"Yes," said Will, quick in finding resources. "I am thinking of the sort of figure I cut the first time I saw you, when you annihilated my poor sketch with your criticism."

25 "My criticism?" said Dorothea, wondering still more. "Surely not. I always feel particularly ignorant about painting."

"I suspected you of knowing so much, that you knew how to say just what was most cutting. You
30 said—I dare say you don't remember it as I do—that the relation of my sketch to nature was quite hidden from you. At least, you implied that." Will could laugh now as well as smile.

"That was really my ignorance," said Dorothea,
35 admiring Will's good-humor. "I must have said so only because I never could see any beauty in the pictures which my uncle told me all judges thought very fine. That always makes one feel stupid. It is painful to be told that anything is very fine and not
40 be able to feel that it is fine—something like being blind, while people talk of the sky."

"Oh, there is a great deal in the feeling for art which must be acquired," said Will. (It was impossible now to doubt the directness of
45 Dorothea's confession.) "Art is an old language with a great many artificial, affected styles, and sometimes the chief pleasure one gets out of knowing them is the mere sense of knowing."

"You mean perhaps to be a painter?" said
50 Dorothea, with a new direction of interest. "You mean to make painting your profession? Mr.

CONTINUE →

Casaubon will like to hear that you have chosen a profession."

"No, oh no," said Will, with some coldness. "I
55 have quite made up my mind against it. It is too one-sided a life. I have been seeing a great deal of the German artists here: I travelled from Frankfurt with one of them. Some are fine, even brilliant fellows—but I should not like to get into their
60 way of looking at the world entirely from the studio point of view."

"That I can understand," said Dorothea, cordially. "But if you have a genius for painting, would it not be right to take that as a guide?
65 Perhaps you might do better things than these—or different, so that there might not be so many pictures almost all alike in the same place."

There was no mistaking this simplicity, and Will was won by it into frankness. "A man must
70 have a very rare genius to make changes of that sort. I am afraid mine would not carry me even to the pitch of doing well what has been done already, at least not so well as to make it worthwhile. And I should never succeed in
75 anything by dint of drudgery. If things don't come easily to me I never get them."

1

Over the course of the passage, the focus of the narrative shifts from

A) Will's appraisal of Mr. Casaubon to his opinions of Dorothea.

B) Will's response to Dorothea's engagement to his thoughts about art and his own shortcomings.

C) Will's admiration of Dorothea from afar to a witty and flirtatious conversation between them.

D) Will's appreciation of art to his internal debate about whether he himself should become an artist.

2

In lines 1-24, Will could best be described as

A) a supportive friend.

B) a horrified relative.

C) a displeased admirer.

D) an amused confidant.

3

Which of the following provides the best evidence for the answer to the previous question?

A) Lines 4-10 ("But the … disgust")

B) Lines 13-16 ("For an … smile")

C) Lines 19-20 ("Dorothea said … you")

D) Lines 21-24 ("I am … criticism")

4

It can be most reasonably inferred that Dorothea is

A) puzzled but pleased by Will's reaction to her news.

B) worried by Will's cold and indifferent manner.

C) offended by Will's comments on art criticism.

D) dismissive of Will's artwork and opinions.

5

Which of the following provides the best evidence for the answer to the previous question?

A) Lines 10-12 ("he was … invective")

B) Lines 17-18 ("Dorothea wondered … too")

C) Lines 49-50 ("You mean … interest")

D) Lines 62-63 ("That I … cordially")

CONTINUE

6

The passage most strongly implies which of the following about Dorothea's taste in art?

A) It comes from years of study in international venues.

B) It stems from her unschooled feelings about the pieces.

C) It is superior to Will's own pedantic taste.

D) It is refined but too artificial to be authentic.

7

As used in line 23, "annihilated" most nearly means

A) eliminated.

B) erased.

C) converted.

D) disparaged.

8

Dorothea makes a comparison in lines 38-41 ("It is … sky") in order to

A) suggest that her sight limits her from appreciating the details in many paintings.

B) illustrate her discomfort and frustration when others discuss elements in art she doesn't understand.

C) show her bored indifference towards the beauty that seems to entrance and delight others.

D) express her hope that she may one day come to understand the more enlightened perspectives of others.

9

As used in line 46, "affected" most nearly means

A) pretentious.

B) deceitful.

C) fake.

D) insincere.

10

In lines 75-76 ("If things … them"), Will is most directly referring to

A) Dorothea's hand in marriage.

B) his potential career as a painter.

C) a proposed trip to Frankfurt.

D) his new foray into art criticism.

CONTINUE

Questions 11-20 are based on the following passage.

This passage is adapted from Shirley Chisolm, "For the Equal Rights Amendment," delivered before the United States Congress in 1970. Chisolm, the first African American woman elected to Congress, was arguing in favor of a Constitutional amendment securing legal equality between men and women.

The resolution before us today, which provides for equality under the law for both men and women, represents one of the most clear-cut opportunities we

Line are likely to have to declare our faith in the
5 principles that shaped our Constitution. It provides a legal basis for attack on the most subtle, most pervasive, and most institutionalized form of prejudice that exists. Discrimination against women, solely on the basis of their sex, is so widespread that
10 is seems to many persons normal, natural, and right.

Legal expression of prejudice on the grounds of religious or political belief has become a minor problem in our society. Prejudice on the basis of race is, at least, under systematic attack. It is time we
15 act to assure full equality of opportunity to those citizens who, although in a majority, suffer the restrictions that are commonly imposed on minorities—women.

The argument that this amendment will not solve
20 the problem of sex discrimination is not relevant. If the argument were used against a civil rights bill, as it has been used in the past, the prejudice that lies behind it would be embarrassing. Of course laws will not eliminate prejudice from the hearts of
25 human beings. But that is no reason to allow prejudice to continue to be enshrined in our laws— to perpetuate injustice through inaction.

What would the legal effects of the equal rights amendment really be? The equal rights amendment
30 would govern only the relationship between the State and its citizens—not relationships between private citizens. The amendment would be largely self-executing, that is, any Federal or State laws in conflict would be ineffective one year after the date
35 of ratification without further action by the Congress

or State legislatures.

Jury service laws not making women equally liable for jury service would have been revised. The selective service law would have to include women,
40 but women would not be required to serve in the Armed Forces where they are not fitted any more than men are required to serve.

Survivorship benefits would be available to husbands of female workers on the same basis as to
45 wives of male workers. Public schools and universities could not be limited to one sex and could not apply different admission standards to men and women. Laws requiring longer prison sentences for women than men would be invalid, and equal
50 opportunities for rehabilitation and vocational training would have to be provided in public correctional institutions.

What would be the economic effects of the equal rights amendment? Direct economic effects would
55 be minor. If any labor laws applying only to women still remained, their amendment or repeal would provide opportunity for women in better-paying jobs in manufacturing. More opportunities in public vocational and graduate schools for women would
60 also tend to open up opportunities in better jobs for women.

Indirect effects could be much greater. The focusing of public attention on the gross legal, economic, and social discrimination against women
65 by hearings and debates in the Federal and State legislatures would result in changes in attitude of parents, educators, and employers that would bring about substantial economic changes in the long run.

This is what it comes down to: artificial
70 distinctions between persons must be wiped out of the law. Legal discrimination between the sexes is, in almost every instance, founded on outmoded views of society and the pre-scientific beliefs about psychology and physiology. It is time to sweep away
75 these relics of the past and set further generations free of them.

The Constitution was designed to protect the rights of white, male citizens. As there were no

CONTINUE

black Founding Fathers, there were no founding
80 mothers—a great pity, on both counts. It is not too
late to complete the work they left undone. Today,
here, we should start to do so.

11

The stance Chisolm takes in the passage is best
described as that of

A) a weary radical.

B) a passionate advocate.

C) an excited politician.

D) an optimistic scholar.

12

According to Chisolm, legal distinctions between
the sexes

A) protect important differences.

B) are usually valid, but occasionally harmful.

C) reflect outdated thinking.

D) have only minimal effects.

13

Which choice provides the best evidence for the
answer to the previous question?

A) Lines 8-10 ("Discrimination against … right")

B) Lines 14-18 ("It is … women")

C) Lines 28-29 ("What would … be")

D) Lines 71-74 ("Legal … and physiology")

14

Chisolm characterizes discrimination against
women as

A) unfortunate but unavoidable.

B) accepted but unjust.

C) embarrassing but necessary.

D) illegal but common.

15

As used in line 11, "expression" most nearly
means

A) assertion.

B) intensity.

C) announcement.

D) emotion.

16

Chisolm recognizes and dismisses which of the
following counterarguments?

A) Legal remedies are insufficient for eradicating
bias.

B) The Constitutional amendment would change
the demographics of the Armed Forces.

C) America is already more equitable than other
countries.

D) The Constitutional amendment would rob
women of certain benefits.

CONTINUE

yontnu

Which choice provides the best evidence for the answer to the previous question?

A) Lines 5-8 ("It provides … exists")

B) Lines 23-25 ("Of course … beings")

C) Lines 29-31 ("The equal … its citizens")

D) Lines 54-55 ("Direct economic … minor")

18

As used in line 41, "fitted" most nearly means

A) contoured.

B) shaped.

C) fixed.

D) suited.

19

The contrast between direct and indirect effects in lines 53-68 serves primarily to

A) argue that although no one knows what the immediate ramifications of the amendment will be, the ultimate effect will be small.

B) imply that while some of the things people fear may come to pass, there will also be unpredictable benefits.

C) suggest that the impact of the amendment will be considerably larger in the future than in the present day.

D) state that certain aspects of people's lives will be changed severely, while other aspects will remain much the same.

20

By "relics of the past," (line 75) Chisolm refers to

A) reliance on the Constitution as the ultimate arbiter of justice.

B) laws with different provisions for men and women.

C) assumptions about women's natural inclinations for homemaking.

D) convoluted legal processes for altering laws.

CONTINUE

PRACTICE TEST 4 | Ivy Global

Questions 21-31 are based on the following passage and supplementary material.

This passage is adapted from Chau Tu, "Can Music Be Used as Medicine?" © 2015 Chau Tu, as first published by The Atlantic Company.

Current research shows that music affects the body and brain to at least some degree, physically and psychologically. For instance, research
Line published in 2005 by Theresa Lesiuk at the
5 University of Windsor, Canada, concluded that music helped to improve the quality and timeliness of office work, as well as increase overall positive attitudes while people were working on those tasks. A review in 2012 by Costas Karageorghis found
10 there was "evidence to suggest that carefully selected music can promote ergogenic and psychological benefits during high-intensity exercise." Meanwhile, Stefan Koelsch in Berlin has found "music can evoke activity changes in the core
15 brain regions that underlie emotion," and physically, "happy" music triggers zygomatic muscle activity— that is, smiling—and "sad" music "leads to the activation of the corrugator muscle"—the frowning muscle in the brow.
20   However, the long-term effects still need to be parsed more thoroughly, and it's still unclear if and how, exactly, music might be used as treatment. "Just because music—or anything else—acts upon a part of the brain, does not mean that mental health
25 can be influenced," Robert Zatorre, a neurologist at McGill University, wrote in an email. "We need far more sophisticated understandings of what is going on in a given disease before we can really answer" the question of whether music can definitively affect
30 mental or physical health. "That said, there are a few promising avenues that people are trying with particular disorders, and hopefully that work will accelerate in future."
One such condition is Parkinson's disease.
35 Jessica Grahn is a neuroscientist at Western University in Ontario who's been studying the relationship between music and movement, and she points to research that has shown that even when

people don't seem to be physically responding to
40 music—by tapping their foot or dancing—fMRI scans reveal that their brains' motor systems are responding internally. "When we look at what happens when someone appears to be very passively listening to music, and they're not doing anything to
45 it, we see quite a lot of the brain responding," she says.
People in these studies, done by Grahn and others, seem to be responding to a song's rhythm. The rhythm, Grahn says, really drives responses in
50 the brain's movement areas, and these responses tend to be stronger with music that has a clear beat that people can follow. Now, the next step for researchers is to find out if rhythm can be used to activate motor brain areas in people who have
55 problems there.
Parkinson's patients, for example, often experience "breaks" or "freezing," and have trouble initiating movement. "It's not entirely clear why freezing happens," Grahn says. But "one thing that
60 people have observed is that if you play music that has a steady beat, or sometimes even just a metronome with a steady beat, these patients seem to have improvements in their walking." Grahn has also observed music seeming effective in elongating
65 and improving the gait of Parkinson's patients, which is often jerky and unsteady.
Still, there are a lot of variables that haven't been studied yet, from figuring out the strength and duration of these apparent effects to whether an
70 individual's musical abilities have an impact. A major boon, Grahn says, would be obtaining data— much, much more of it, and from patients in real-world situations.
"Patients really vary; some have a very fast
75 progression in the disease, some have a slow progression," she says. "It's impossible to test enough patients to really capture every kind of patient with every kind of musical ability in the lab."

CONTINUE

Effect of Music Intervention

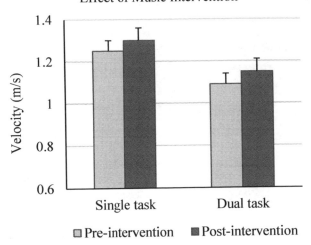

□ Pre-intervention   ■ Post-intervention

This graph shows the walking velocity of a group of patients with Parkinson's disease, first while walking without music then while walking with music. The patients either walked (single task), or walked while simultaneously doing something else (dual task).

21

The passage primarily focuses on which of the following aspects of music?

A) Its physiological effects on facial musculature in humans

B) Its impressive ability to improve productivity in office settings

C) Its potential effects on patients with health conditions

D) Its lasting impact on the moods of people with Parkinson's disease

22

Which of the following best describes the structure of the passage as a whole?

A) An overview of diverse results followed by a discussion of a particular avenue of research

B) A series of related anecdotes followed by a scientific theory that unites them all

C) An interview with a doctor conducting research followed by descriptions of her patients

D) An explanation of basic principles followed by an exploration of their potential application

23

As used in line 7, "positive" most nearly means

A) favorable.

B) definite.

C) unequivocal.

D) beneficial.

CONTINUE

24

How do the studies in the first paragraph relate to the rest of the passage?

A) They lay out the prevailing scientific consensus about music and the body, while the rest of the passage argues that new evidence suggests the truth is more complicated.

B) They introduce the topic of music's effects on the body, while the rest of the passage discusses a potential manifestation of that phenomenon.

C) They demonstrate the wide range of opinions that exists about Parkinson's treatment, while the rest of the passage advocates a specific treatment for the illness.

D) They emphasize the difficulty of securing funding for scientific research, while the rest of the passage talks about the benefits of well-funded experiments.

25

As used in line 34, "condition" most nearly means

A) illness.

B) situation.

C) environment.

D) requirement.

26

The passage most strongly suggests that

A) music therapy has been a significant breakthrough in Parkinson's treatments.

B) the effects of music on the brain are confusing and difficult to study.

C) while some support researching the effects of music of the brain, others are scornful.

D) music may have significant effects for some patients, but it's too early to tell.

27

Which choice provides the best evidence for the answer to the previous question?

A) Lines 26-30 ("We need … health")

B) Lines 47-48 ("People in … rhythm")

C) Lines 59-63 ("But … their walking")

D) Lines 76-78 ("It's impossible … lab")

28

It is reasonable to conclude that one reason Grahn would like significantly more data about the effect of music on patients with Parkinson's is that more data would

A) make her argument more convincing to scientific authorities.

B) allow her to begin testing out different types of treatments on patients.

C) clarify how individual factors might affect patients' responses to music.

D) demonstrate her need for significantly more funding to conduct her research.

CONTINUE

29

Which choice provides the best evidence for the answer to the previous question?

A) Lines 35-37 ("Jessica Grahn ... movement")

B) Lines 49-52 ("The rhythm ... follow")

C) Lines 63-66 ("Grahn has ... unsteady")

D) Lines 67-70 ("Still ... impact")

30

Based on the graph, Parkinson's patients who listened to music while walking moved

A) faster than patients who did not listen to music.

B) faster than they did without listening to music.

C) slower than patients who did not listen to music.

D) slower than they did without listening to music.

31

Data in the graph provide most direct support for which assertion in the passage?

A) Lines 13-19 ("Meanwhile ... the brow")

B) Lines 42-46 ("When we ... says")

C) Lines 59-63 ("But ... their walking")

D) Lines 74-76 ("Patients really ... says")

Questions 32-41 are based on the following passage and supplementary material.

This passage is adapted from Kelly McGonigal, "Use Stress to Your Advantage." © 2015 by Dow Jones and Company.

When Harvard Business School professor Alison Wood Brooks asked hundreds of people if they should try to calm down or try to feel excited in
Line stressful situations, the responses were nearly
5 unanimous: 91% thought that the best advice was to try to calm down. But is it true?

Prof. Brooks designed an experiment to find out. For a research paper published last year in the *Journal of Experimental Psychology*, she recruited
10 140 people to give a speech. She told part of the group to relax and to calm their nerves by saying to themselves, "I am calm." The others were told to embrace their anxiety and to tell themselves, "I am excited."
15 Members of both groups were still nervous before the speech, but the participants who had told themselves "I am excited" felt better able to handle the pressure and were more confident in their ability to give a good talk. Not only that, but observers who
20 rated the talks found the excited speakers more persuasive, confident and competent than the participants who had tried to calm down. With this one change in mind-set, the speakers had transformed their anxiety into energy that helped
25 them to perform under pressure.

"We're bombarded with information about how bad stress is," says Jeremy Jamieson, a professor of psychology at the University of Rochester who specializes in stress. But the conventional view, he
30 says, fails to appreciate the many ways in which physical and psychological tension can help us to perform better.

In research published in the *Journal of Experimental Social Psychology* in 2010, Prof.
35 Jamieson tested his theory with college students who were preparing to take the Graduate Record Examination. He invited 60 students to take a practice GRE and collected saliva samples from them beforehand to get baseline measures of their

CONTINUE

levels of alpha-amylase, a hormonal indicator of stress. He told them that the goal of the study was to examine how the physiological stress response affects performance.

He then gave half the students a brief pep talk to help them rethink their pre-exam nervousness. "People think that feeling anxious while taking a standardized test will make them do poorly," he told them. "However, recent research suggests that stress doesn't hurt performance on these tests and can even help performance. People who feel anxious during a test might actually do better.... If you find yourself feeling anxious, simply remind yourself that your stress could be helping you do well."

It worked: students who received the mind-set intervention scored higher on the practice exam than those in the control group. The difference in GRE scores could not be attributed to differences in ability: students had been randomly assigned to the two groups and didn't differ, on average, in their SAT scores or college GPAs.

Prof. Jamieson wondered about another possible explanation: perhaps his pep talk had simply calmed the students down instead of helping them to use their stress. To test this proposition, he took a second saliva sample from students after the exam. The group that had received the mind-set message showed higher, not lower, levels of salivary alpha-amylase—in other words, they were more stressed after the exam, not less.

Interestingly, he also found that stress by itself, as measured by the saliva sample, was not the key to better performance. For students who had received the pep talk, a stronger physical stress response was associated with higher scores. In contrast, there was no relationship between stress hormones and performance in the control group. The stress response by itself had not helped or hurt their test-taking in any predictable way.

What makes such mind-set interventions so promising, says Prof. Jamieson, is that when they work, they do not just have an immediate, one time effect—they stick. He delivered his pep talk days

before the actual exam, but the students had somehow internalized its message.

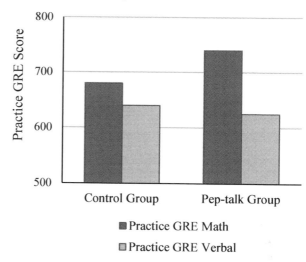

Effect of Pep Talk on Practice GRE Scores

■ Practice GRE Math
□ Practice GRE Verbal

32

The passage is written from the perspective of someone who is

A) an expert on physiological symptoms of stress in humans.

B) interested in recent research about different ways people respond to stress.

C) an advocate for decreasing the stressfulness of graduate school admissions.

D) passionate about helping young people lower their stress levels.

33

As used in line 13, "embrace" most nearly means

A) hold.

B) adopt.

C) accept.

D) comprise.

CONTINUE

34

Which statement best summarizes lines 1-25?

A) A researcher found that the best strategy for dealing with stress was counterintuitive to most of the people she surveyed.

B) A student discovered that she would need to learn to manage her stress better in order to keep her GPA at a satisfactory level.

C) A pair of experts provided their opinions on how to deal with stress and agreed that stress can be beneficial.

D) A public speaking coach offered tips on handling anxiety gleaned from a long career of helping others succeed.

35

Based on the passage, Prof. Brooks found that participants told to embrace their anxiety

A) rated themselves as more confident and performed at a similar level.

B) received higher ratings from observers of the talks.

C) remained anxious, but impressed viewers with their apparent calm.

D) varied too much in their responses to provide conclusive evidence.

36

Which choice provides the best evidence for the answer to the previous question?

A) Lines 5-6 ("91% ... calm down")

B) Line 7 ("Prof. Brooks ... out")

C) Lines 12-14 ("The others ... excited")

D) Lines 19-22 ("Not only ... down")

37

As used in line 29, "conventional" most nearly means

A) orthodox.

B) plain.

C) standard.

D) customary.

38

Based on the passage, Prof. Jamieson is most impressed by the fact that encouraging students to embrace their anxiety

A) raises their test scores.

B) decreases their anxiety.

C) has long-lasting effects.

D) affects everyone differently.

39

Which choice provides the best evidence for the answer to the previous question?

A) Lines 33-37 ("In research ... Examination")

B) Lines 46-48 ("People think ... them")

C) Lines 70-72 ("Interestingly ... better performance")

D) Lines 79-82 ("What makes ... stick")

CONTINUE

40

Which statement best summarizes the information presented in the graph?

A) On average, students who were more stressed did better on the practice GRE.

B) On average, students who were less stressed did better on the practice GRE.

C) On average, students who were told to think of their anxiety positively did better on the practice GRE.

D) On average, students who were told to think of their anxiety positively did worse on the practice GRE.

41

Which of the following is supported by the passage and the graph?

A) Studying harder before the test was linked to more stress while taking it, but made no difference in scores.

B) Being told to embrace their anxiety was linked to higher scores on the practice GRE math section, but not on the verbal.

C) A strong physiological stress response was predictive of top scores on the practice GRE verbal section, but not on the math.

D) People think stress is only harmful, but it often has more positive than negative effects.

Questions 42-52 are based on the following passages.

Passage 1 is adapted from Merlin Crossley, "Explainer: what is genome editing?" © 2015 Merlin Crossley. Passage 2 is adapted from Anthony Wrigley and Ainsley Newson, "Genome editing poses ethical problems that we cannot ignore." © 2015 by Anthony Wrigley and Ainsley Newson.

Passage 1

Mistakes in the paper version of the Encyclopedia Britannica took a long time to correct—years often passed between revised
Line editions—but these days editing information is much
5 easier. In electronic sources, like Wikipedia, anyone can log on and use simple web-based tools to make corrections or even improvements. Human genomes also contain various errors or mutations. Many are relatively harmless but some cause life-threatening
10 genetic diseases. Today, some of these errors can also be corrected using modern technology.

In a few cases, patients have been treated by conventional gene therapy; new genes have been carried in by viruses. These can then compensate for
15 defective genes. But so far few—if any—patients have had their mutations corrected by genomic editing. This may all change now that new editing tools have come on the scene. A quiet revolution is occurring in our ability to modify living genomes.
20 The affordable sequencing of human genomes has allowed the ready identification of myriad harmful mutations. Conversely, in agriculturally important organisms, new beneficial gene variants have been identified. Thus, it is becoming more and
25 more relevant to think about editing such variants in or out. At the same time, the improvements in sequencing also mean that one can readily re-sequence after editing. One can check whether any unintended errors have been introduced.
30 There are two reasons few people are talking about genomic editing. First, the revolution has crept up on us because the breakthrough really revolves around better and cheaper tools rather than new ideas or concepts. Genomic editing was already
35 possible in simple organisms and it was feasible but

CONTINUE

expensive to make mice with added or deleted genes. But it was slow and laborious. Now it is easier.

40 The other point concerns specificity. We know we can make the desired changes but we do not know how many other unintended changes are also being introduced. In agriculture, if the sum of all changes results in the desired outcome, other unintended changes may not matter. But before

45 anyone embarks on human genomic editing we will want to know about any off-target effects. With the availability of affordable genomic sequencing this should be possible and it is reasonable to be optimistic that refinements in specificity and editing

50 processes will, one day, make genomic editing a useful new therapeutic tool.

Passage 2

Genome editing presents us with the very real possibility that any aspect of the human genome could be manipulated as we desire. This could mean

55 eliminating harmful genetic conditions, or enhancing traits deemed advantageous, such as resistance to diseases. But this ability may also open the door to eugenics, where those with access to the technology could select for future generations based on traits

60 considered merely desirable: eye, skin, or hair color, or height.

The concern prompting the US academics' call for a moratorium is the potential for altering the human germ-line, making gene alterations

65 inheritable by our children. Gene therapies that produce non-inheritable changes in a person's genome are ethically accepted, in part because there is no risk for the next generation if things go wrong. However, to date only one disease—severe

70 combined immunodeficiency—has been cured by this therapy.

Germ-line alternations pose much greater ethical concerns. A mistake could harm future individuals by placing that mistake in every cell. Of course the

75 flip-side is that, if carried out safely and as intended,

germ-line alterations could also provide potentially permanent solutions to genetic diseases. No research is yet considering this in humans, however.

Nevertheless, even if changes to the germ-line

80 turn out to be safe, the underlying ethical concerns of scope and scale that genome editing brings will remain. If a technique can be used widely and efficiently, without careful oversight governing its use, it can readily become a new norm or an

85 expectation. Those unable to access the desired genetic alterations, be they humans with diseases, humans without enhanced genetic characteristics, or farmers without genetically modified animals or crops, may all find themselves gravely and unfairly

90 disadvantaged.

42

The author of Passage 1 refers to mistakes in the paper version of the Encyclopedia Britannica primarily to

A) encourage people to read even the most authoritative sources critically.

B) emphasize the difference in speed that modern technology can achieve for some processes.

C) enumerate the advantages of digital tools across different domains.

D) explain that the paper version of the Encyclopedia Britannica misrepresented the facts about genome editing.

43

The author of Passage 1 attributes the sudden feasibility of genome editing to

A) revolutionary theoretical breakthroughs.

B) changes in the political landscape.

C) improvements in relevant technologies.

D) shifting environmental concerns.

CONTINUE

44

Which choice provides the best evidence for the answer to the previous question?

A) Lines 18-19 ("A quiet ... genomes")

B) Lines 28-29 ("One can ... introduced")

C) Lines 31-34 ("First, the ... concepts")

D) Lines 39-42 ("We know ... introduced")

45

As used in line 51, "therapeutic" most nearly means

A) curative.

B) remedial.

C) positive.

D) tonic.

46

If genome editing could be proven to be safe, the authors of Passage 2 would most likely

A) cautiously embrace it as a benefit for humanity.

B) argue that it is too expensive to be practical.

C) continue to worry about its ethical implications.

D) reject it for being too abnormal.

47

Which choice provides the best evidence for the answer to the previous question?

A) Lines 54-57 ("This could ... diseases")

B) Lines 62-65 ("The concern ... children")

C) Lines 77-78 ("No research ... however")

D) Lines 79-82 ("Nevertheless ... will remain")

48

Which situation is most similar to the one described in lines 72-74 ("Germ-line ... cell")?

A) A city is hit by an epidemic which gives scars to many citizens.

B) A computer virus infects people using their email contact lists.

C) A model for a mold is misshapen, causing every mold made from it to be defective.

D) A machine at a manufacturing plant creates dangerous working conditions.

49

As used in line 72, "pose" most nearly means

A) arrange.

B) model.

C) position.

D) raise.

50

Which choice best states the relationship between the two passages?

A) Passage 1 outlines the political implications of the technology described by Passage 2.

B) Passage 2 raises additional concerns about a scientific breakthrough outlined in Passage 1.

C) The author of Passage 1 is conducting the sort of research the authors of Passage 2 are arguing against.

D) The author of Passage 1 is a dedicated opponent of the reforms the authors of Passage 2 cautiously support.

CONTINUE ➤

51

Which of the following issues with genome editing is discussed only by Passage 2?

A) That it could exacerbate existing inequalities between groups of people

B) That consuming genetically modified crops could pose health risks

C) That it will be too expensive to ever be feasible in humans

D) That even correctly executed modifications could have unforeseen effects

52

Which choice would best support the claim that the author of Passage 1 has a more favorable view of genome editing than the authors of Passage 2?

A) Lines 8-10 ("Many are … diseases")

B) Lines 17-18 ("This may … scene")

C) Lines 24-26 ("Thus … or out")

D) Lines 46-51 ("With the … tool")

STOP

If you complete this section before the end of your allotted time, check your work on this section only. Do NOT use the time to work on another section.

Section 2

Writing and Language Test

35 MINUTES, 44 QUESTIONS

Turn to Section 2 of your answer sheet to answer the questions in this section.

Every passage comes with a set of questions. Some questions will ask you to consider how the writer might revise the passage to improve the expression of ideas. Other questions will ask you to consider correcting potential errors in sentence structure, usage, or punctuation. There may be one or more graphics that you will need to consult as you revise and edit the passage.

Some questions will refer to a portion of the passage that has been underlined. Other questions will refer to a particular spot in a passage or ask that you consider the passage in full.

After you read the passage, select the answers to questions that most effectively improve the passage's writing quality or that adjust the passage to follow the conventions of standard written English. Many questions give you the option to select "NO CHANGE." Select that option in cases where you think the relevant part of the passage should remain as it currently is.

Questions 1-11 are based on the following passage.

What Do Professors Do?

There is no such thing as a "typical day" in the life of a college professor. That's part of the appeal of this **1** career. Each day offers unique opportunities and unique challenges. Add in the fact that **2** there are approximately 1.7 million professors in the United States and many professors feel they've won the career lottery.

1

Which choice correctly combines the sentences at the underlined portion?

A) career each,

B) career each

C) career, each

D) career: each

2

Which detail best supports the assertion at the end of this sentence?

A) NO CHANGE

B) most professors teach the subject they love

C) most professors are experts in their fields

D) everyone likes jobs that offer variety

CONTINUE

[3] Becoming a professor requires many years of study in a specific discipline. A master's degree is the minimum educational requirement, but most tenure-track positions require a doctoral degree. Anne Swanson, who teaches English at a small independent university, explains, "to become a professor, I first earned a B.A. in English, followed by a Ph.D. in Rhetoric and Composition." That took Anne six years of advanced studies, including becoming [4] affluent in two foreign languages.

While some might think that all professors [5] would have done is lecture a few times a week and assign some homework, that's not all Prof. Swanson does. "The reality is that for every hour I spend in the classroom, I spend a minimum of two hours on planning and grading," she says. That planning begins well before the semester does. Over the summer, when most students are returning home, studying abroad, or taking summer jobs, [6] she works on syllabi, along with reviewing the textbook and developing a preliminary schedule of lesson plans and assignments.

3

A) NO CHANGE

B) I had to study a lot of specific things before I became a professor.

C) It is said that becoming a professor requires many years of study in a discipline.

D) It's not like you can just be a professor straight out of undergrad, though.

4

A) NO CHANGE

B) effluent

C) fluent

D) fluid

5

A) NO CHANGE

B) do

C) did

D) would do

6

A) NO CHANGE

B) she is working on syllabi, reviewing the textbook, and developing

C) she works to create syllabi, she reviews the textbook, and she develops

D) she is reviewing the textbook, and developing syllabi and

CONTINUE

[1] Once the semester begins, Prof. Swanson works on her lectures, reviews and revises the lesson plans and assignments, and holds office hours. [2] "I meet with students to review assignments," she says. [3] In addition, she advises students about their courses and even what major to choose. [4] That is not all they talk about, though. [5] "Sometimes a student comes in to talk about something class-related and we end up talking about other things, like time management or even a problem with a roommate," she says. **7**

When she's not meeting with students, participating in committees, and planning, Prof. Swanson is grading papers submitted by her students **8** with the online classroom through the Internet. "Sometimes I wish I taught math because then the answers are right or wrong," **9** she says. "Grading writing assignments means I make note of such issues as incorrect punctuation and grammar, but I spend far more time writing comments in the margins. The good news is I can grade papers anywhere I have access to the website—mostly I do grading at home."

7

For the sake of cohesion of this paragraph, sentence 1 should be placed

A) where it is now.

B) after sentence 2.

C) before sentence 4.

D) before sentence 5.

8

A) NO CHANGE

B) using the university's online classroom

C) which are submitted using her university's virtual classroom

D) DELETE the underlined portion

9

A) NO CHANGE

B) one says

C) I say

D) they say

Her job also includes participating in English department meetings and **10** <u>staging</u> other services for the university. Prof. Swanson is on her institution's faculty salary committee and a committee devoted to social justice issues; these committees meet year-round, even in summer.

During most weeks Prof. Swanson spends just nine hours in the classroom and another nine creating lesson plans and lectures. **11** "The bottom line is that I work all year long, and I work a lot more than 40 hours a week. But I love being a professor. It's the best job ever."

10

A) NO CHANGE

B) achieving

C) discharging

D) performing

11

At this point the writer is considering adding the following sentence

> Office hours and committee and faculty meetings take up about eighteen hours, and she can spend as much as sixteen hours grading papers.

Should the writer make this addition here?

A) Yes, because it supports the statement about how many hours Prof. Swanson works.

B) Yes, because it explains what all professors have to do in addition to teaching.

C) No, because the number of hours Prof. Swanson spends on grading is only approximate.

D) No, because Prof. Swanson doesn't always teach summer classes.

CONTINUE

Questions 12-22 are based on the following passage.

The Midnight Ride of Sybil Ludington

Paul Revere's midnight ride is legendary, but the story of a similar ride made by a teenaged girl named Sybil Ludington is less well-known. **12** Her journey through the rough countryside of Putnam County, New York, was of equal importance to the Continental Army during the Revolutionary War. **13** Though her ride helped win a battle, General George Washington visited her family farm to personally thank the brave girl.

12

Which choice would most effectively develop the main topic of this passage?

A) NO CHANGE

B) Sybil Ludington rode a horse, named "Star," married a man named Edmund Ogden, and lived to the age of 77.

C) During the Revolutionary War, a number of people rode through the night to warn about impending battles.

D) Paul Revere went on to serve in the militia, and become a successful entrepreneur.

13

A) NO CHANGE

B) Whereas

C) Insofar as

D) Because

CONTINUE

Before the Revolutionary War **14** inaugurated, Sybil Ludington led a fairly stable and secure life. Her father, Henry Ludington, was a successful farmer and businessman. He had also served the British crown in the French and Indian War, and he remained a Loyalist **15** until 1773, when he joined the rebel cause. Because of his extensive military experience, Henry Ludington was named a Colonel and commissioned to lead a regiment of the Continental Army made up of local men.

[1] In late April of 1777, British General William Tryon led a company of 2,000 men in an attack on Danbury, Connecticut, some 20 plus miles away from the Ludington home. [2] Riders were dispatched to find help in battling Tryon's soldiers. [3] The British destroyed the munitions stored **16** they're by the Continental Army before setting all the homes owned by revolutionaries on fire. [4] On the night of April 26, 1777, one of these riders arrived at the Ludington farm. [5] Because it was planting season, Colonel Ludington's regiment had disbanded; someone would have to spread the word that they must regroup. [6] The rider from Danbury was exhausted and the Colonel had to prepare for battle, so it was decided that Sybil, then 16, would go. **17**

14

A) NO CHANGE
B) initiated
C) broke out
D) blew up

15

A) NO CHANGE
B) until 1773 when he
C) until 1773. When he
D) until, 1773, when he

16

A) NO CHANGE
B) their
C) there
D) they are

17

For the sake of cohesion of the paragraph, sentence 2 should be placed

A) where it is now.
B) after sentence 3.
C) after sentence 4.
D) before sentence 6.

CONTINUE

She saddled her horse Star and set off into the dark [18] night, made even darker, by a powerful rainstorm. Riding over muddy roads that ran through deep woods, Sybil stopped at the farmhouses of the militiamen and [19] shouts, "The British are burning Danbury; muster at Ludington's!" By the time Sybil returned home the next morning, she had ridden 40 miles and most of the 400 members of her father's regiment were assembled at the farm. [20] By this time, Sybil's clothes were completely wet and muddy. They set off in pursuit of Tryon's troops, whom they encountered in Ridgefield, Connecticut. As a result of that battle, Tryon withdrew his troops from Connecticut, never to return.

18

A) NO CHANGE

B) night made even darker by

C) night made even darker, by

D) night, made even darker by

19

A) NO CHANGE

B) shouting

C) to shout

D) shouted

20

The writer is considering deleting this sentence. It should be

A) kept, because it makes sense that Sybil would have been soaked after riding through the rain.

B) kept, because it helps to explain why Sybil made her ride so quickly and how she inspired the assembled troops.

C) deleted, because it interrupts the transition from information about assembled troops to their action with extraneous information.

D) deleted, because Sybil's personal comfort is not relevant to the story of her ride.

CONTINUE

Shortly thereafter, General Washington visited the Ludington home to thank Sybil for [21] one's courageous ride. Although she rode twice as far as he did, Sybil never became as famous as Paul Revere. [22] As a result, she has been honored for her role in history: there is a statue of her near the location of the farm in Carmel, New York, and the U.S. Postal Service also honored her with a stamp in 1975.

21

A) NO CHANGE
B) her
C) she
D) their

22

A) NO CHANGE
B) However,
C) Therefore,
D) In addition,

CONTINUE

Questions 23-33 are based on the following passage.

After The Fall

Sometime around 1560, the Dutch Renaissance painter Pietcr Bruegel the Elder painted a work known as "The Fall of Icarus." Acquired by the Musées Royaux des Beaux-Arts in Brussels, Belgium, the painting depicts the fate of Icarus, the son of Daedelus, who flew too close to the sun.

According to myth, **23** Daedelus, and Icarus were imprisoned after Daedelus betrayed King Minos of Crete. **24** Although Daedelus warned him not to fly too close the sun, Icarus was overcome with the thrill of flight and flew too high. The wax melted, rendering the wings useless, and the young lad fell into the sea where he drowned.

23

A) NO CHANGE
B) Daedelus and Icarus
C) Daedelus; and Icarus
D) Daedelus—and Icarus

24

Which sentence, inserted here, would most effectively develop the series of events described in the paragraph?

A) Icarus was unjustly accused for a crime he didn't commit, which made his father absolutely furious.
B) To escape, the father and son flew to freedom using wings they had built from bird feathers held together with wax.
C) King Minos was a cruel man who imprisoned a number of his subjects for no reason.
D) Because Daedelus was an inventor, he made wings out of wax, wood, and some bird feathers.

CONTINUE

"The Fall of Icarus" has [25] induced the work of poets and captured the imagination of countless art scholars. Despite this—or perhaps because of this—there seems to be some argument about how to interpret its meaning. In spite of the title, the painting does not focus on [26] Icarus spectacular fall into the sea; all we see of this tragic youth are his legs flailing just above the water's surface. The central figure is actually a farmer plowing his [27] field. Other figures include a shepherd, a fisherman, and a merchant ship. All of these figures are simply going about their day, paying no attention to the drowning Icarus.

25

A) NO CHANGE
B) driven
C) provoked
D) inspired

26

A) NO CHANGE
B) Icaruses
C) Icarus's
D) that of Icarus

27

Which choice most effectively combines the sentences at the underlined portion?

A) field, other
B) field, but other
C) field; other
D) field: other

[1] After viewing the painting in 1938, W. H. Auden was inspired to write the poem "Musée des Beaux Arts." [2] **28** <u>They</u> wrote, "... how everything turns away / Quite leisurely from the disaster; the ploughman may / Have heard the splash, the forsaken cry, / But for him it was not an important failure. ..." [3] It's so tragic. [4] **29** <u>As an allegory, Auden clearly interpreted the painting as</u> about the nature of suffering and human indifference to that suffering. **30**

William Carlos Williams mentions the genre of the painting in the title of his poem "Landscape with the Fall of Icarus," though the last lines of the poem discuss the fall: "unsignificantly / off the coast / there was / a splash quite unnoticed / this was / Icarus drowning." **31** <u>By adding the word "Landscape" as an addition to</u> the title of the painting, Williams subordinates the fall, just as Bruegels did.

28

A) NO CHANGE

B) He

C) Him

D) One

29

A) NO CHANGE

B) Auden clearly interpreted the painting as an allegory

C) Auden, as an allegory, clearly interpreted the painting as

D) Clearly, Auden interpreted as an allegory the painting

30

The writer is considering deleting one of the sentences in this paragraph. Which deletion would most improve the focus of the paragraph?

A) DELETE Sentence 1

B) DELETE Sentence 2

C) DELETE Sentence 3

D) DELETE Sentence 4

31

A) NO CHANGE

B) By revising the name of

C) By adding the word "Landscape" to

D) By adding to the title the word "landscape"

CONTINUE

Though both commenting on Bruegels's work, Auden and Williams offer different interpretations. While Auden recognizes the problem with the human tendency to become preoccupied by the demands of everyday life, the poem by Williams intensifies the lack of concern and seems almost like a protest against privileging the ordinary over the catastrophic. **32** <u>Each artist offers his own view.</u> Because Bruegels remained **33** <u>moot</u> about his intentions for this painting, each viewer is free to offer his or her own interpretation.

32

The writer is considering deleting the underlined sentence. Should the sentence be kept or deleted?

A) Kept, because it provides a detail that supports the main topic of the paragraph.

B) Kept, because it supports the main argument of the passage.

C) Deleted, because it unnecessarily repeats information that has been provided earlier in the paragraph.

D) Deleted, because it fails to support the main argument of the passage as introduced in the first paragraph.

33

A) NO CHANGE

B) mood

C) mute

D) mused

CONTINUE

Questions 34-44 are based on the following passage.

Frozen Smoke

What is 1,000 times less dense than [34] glass has been used as insulation on the Mars Exploration Rover and thermal sports bottles, and can collect interstellar dust? The answer is aerogel, a material that can be made of silica, carbon, iron oxide, organic polymers, semiconductor nanostructures, gold, copper, and up to 99.8% air. An aerogel made from graphene is the least dense material in the world, but all aerogels are very light and have other remarkable properties.

Though it sounds like [35] an impossible invention in some book, aerogel is very real. Aerogel is made by [36] creating a gel in a solution, then the slow removal of the liquid component using high temperatures, effectively drying the gel so that it maintains its structural shape. The liquid is then replaced by air. The resulting foam is as [37] slim as a cloud, but strong enough to survive the force of a rocket launch.

34

A) NO CHANGE
B) glass, has
C) glass; has
D) glass. Has

35

A) NO CHANGE
B) some stuff that just got made up
C) it's just plain made up
D) the stuff of science fiction

36

A) NO CHANGE
B) creation of a gel in a solution, then the slow removing of
C) creating a gel in a solution, then slowly removing
D) creating a gel in a solution, then you remove

37

A) NO CHANGE
B) emaciated
C) frail
D) wispy

CONTINUE

Because of its unique properties, NASA used aerogel for its "Stardust" mission, 38 which collected dust from the "Wild 2" comet. The aerogel trapped the fragile particles without damaging them, even though the dust travels through space at about 6 times the speed of a rifle bullet. It is so porous that it slows the dust to a stop gradually, without creating heat that could alter the dust.

[1] It can either be injected into existing cavities in older buildings, or 39 it is manufactured as insulating boards for new construction. [2] Aerogel also has more mundane applications, thanks to certain thermal properties. [3] "R-value" is a standard measure of thermal resistance, and 40 aerogel's r-value is higher than those of all other forms of insulation. [4] Because it has such high thermal resistance, aerogel is a valuable form of insulation. [5] An aerogel-based plaster has even been developed for use in historic buildings that must appear authentic while being made energy efficient. 41

R-Values of Various Insulators

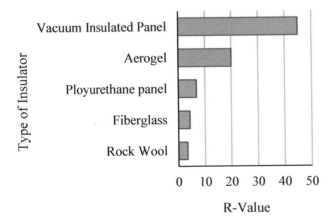

38

A) NO CHANGE
B) who
C) what
D) whom

39

A) NO CHANGE
B) by being manufactured
C) by manufacturing it
D) it can be manufactured

40

Which choice most accurately and effectively represents the information in the graph?

A) NO CHANGE
B) the r-value of aerogel is lower than that of either rock wool or fiberglass.
C) aerogel has a higher r-value than do traditional forms of insulation, like rock wool.
D) aerogel is a better choice of insulation than vacuum insulated panels for most buildings.

41

For the sake of cohesion of the paragraph, sentence 1 should be placed

A) where it is now.
B) after sentence 2.
C) after sentence 3.
D) after sentence 4.

42 Researchers at the University of Wisconsin-Madison are currently exploring ways that aerogels may be developed for cleaning up oil and chemical spills. The specific aerogel these researchers are working with is made of cellulose nanofibrils and an environmentally friendly polymer. Even the process is environmentally friendly, using freeze-drying to **43** avoid the use of potentially harmful organic solvent.

The wide range of current applications for aerogels promises to become even wider as ongoing improvements to the manufacturing process produce **44** aerogels with greater strength, lower density, or other novel properties.

Which choice most effectively establishes the main point of the paragraph?

A) The researchers at University of Wisconsin-Madison know how to freeze-dry cellulose and use safer polymers.

B) Beyond its use as an effective insulator, aerogel may have additional environmentally beneficial uses.

C) Aerogel is made in Wisconsin using eco-friendly materials like polymers and nanofibrils.

D) The way aerogel is currently manufactured makes it hard on the environment and useless for tasks like cleaning up oil spills.

43

A) NO CHANGE

B) dodge

C) foreswear

D) renounce

44

A) NO CHANGE

B) aerogels; with greater strength; lower density; or other

C) aerogels with: greater strength, lower density, or other

D) aerogels with greater strength lower density or other

STOP

If you complete this section before the end of your allotted time, check your work on this section only. Do NOT use the time to work on another section.

Section 3

Math Test – No Calculator

25 MINUTES, 20 QUESTIONS

Turn to Section 3 of your answer sheet to answer the questions in this section.

DIRECTIONS

Questions **1-15** ask you to solve a problem, select the best answer among four choices, and fill in the corresponding circle on your answer sheet. Questions **16-20** ask you to solve a problem and enter your answer in the grid provided on your answer sheet. There are detailed instructions on entering answers into the grid before question 16. You may use your test booklet for scratch work.

NOTES

1. You **may not** use a calculator.
2. Variables and expressions represent real numbers unless stated otherwise.
3. Figures are drawn to scale unless stated otherwise.
4. Figures lie in a plane unless stated otherwise.
5. The domain of a function f is defined as the set of all real numbers x for which $f(x)$ is also a real number, unless stated otherwise.

REFERENCE

$$A = \frac{1}{2}bh$$

$$a^2 + b^2 = c^2$$

Special Triangles

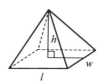

$$V = \frac{1}{3}lwh$$

$$V = \frac{1}{3}\pi r^2 h$$

$$A = lw$$

$$V = lwh$$

$$V = \pi r^2 h$$

$$A = \pi r^2$$
$$C = 2\pi r$$

$$V = \frac{4}{3}\pi r^3$$

There are 360° in a circle.

The sum of the angles in a triangle is 180°.

The number of radians of arc in a circle is 2π.

CONTINUE

1

If 20 less than $3x$ is 40, then what is the value of x?

A) 3

B) 20

C) 30

D) 40

2

$$y = 5n + 6$$
$$y = n^2 - 2n - 24$$

For which value of n are the equations above equivalent?

A) 0

B) 5

C) 10

D) 15

3

If $\dfrac{x-5}{4} = y$ and $y = 6$, what is the value of x?

A) 5

B) 10

C) 29

D) 36

4

An anthropologist proposes that the change in a certain population can be modeled by the expression $\sqrt{9x^2} - 7x$. If x is positive, this expression is equivalent to which of the following?

A) $2x$

B) $-4x$

C) $3x^2 - 7x$

D) $3x - \sqrt{7x}$

5

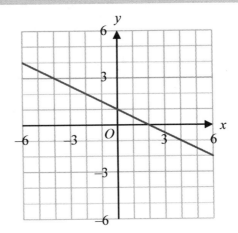

What is the slope of the function in the graph above?

A) $-\dfrac{1}{2}$

B) $\dfrac{1}{2}$

C) 2

D) 4

CONTINUE

6

A line in the *xy*-plane passes through the point $(1, 1)$ and has a slope of $\frac{1}{3}$. Which of the following points lies on the line?

A) $(0, 0)$

B) $(4, 3)$

C) $(6, 3)$

D) $(7, 3)$

7

What is the value of i^8? (Note: $i = \sqrt{-1}$.)

A) -1

B) $-i$

C) 1

D) i

8

A computer programmer can write 3 pages of HTML code in 5 hours and 2 pages of JavaScript code in 3 hours. How long will it take her to create 6 new websites, each consisting of one page of HTML code and one page of JavaScript?

A) 18 hours

B) 19 hours

C) 20 hours

D) 21 hours

9

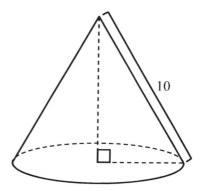

Note: figure is not drawn to scale.

What is the volume of the cone in the diagram above if the diameter of the base is 16?

A) 32π

B) 96π

C) 128π

D) 192π

CONTINUE

10

The expression $(n^3 - 3n^2 + 5)(n^2 - n)$ is equivalent to which of the following?

A) $n^5 - 4n^4 + 3n^3 + 5n^2 - 5n$

B) $n^5 - n^4 - 3n^3 + 8n^2 - 5n$

C) $n^5 - 3n^4 + 5n^2$

D) $n^5 - 4n^4 + 3n^3$

11

$$\frac{2x}{y} = 12$$

$$8(y + 2) = x$$

If (x, y) is the solution to the system of equations above, what is the value of y?

A)   8

B)   4

C) −4

D) −8

12

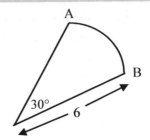

Note: figure is not drawn to scale.

What is length of arc AB in the figure above?

A) 180

B)   90

C) π

D) $\dfrac{\pi}{2}$

13

Carlos bought an iPad online at 15 percent off the original price. The total amount he paid was d dollars including a 6 percent sales tax on the discounted price. Which of the following expressions represents the original price of the iPad in terms of d?

A) $\dfrac{d}{(1.06)(0.85)}$

B) $\dfrac{d(1.06)}{0.85}$

C) $\dfrac{d}{0.85 + 1.06}$

D) $\dfrac{d}{0.85}$

CONTINUE

14

A certain subatomic particle's energy, e, increases as its distance, d, from a set point increases. Which of the following expressions could model this behavior?

A) $e = d - 12^d + 12$

B) $e = -d^2 + 100d + 9$

C) $e = 5d^3 + 50d - 20$

D) $e = 10d^2 - 10^d + 80$

15

The force of gravity between two objects, F, can be modeled by the equation $F = G\dfrac{m_1 m_2}{d^2}$, where G is a constant, m_1 and m_2 are the masses of the two objects, and d is the distance between them. If the distance between the two objects were to double, what would happen to the force of gravity between them?

A) It would double

B) It would decrease by half

C) It would quadruple

D) It would decrease by three quarters

CONTINUE

DIRECTIONS

Questions **16-20** ask you to solve a problem and enter your answer in the grid provided on your answer sheet. When completing grid-in questions:

1. You are required to bubble in the circles for your answers. It is recommended, but not required, that you also write your answer in the boxes above the columns of circles. Points will be awarded based only on whether the circles are filled in correctly.

2. Fill in only one circle in a column.

3. You can start your answer in any column as long as you can fit in the whole answer.

4. For questions 16-20, no answers will be negative numbers.

5. **Mixed numbers,** such as $4\frac{2}{5}$, must be gridded as decimals or improper fractions, such as 4.4 or as 22/5. "42/5" will be read as "forty-two over five," not as "four and two-fifths."

6. If your answer is a **decimal** with more digits than will fit on the grid, you may round it or cut it off, but you must fill the entire grid.

7. If there are **multiple correct solutions** to a problem, all of them will be considered correct. Enter only **one** on the grid.

CONTINUE →

16

In the *xy*-plane, lines *k* and *j* are perpendicular. Line *k* is represented by $y = -\frac{2}{3}x + 1$. What is the slope of line *j*?

17

Amelie leaves her house and runs south at a constant speed of 5 miles per hour. If her brother leaves the same house two hours later and skateboards south at a constant speed of 15 miles per hour, how long will it take him, in hours, to reach Amelie?

18

If $f(x) = x^3 - 10x + 1$ and $g(x) = f(2x)$, what is $g(3)$?

19

Charlie lives 15 miles downhill from the summit of the dormant Haleakala volcano. Charlie leaves his home, bikes to the top of Haleakala, and then bikes back. If Charlie ascends at 12 miles per hour and descends at 36 miles per hour, how many minutes will it take Charlie to make a round trip from his home to the volcano and back?

20

Sarah has 15 pairs of shoes, and the size of her collection doubles every 5 years. If Sarah decides to donate 10 percent of her shoes after 15 years, how many pairs of shoes will she have left after the donation?

STOP

If you complete this section before the end of your allotted time, check your work on this section only. Do NOT use the time to work on another section.

Section 4

Math Test – Calculator

55 MINUTES, 38 QUESTIONS

Turn to Section 4 of your answer sheet to answer the questions in this section.

Questions **1-30** ask you to solve a problem, select the best answer among four choices, and fill in the corresponding circle on your answer sheet. Questions **31-38** ask you to solve a problem and enter your answer in the grid provided on your answer sheet. There are detailed instructions on entering answers into the grid before question 31. You may use your test booklet for scratch work.

1. You **may** use a calculator.
2. Variables and expressions represent real numbers unless stated otherwise.
3. Figures are drawn to scale unless stated otherwise.
4. Figures lie in a plane unless stated otherwise.
5. The domain of a function f is defined as the set of all real numbers x for which $f(x)$ is also a real number, unless stated otherwise.

$$A = \frac{1}{2}bh$$

$$a^2 + b^2 = c^2$$

 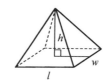

Special Triangles

$$V = \frac{1}{3}lwh$$

$$V = \frac{1}{3}\pi r^2 h$$

$$A = lw$$

$$V = lwh$$

$$V = \pi r^2 h$$

$$A = \pi r^2$$
$$C = 2\pi r$$

$$V = \frac{4}{3}\pi r^3$$

There are 360° in a circle.

The sum of the angles in a triangle is 180°.

The number of radians of arc in a circle is 2π.

CONTINUE

1

Every thirty minutes the mass of a substance increases by forty-eight grams. If the substance weighs 111 grams after an hour, how many grams did it originally weigh?

A) 0

B) 8

C) 15

D) 71

2

Day	Number of Manuscripts Edited
Tuesday	x
Wednesday	$2.5x$
Thursday	$3.5x$
Friday	$4x$

Bartleby edits manuscripts at a rate according to x, as defined in the chart above. If he works every day, begins editing on Tuesday, and edits 33 manuscripts by the end of the day on Friday, what is the value of x?

A) 2

B) 3

C) 4

D) 5

3

Skye spends $1.75 per day on her online newspaper subscriptions. How much does she spend for the months of July, August, and September? (July and August each have 31 days and September has 30 days.)

A) $52.50

B) $108.50

C) $161.00

D) $161.50

4

If $\dfrac{x}{y} = 4$, what is the value of $\dfrac{6x}{y}$?

A) 6

B) 16

C) 24

D) 36

CONTINUE

5

Which of the expressions shown below is equivalent to $5x^2 + 13x - 6$?

I. $(5x - 2)(x + 3)$
II. $(x - 2)(5x + 3)$
III. $5(x - 2)(x + 3)$

A) I only

B) II only

C) III only

D) I, II, and III

6

Traffic Regulation Survey Results			
Age	Support	Oppose	Total
18-34	24	53	77
35-54	62	32	94
55-74	71	32	103
75 and older	44	18	62
Total	201	135	336

A city is considering a new traffic regulation. City planners conducted a survey of a random sample of adult residents about their position on the new regulation. The results of the survey are summarized in the chart above. Which of the following statements is supported by the chart's data?

A) A person between 35 and 54 years old is less likely to oppose the regulation than a person between 55 and 74 years old.

B) A person between 35 and 54 years old is equally likely to oppose the regulation as a person between 55 and 74 years old.

C) A person between 18 and 34 years old is more likely to oppose the regulation than a person between 55 and 74 years old.

D) The data is insufficient to support any of the statements above.

CONTINUE

7

$$y = x^2 + 5x - 4$$
$$y = 6x + 2$$

If (x, y) is the solution to the system of equations above, which of the following is a possible value of the product xy?

A) −200

B) −20

C) 6

D) 60

8

In the xy-plane, the line $mx - 6y = 24$ passes through the point $(3, 6)$. What is the value of m?

A) 6

B) 12

C) 20

D) 60

9

$$3(x + 5) + 7 = 22$$

What is the value of x in the equation above?

A) 0

B) $\dfrac{3}{7}$

C) $\dfrac{7}{3}$

D) 11

10

$$|x - 4| \le 6$$

Which of the following inequalities is equivalent to the inequality above?

A) $-2 \le x \le 10$

B) $-4 \le x \le 10$

C) $x \le 4$ or $x \ge 10$

D) $x \le -10$ or $x \ge 2$

CONTINUE

11

x	0	3	6	9
$f(x)$	2	6	10	14

Which of the following equations defines $f(x)$ in the table above?

A) $f(x) = \dfrac{4}{3}x + 2$

B) $f(x) = \dfrac{3}{4}x + 1$

C) $f(x) = -\dfrac{4}{3}x$

D) $f(x) = 4x + 2$

12

Which of the following scenarios could be modeled by y in the equation $y = t^2 + 4t + 10$, where t represents time?

A) A population of ladybugs that doubles every four weeks

B) The height of a rock that is dropped off a ten-foot cliff

C) The height of a hot air balloon that accelerates as it rises

D) The value of an investment that increases by 5% every quarter

13

Employment Status of Residents in Franklin County			
Education Level	Employed	Unemployed or Not in Labor Force	Total
Less than High School Diploma	198	164	362
High School Graduate	510	318	828
Some College	367	153	520
College Graduate	707	216	923
Total	1782	851	2633

The table above shows data from a survey of the employment status of residents in Franklin County. The participants were randomly selected from all residents over the age of 25 years old. Based on the given data, what is the likelihood that an employed worker over the age of 25 has not attended college?

A) 28.6%

B) 39.7%

C) 54.7%

D) 59.5%

CONTINUE

14

Genetic Divergence of Species

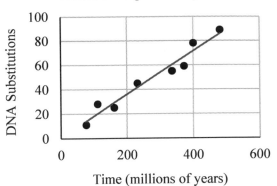

Time (millions of years)

The number of differences in two species' DNA sequences can be used to estimate when those species branched off from a common ancestor. The plot above shows the number of substitutions, S, in the DNA sequence of certain animals compared to the human DNA sequence. The time, T, since the species shared a common ancestor is measured in millions of years. Which of the following equations is the best estimate for the plot's line of best fit?

A) $S = 0.2T$

B) $S = 0.2T + 10$

C) $S = 5.5T$

D) $S = 5.5T + 10$

15

$$x^2 + 2x - 2$$
$$3x^2 - x - 1$$

What is the product of the expressions above?

A) $3x^4 + 5x^3 - 9x^2 + 2$

B) $3x^4 + 5x^3 - 9x^2 + 2x$

C) $3x^4 + 5x^3 - 8x^2 + 2x$

D) $3x^4 + 5x^3 - 8x^2 + 2x + 2$

CONTINUE

Questions 16 and 17 refer to the following information.

The nine-banded armadillo, frequently found in the southern United States, eats about 500 different kinds of food. Around 10% of its daily intake consists of plants. Female armadillos over 1 year of age commonly give birth to quadruplets and may give birth to over 50 young in a lifetime. The chart below shows the population of the nine-banded armadillo in a rural district from 2012-2014. The population counts were taken at the beginning of each year.

Armadillos in Rural District

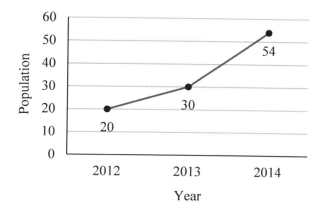

16

If the average nine-banded armadillo eats 3 lbs of food per day, what is the approximate weight of plant matter, in pounds, consumed by three armadillos in one week?

A) 2.1

B) 6.3

C) 21

D) 63

17

Five females had litters in 2012, and 12 females had litters in 2013. Assuming that four baby armadillos were born with every litter, how many armadillos did not survive between 2012 and 2014?

A) 24

B) 34

C) 40

D) 54

CONTINUE

18

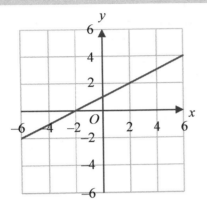

Which of the following functions represents the graph above?

A) $f(x) = \dfrac{1}{2}x + 1$

B) $f(x) = -\dfrac{1}{2}x + 1$

C) $f(x) = 2x - 1$

D) $f(x) = -\dfrac{1}{2}x - 1$

19

Data Set A: 1, 1, 2, 4, 4, 6
Data Set B: 2, 2, 3, 3, 5

Which of the following statements is supported by the information provided above?

A) Data Set A has a larger mean than Data Set B; Data Set A has a larger standard deviation than Data Set B.

B) Data Set A has a larger mean than Data Set B; Data Set A has a smaller standard deviation than Data Set B.

C) Data Set A and Data Set B have the same mean; Data Set A has a larger standard deviation than Data Set B.

D) Data Set A and Data Set B have the same mean; Data Set A has a smaller standard deviation than Data Set B.

CONTINUE

20

Package 1   Package 2

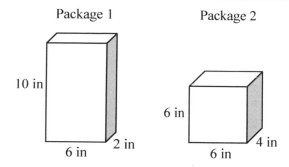

10 in

6 in

2 in

6 in

6 in

4 in

6 in

The figures above show two options for packaging. The material required for Package 1 is 184 in², and the material required for Package 2 is 168 in². A company measures package efficiency as package volume per square inch of packaging material. If both packages are filled completely with a uniform liquid, which of the following statements is true?

A) Package 1 is more efficient than Package 2 by approximately 0.20 in³ per in².

B) Package 1 is more efficient than Package 2 by approximately 0.37 in³ per in².

C) Package 2 is more efficient than Package 1 by approximately 0.20 in³ per in².

D) Package 2 is more efficient than Package 1 by approximately 0.37 in³ per in².

21

An auto dealership is offering a deal on used cars. The final sale price of each car is 5% off the pre-sale price, plus an additional 1% off the pre-sale price for every 10,000 miles on the car's odometer.

Kara is considering two cars at the dealership. Car 1 has a pre-sale price of \$4,500 with 80,000 miles on its odometer and Car 2 has a pre-sale price of \$5,200 with 20,000 miles on its odometer. What is the difference, rounded to the nearest dollar, between the sale prices of Car 1 and Car 2?

A) \$903

B) \$908

C) \$921

D) \$926

22

$$2y = \frac{x}{5} - 1$$

$$y = \frac{2x + 8}{3}$$

What is the solution of the system of equations above?

A) No solutions

B) $\left(-\dfrac{95}{17}, -\dfrac{18}{17}\right)$

C) $\left(-\dfrac{85}{19}, -\dfrac{18}{19}\right)$

D) Infinitely many solutions

CONTINUE

23

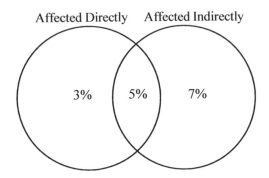

Affected Directly   Affected Indirectly

3%   5%   7%

The chart above shows data on how an increase in the number of school music programs affects students in schools. At Shelby High School, 56 students, 8% of the total student population, have indicated that they are directly affected by an increase in the school's music programs. Based on the data above, what is the best estimate for the number of students who are only affected indirectly by an increase in the school's music programs?

A)   49

B)   79

C)   84

D)   141

24

If $f(x) = 5x^2 + 8x - 4$ and $g(x) = x + 2$, what is $\dfrac{f(n)}{g(n)}$ when $n = 3$?

A) 65

B) 26

C) 15

D) 13

25

Change in Teens' Physical Activity

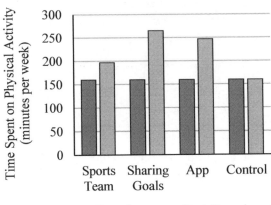

■ Pre-Experiment   ■ Post-Experiment

A psychologist conducted a study to compare different methods of encouraging teenagers to participate in physical activities. The three methods studied were obligatory participation on a sports team, sharing personal goals with a friend, and recording physical activity on an interactive smartphone app. Participants were randomly assigned to one of these methods or a control group. The study measured the participants' increase in physical activity one month after the experiment. The results are shown in the bar graph above.

Which of the following statements is supported by the data?

A)   Participation on a sports team was the most effective of the studied methods for increasing physical activity.

B)   Every method that was studied increased teens' physical activity at the time of the post-study measurement.

C)   Teens' physical activity will decline over time if no method is employed to encourage it.

D)   Joining a sports team helped teens find time for physical activity.

CONTINUE

Questions 26 and 27 refer to the following information.

Results from the 2007 census for the Mining, Quarrying, and Oil and Gas Extracting sector of the U.S. economy are compared to census results from 1997 and 2002. The comparison of the sector based on establishments with more than one employee is summarized in the table below.

Mining, Quarry, and Oil and Gas Extracting Economic Sector for the U.S.			
	1997	2002	2007
Number of Establishments	25,000	24,087	22,667
Value of Shipments ($ Millions)	173,985	182,911	413,525
Annual Payroll ($ Millions)	20,798	21,174	40,687
Total Employment	509,006	477,840	730,433
Payroll Per Employee ($)	40,861	44,312	55,703
US Total Population	272,646,925	287,625,193	301,231,207
US Population Per Establishment	10,906	11,941	13,289

26

Which of the following statements is true for the period from 2002 to 2007?

A) Fewer establishments resulted in lower shipment values for the sector.

B) Overall, the value of shipments in the sector per U.S. person more than doubled.

C) With a greater number of people employed in the sector, the average person was paid less.

D) With fewer establishments, there were fewer people employed in the sector.

27

An analyst compared the ratio of the value of shipments to annual payroll from 1997 to 2007. What is the approximate percentage growth, to the nearest tenth of a percent, of this ratio during this period?

A) 21.5%

B) 95.6%

C) 237.7%

D) 836.5%

CONTINUE

28

Salbutamol, a chemical used to treat asthma, has a biological half-life of 1.6 hours, which means that after 1.6 hours in the body, salbutamol loses half of its therapeutic activity. If salbutamol's therapeutic activity starts at a value of 480, what is its value of therapeutic activity after the chemical has been in the body for 480 minutes?

A) 7

B) 15

C) 30

D) 60

29

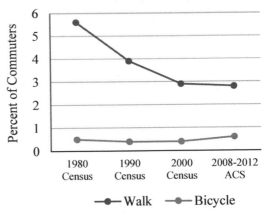

Walking and Bicycling to Work: 1980 to 2008-2012

Sources: U.S. Census Bureau, Decennial Census, 1980, 1990, 2000; American Community Survey, 2008-2012.

Researchers conducted a study on commuters' choice of transportation to work. The chart above displays some of the data they collected. Which of the following statements is supported by the chart?

A) Walking was the most popular mode of transportation for commuters between 1980 and 2012.

B) The number of commuters who bicycled to work decreased from 1980 to 2000.

C) The percentage of commuters who walked to work decreased more slowly between 1980 and 1990 than between 1990 and 2000.

D) In 2000, about 6 times as many commuters walked to work as biked to work.

CONTINUE

30

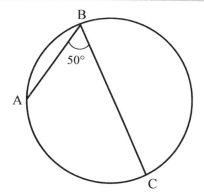

Note: figure is not drawn to scale.

In the diagram above, what is the length, in radians, of arc AC if the radius of the circle is 10 and BC is the diameter?

A) $\dfrac{25\pi}{18}$

B) $\dfrac{25\pi}{9}$

C) $\dfrac{50\pi}{9}$

D) $\dfrac{100\pi}{9}$

CONTINUE

DIRECTIONS

Questions **31-38** ask you to solve a problem and enter your answer in the grid provided on your answer sheet. When completing grid-in questions:

1. You are required to bubble in the circles for your answers. It is recommended, but not required, that you also write your answer in the boxes above the columns of circles. Points will be awarded based only on whether the circles are filled in correctly.

2. Fill in only one circle in a column.

3. You can start your answer in any column as long as you can fit in the whole answer.

4. For questions 31-38, no answers will be negative numbers.

5. **Mixed numbers,** such as $4\frac{2}{5}$, must be gridded as decimals or improper fractions, such as 4.4 or as 22/5. "42/5" will be read as "forty-two over five," not as "four and two-fifths."

6. If your answer is a **decimal** with more digits than will fit on the grid, you may round it or cut it off, but you must fill the entire grid.

7. If there are **multiple correct solutions** to a problem, all of them will be considered correct. Enter only **one** on the grid.

CONTINUE

31

$$y = 0.25x + 5$$

In the equation above, what is the value of x if $y = 6$?

32

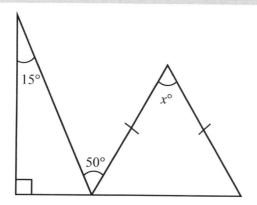

Note: figure is not drawn to scale.

In the diagram above, what is the value of x?

33

A farmer transports oranges in crates that each contain 5 pounds of oranges. The farmer can fit 16 crates in her truck, and the total revenue from one truckload of oranges is $96. What is the price of the oranges in dollars per pound?

34

If $f(x) = 6x + 1$ and $g(x) = 2x - 1$, what is the value of $\dfrac{f(3)}{g(f(0))}$?

35

The Earth's speed of rotation is slowly decreasing. 900 million years ago, one day was 18 hours long, whereas today it is 24 hours long, and there are 365 days in a year. Assuming the Earth took the same amount of time to orbit the sun as it does today, how many days did one year contain 900 million years ago? Round your answer to the nearest whole number.

36

An object's mass in kilograms, m, is represented by the equation $3\sqrt{m} - \sqrt{162} = 0$. What is the object's mass in kilograms?

CONTINUE

Questions 37 and 38 refer to the following information.

Boyle's law asserts that at a constant temperature, the pressure and volume of any gas are inversely proportional. The law is written according to the equation $PV = k$, where P is the pressure of a gas, V is the volume of a gas, and k is a constant.

37

A gas is contained within a cylindrical syringe with a rubber stopper, as shown in the diagram below. The gas in the syringe initially has a pressure of 78 kilopascals, and takes up 30 cm^2. If the stopper is then pushed down so that the gas takes up 20 cm^2 what is the new pressure of the gas in kilopascals?

Gas

38

A second gas is held in a separate container with a pressure of 15.6 kilopascals and an initial volume of 50 cm^2. If the volume of the gas's container is decreased by 40%, what is the new pressure of the gas, in kilopascals?

STOP

If you complete this section before the end of your allotted time, check your work on this section only. Do NOT use the time to work on another section.

Essay

Essay (Optional)

50 MINUTES

Turn to the lined pages of your answer sheet to write your essay.

DIRECTIONS

This essay is optional. It is a chance for you to demonstrate how well you can understand and analyze a written passage. Your essay should show that you have carefully read the passage and should be a concisely written analysis that is both logical and clear.

You must write your entire essay on the lines in your answer booklet. No additional paper will be provided aside from the Planning Page inside your answer booklet. You will be able to write your entire essay in the space provided if you make use of every line, keep tight margins, and write at a suitable size. Don't forget to keep your handwriting legible for the readers evaluating your essay.

You will have 50 minutes to read the passage in this booklet and to write an essay in response to the prompt provided at the end of the passage.

REMINDERS

- What you write in this booklet will not be evaluated. Write your essay in the answer booklet only.

- Essays that are off-topic will not be evaluated.

As you read the following passage, consider how Christine Porath uses

- evidence, like examples or facts, to support her arguments.
- logical reasoning to develop her ideas and to connect her claims to her evidence.
- stylistic or persuasive techniques, such as the choice of particular words or appeals to her readers' emotions, to give power to the ideas put forth.

Adapted from Christine Porath, "No Time to Be Nice at Work." © 2015 by The New York Times Company. Originally published June 19, 2015.

1   Rudeness and bad behavior have all grown over the last decades, particularly at work. For nearly 20 years I've been studying, consulting, and collaborating with organizations around the world to learn more about the costs of this incivility. How we treat one another at work matters. Insensitive interactions have a way of whittling away at people's health, performance and souls.

2   Robert M. Sapolsky, a Stanford professor and the author of *Why Zebras Don't Get Ulcers*, argues that when people experience intermittent stressors like incivility for too long or too often, their immune systems pay the price. We also may experience major health problems, including cardiovascular disease, cancer, diabetes and ulcers.

3   Intermittent stressors—like experiencing or witnessing uncivil incidents or even replaying one in your head—elevate levels of hormones called glucocorticoids throughout the day, potentially leading to a host of health problems, including increased appetite and obesity. A study published in 2012 that tracked women for 10 years concluded that stressful jobs increased the risk of a cardiovascular event by 38 percent.

4   I've surveyed hundreds of people across organizations spanning more than 17 industries, and asked people why they behaved uncivilly. Over half of them claim it is because they are overloaded, and more than 40 percent say they have no time to be nice. But respect doesn't necessarily require extra time. It's about how something is conveyed; tone and nonverbal manner are crucial.

5   Incivility also hijacks workplace focus. According to a survey of more than 4,500 doctors, nurses and other hospital personnel, 71 percent tied disruptive behavior, such as abusive, condescending or insulting personal conduct, to medical errors, and 27 percent tied such behavior to patient deaths.

6   My studies with Amir Erez, a management professor at the University of Florida, show that people working in an environment characterized by incivility miss information that is right in front of them. They are no longer able to process it as well or as efficiently as they would otherwise.

7   In one study, the experimenter belittled the peer group of the participants, who then performed 33 percent worse on anagram word puzzles and came up with 39 percent fewer creative ideas during a brainstorming task focused on how they might use a brick. In our second study, a stranger—a "busy professor" encountered en route to the experiment—was rude to participants by

admonishing them for bothering her. Their performance was 61 percent worse on word puzzles, and they produced 58 percent fewer ideas in the brick task than those who had not been treated rudely. We found the same pattern for those who merely witnessed incivility: they performed 22 percent worse on word puzzles and produced 28 percent fewer ideas in the brainstorming task.

8   Even though a growing number of people are disturbed by incivility, I've found that it has continued to climb over the last two decades. A quarter of those I surveyed in 1998 reported that they were treated rudely at work at least once a week. That figure rose to nearly half in 2005, then to just over half in 2011.

9   Although in surveys people say they are afraid they will not rise in an organization if they are really friendly and helpful, the civil do succeed. My recent studies with Alexandra Gerbasi and Sebastian Schorch at the Grenoble École de Management, published in the *Journal of Applied Psychology*, show that behavior involving politeness and regard for others in the workplace pays off. In a study in a biotechnology company, those seen as civil were twice as likely to be viewed as leaders.

10   Civility pays dividends. J. Gary Hastings, a retired judge in Los Angeles, told me that when he informally polled juries about what determined their favor, he found that respect—and how attorneys behaved—was crucial. Juries were swayed based on thin slices of civil or arrogant behavior.

11   Across many decisions—whom to hire, who will be most effective in teams, who will be able to be influential—civility affects judgments and may shift the balance toward those who are respectful.

12   Given the enormous cost of incivility, it should not be ignored. We all need to reconsider our behavior. You are always in front of some jury. In every interaction, you have a choice: Do you want to lift people up or hold them down?

Write an essay explaining how Christine Porath builds her argument to persuade her audience that civility should be more highly valued than it currently is. Analyze how Porath utilizes at least one of the features in the box above, or features of your own choosing, to make her argument more logical and persuasive. Your analysis should focus on the most relevant features of the passage.

You should not explain whether you agree with Porath's argument; rather, your essay should explain how Porath builds an argument to persuade her readers.

Chapter 3
Answers and Scoring

PRACTICE TEST 1 ANSWERS
PART 1

SECTION 1

1. C	14. D	27. A	40. C
2. B	15. B	28. C	41. A
3. A	16. A	29. B	42. B
4. A	17. A	30. B	43. B
5. D	18. C	31. C	44. B
6. B	19. B	32. D	45. A
7. C	20. D	33. D	46. C
8. D	21. D	34. D	47. A
9. C	22. B	35. A	48. B
10. D	23. B	36. B	49. C
11. A	24. B	37. A	50. D
12. B	25. C	38. B	51. D
13. B	26. A	39. C	52. C

SECTION 2

1. A	12. C	23. B	34. B
2. C	13. C	24. C	35. A
3. B	14. B	25. C	36. C
4. C	15. C	26. B	37. D
5. D	16. A	27. D	38. C
6. B	17. D	28. A	39. A
7. B	18. C	29. D	40. D
8. B	19. C	30. B	41. D
9. C	20. D	31. A	42. C
10. C	21. D	32. B	43. B
11. D	22. A	33. B	44. B

Section 3

1. C	6. B	11. B	16. 3
2. C	7. A	12. B	17. 10
3. B	8. B	13. D	18. 17/2
4. C	9. C	14. A	19. 6
5. D	10. A	15. B	20. 6

Section 4

1. B	11. B	21. B	31. 18
2. B	12. D	22. A	32. 142
3. B	13. C	23. B	33. 18
4. B	14. D	24. C	34. 3
5. D	15. D	25. C	35. 16
6. B	16. C	26. C	36. 4
7. D	17. C	27. C	37. 12
8. B	18. D	28. A	38. 8
9. C	19. C	29. A	
10. A	20. B	30. C	

PRACTICE TEST 2 ANSWERS
PART 2

SECTION 1

1. C	14. D	27. B	40. C
2. B	15. A	28. B	41. A
3. C	16. D	29. D	42. C
4. D	17. D	30. B	43. D
5. D	18. D	31. B	44. C
6. C	19. A	32. B	45. B
7. D	20. B	33. C	46. D
8. A	21. B	34. A	47. D
9. D	22. A	35. C	48. C
10. D	23. A	36. A	49. A
11. B	24. C	37. B	50. C
12. C	25. D	38. C	51. B
13. A	26. D	39. A	52. A

SECTION 2

1. A	12. D	23. B	34. D
2. D	13. B	24. A	35. C
3. A	14. C	25. B	36. B
4. B	15. C	26. B	37. C
5. C	16. A	27. A	38. C
6. C	17. D	28. B	39. A
7. D	18. B	29. B	40. C
8. B	19. B	30. D	41. C
9. C	20. A	31. C	42. D
10. A	21. B	32. B	43. A
11. D	22. D	33. C	44. C

SECTION 3

1. B
2. B
3. A
4. C
5. B

6. A
7. B
8. A
9. D
10. C

11. B
12. D
13. D
14. A
15. B

16. 1
17. $\frac{1}{5} \leq x \leq 1$
18. 7
19. 3
20. 18

SECTION 4

1. B
2. A
3. B
4. B
5. B
6. A
7. B
8. D
9. C
10. A

11. A
12. D
13. B
14. B
15. A
16. A
17. A
18. C
19. C
20. D

21. C
22. B
23. D
24. A
25. D
26. B
27. B
28. B
29. C
30. A

31. 8
32. 32
33. 6
34. 15
35. 1/29
36. 40
37. 10
38. 17

PRACTICE TEST 3 ANSWERS

PART 3

SECTION 1

1. B	14. A	27. A	40. B
2. C	15. D	28. B	41. A
3. A	16. D	29. A	42. B
4. D	17. A	30. D	43. C
5. D	18. C	31. C	44. A
6. A	19. D	32. C	45. C
7. B	20. A	33. C	46. D
8. D	21. A	34. C	47. A
9. C	22. C	35. D	48. B
10. B	23. B	36. C	49. B
11. C	24. B	37. C	50. D
12. D	25. D	38. B	51. A
13. D	26. A	39. B	52. C

SECTION 2

1. C	12. C	23. D	34. D
2. D	13. A	24. A	35. B
3. A	14. B	25. C	36. A
4. D	15. D	26. D	37. C
5. B	16. D	27. B	38. A
6. D	17. C	28. D	39. D
7. B	18. C	29. C	40. C
8. C	19. B	30. B	41. B
9. A	20. C	31. D	42. C
10. D	21. A	32. C	43. C
11. B	22. C	33. D	44. D

SECTION 3

1. B	6. C	11. C	16. 10
2. D	7. B	12. C	17. 5
3. D	8. C	13. A	18. 0
4. B	9. C	14. A	19. 16
5. A	10. B	15. B	20. 48

SECTION 4

1. C	11. D	21. A	31. 18
2. A	12. B	22. C	32. 10
3. A	13. C	23. C	33. 5
4. B	14. B	24. B	34. 45
5. C	15. B	25. D	35. 233
6. A	16. C	26. B	36. 10
7. C	17. D	27. A	37. 30
8. D	18. D	28. D	38. 12
9. A	19. C	29. C	
10. C	20. C	30. D	

PRACTICE TEST 4 ANSWERS
PART 4

SECTION 1

1. B	14. B	27. A	40. C
2. C	15. A	28. C	41. B
3. A	16. A	29. D	42. B
4. A	17. B	30. B	43. C
5. B	18. D	31. C	44. C
6. B	19. C	32. B	45. A
7. D	20. B	33. C	46. C
8. B	21. C	34. A	47. D
9. A	22. A	35. B	48. C
10. B	23. A	36. D	49. D
11. B	24. B	37. C	50. B
12. C	25. A	38. C	51. A
13. D	26. D	39. D	52. D

SECTION 2

1. D	12. A	23. B	34. B
2. B	13. D	24. B	35. D
3. A	14. C	25. D	36. C
4. C	15. A	26. C	37. D
5. B	16. C	27. C	38. A
6. B	17. B	28. B	39. D
7. A	18. D	29. B	40. C
8. B	19. D	30. C	41. D
9. A	20. C	31. C	42. B
10. D	21. B	32. C	43. A
11. A	22. B	33. C	44. A

Section 3

1. B	6. D	11. D	16. 3/2
2. C	7. C	12. C	17. 1
3. C	8. B	13. A	18. 157
4. B	9. C	14. C	19. 100
5. A	10. A	15. D	20. 108

Section 4

1. C	11. A	21. C	31. 4
2. B	12. C	22. B	32. 70
3. C	13. B	23. A	33. 1.2
4. C	14. A	24. D	34. 19
5. A	15. A	25. B	35. 487
6. C	16. B	26. B	36. 18
7. D	17. B	27. A	37. 117
8. C	18. A	28. B	38. 26
9. A	19. C	29. D	
10. A	20. C	30. C	

THE SCORING SYSTEM
PART 5

The new SAT will have three test scores on a scale from 10 to 40. There will be one test score for each test: the Reading Test, the Writing and Language Test, and the Math Test. The Reading Test score and the Writing and Language Test score will be added together and converted to a single area score in Evidence-Based Reading and Writing; there will also be an area score in Math based on the Math Test Score.

The area scores will be on a scale from 200 to 800. Added together, they will form the composite score for the whole test, on a scale from 400 to 1600. The Essay will be scored separately and will not affect your scores in other areas.

SAT Scoring	
Test Scores (10 to 40)	• Reading Test • Writing and Language Test • Math Test
Area Scores (200 to 800)	• Evidence-Based Reading and Writing • Math
Composite Score (400 to 1600)	• Math (Area Score) + Evidence-Based Reading and Writing (Area Score)
Essay Scores (1 to 4)	• Reading • Analysis • Writing

The College Board will also be reporting new types of scores. **Cross-test scores** for **Analysis in Science** and **Analysis in History/Social Studies** will be based on performance on specific questions across different tests relating to specific types of content. For example, your cross-test score in Analysis in Science will be based on your performance on questions relating to science passages on the Reading Test as well as questions using scientific data on the Math Test. These scores will be on a scale from 10 to 40.

There will also be seven **subscores** based on particular question types within each test section. Subscores will be reported on a scale from 1 to 15. Four will be related to particular questions in the Reading and Writing and Language Test: Words in Context, Command of Evidence, Expression of Ideas, and Standard English Conventions. The other three relate to specific types of questions on the Math Test: Heart of Algebra, Problem Solving and Data Analysis, and Passport to Advanced Math.

CROSS-TEST SCORES AND SUBSCORES

You will receive **cross-test scores** for Analysis in Science and Analysis in History/Social Studies. The scores are based on your performance on questions in their respective subject domains across all sections of the exam. These scores will be reported on a scale of 10-40.

You will also receive **subscores** based on your performance on certain question types within each test section. Subscores will be reported on a scale of 1-15. There will be seven subscores, for the following areas:

- **Words in Context:** this subscore will be based on your performance on questions related to determining the meanings of words in the context of a passage in the Reading and Writing and Language tests.

- **Command of Evidence:** this subscore will be based on your performance on questions that ask you to identify the best evidence in the Reading and Writing and Language tests.

- **Expression of Ideas:** this subscore will be based on your performance on questions that ask you to identify clear, stylistically appropriate choices in Writing passages.

- **Standard English Conventions:** this subscore will be based on your performance on questions that ask you to identify and correct errors of grammar, punctuation, usage, and syntax in Writing passages.

- **Heart of Algebra:** this subscore will be based on your performance on Math questions testing key concepts in Algebra.

- **Problem Solving and Data Analysis**: this subscore will be based on your performance on Math questions testing your ability to analyze sets of data, the meanings of units and quantities, and the properties of different objects and operations.

- **Passport to Advanced Math:** this subscore will be based on your performance on Math questions that test the skills you'll build on as you continue to learn more advanced math including rewriting expressions, solving quadratic equations, working with polynomials and radicals, and solving systems of equations.

For detailed scoring information, visit:

ivyglobal.com/study

SCORING YOUR TEST
PART 6

To score your tests, first use the answer key to mark each of your responses right or wrong. Then, calculate your **raw score** for each section by counting up the number of correct responses. Use the tables below to help you calculate your scores:

Raw Score (# of Questions Correct)

Section	Test 1	Test 2	Test 3	Test 4
1. Reading	_____	_____	_____	_____
2. Writing and Language	_____	_____	_____	_____
3. Math: No-Calculator	_____	_____	_____	_____
4. Math: Calculator	_____	_____	_____	_____
Raw Score for Reading (Section 1)	_____	_____	_____	_____
Raw Score for Writing and Language (Section 2)	_____	_____	_____	_____
Raw Score for Math (Section 3 + 4)	_____	_____	_____	_____

SCALED SCORES

Once you have found your raw score for each section, convert it into an approximate **scaled test score** using the following chart. To find a scaled test score for each section, find the row in the Raw Score column which corresponds to your raw score for that section, then check the column for the section you are scoring in the same row. For example, if you had a raw score of 48 for Reading, then your scaled Reading test score would be 39. Keep in mind that these scaled scores are estimates only. Your actual SAT score will be scaled against the scores of all other high school students taking the test on your test date.

Raw Score	Math Scaled Score	Reading Scaled Score	Writing Scaled Score	Raw Score	Math Scaled Score	Reading Scaled Score	Writing Scaled Score
58	40			28	23	26	25
57	40			27	22	25	24
56	40			26	22	25	24
55	39			25	21	24	23
54	38			24	21	24	23
53	37			23	20	23	22
52	36	40		22	20	22	21
51	35	40		21	19	22	21
50	34	40		20	19	21	20
49	34	39		19	18	20	20
48	33	39		18	18	20	19
47	33	38		17	17	19	19
46	32	37		16	16	19	18
45	32	36		15	15	18	18
44	31	35	40	14	14	17	17
43	30	34	39	13	13	16	16
42	30	34	38	12	12	16	15
41	29	33	37	11	11	14	14
40	29	33	35	10	10	13	13
39	28	32	34	9	10	12	12
38	28	31	33	8	10	11	11
37	27	31	32	7	10	10	10
36	27	30	31	6	10	10	10
35	26	30	30	5	10	10	10
34	26	29	29	4	10	10	10
33	25	29	28	3	10	10	10
32	25	28	27	2	10	10	10
31	24	28	27	1	10	10	10
30	24	27	26	0	10	10	10
29	23	26	26				

Use the table below to record your scaled scores:

Scaled Scores

Section	Test 1	Test 2	Test 3	Test 4
Reading (Out of 40)	_____	_____	_____	_____
Writing and Language (Out of 40)	_____	_____	_____	_____
Math (Out of 40)	_____	_____	_____	_____

ESSAY SCORE

Estimate your essay score by assigning your essay a score out of 1-4 in each scoring area listed below. Have a trusted reader check your work. For more information on essay scoring criteria, see Chapter 4 of Ivy Global's New SAT Guide.

Essay Score

Scoring Area	Reading		Analysis		Writing	
	Reader 1	Reader 2	Reader 1	Reader 2	Reader 1	Reader 2
Test 1	_____	_____	_____	_____	_____	_____
Test 2	_____	_____	_____	_____	_____	_____
Test 3	_____	_____	_____	_____	_____	_____
Test 4	_____	_____	_____	_____	_____	_____

AREA SCORE CONVERSION

You can look up your area score out of 800 below. To find your overall score, combine your area score for Reading + Writing with your area score for Math to get your total score out of 1600.

READING + WRITING

Scaled Score	Area Score	Scaled Score	Area Score	Scaled Score	Area Score
80	760-800	59	550-630	39	350-430
79	750-800	58	540-620	38	340-420
78	740-800	57	530-610	37	330-410
77	730-800	56	520-600	36	320-400
76	720-800	55	510-590	35	310-390
75	710-790	54	500-580	34	300-380
74	700-780	53	490-570	33	290-370
73	690-770	52	480-560	32	280-360
72	680-760	51	470-550	31	270-350
71	670-750	50	460-540	30	260-340
70	660-740	49	450-530	29	250-330
69	650-730	48	440-520	28	240-320
68	640-720	47	430-510	27	230-310
67	630-710	46	420-500	26	220-300
66	620-700	45	410-490	25	210-290
65	610-690	44	400-480	24	200-280
64	600-680	43	390-470	23	200-270
63	590-670	42	380-460	22	200-260
62	580-660	41	370-450	21	200-250
61	570-650	40	360-440	20	200-240
60	560-640				

MATH

Total Points	Area Score	Total Points	Area Score
40	760-800	24	440-520
39	740-800	23	420-500
38	720-800	22	400-480
37	700-780	21	380-460
36	680-760	20	360-440
35	660-740	19	340-420
34	640-720	18	320-400
33	620-700	17	300-380
32	600-680	16	280-360
31	580-660	15	260-340
30	560-640	14	240-320
29	540-620	13	220-300
28	520-600	12	200-280
27	500-580	11	200-260
26	480-560	10	200-240
25	460-540		

Use the table below to record your area scores and to calculate your overall score:

	Reading + Writing Area Score		Math Area Score		Overall Score (400-1600)
Test 1	_____	+	_____	=	_____
Test 2	_____	+	_____	=	_____
Test 3	_____	+	_____	=	_____
Test 4	_____	+	_____	=	_____

Ivy Global

The World's Most Comprehensive Prep for the New SAT

Order on sat.ivyglobal.com or amazon.com

New SAT Guide

The first comprehensive SAT Guide to address the changes to the new SAT in 2016, with effective strategies and extensive practice material.

Teacher's Guide

Our all-encompassing companion to the New SAT Guide offers a variety of class curricula and extensive training for teachers.

3 Practice Tests for the New PSAT

The first book of practice tests that addresses the changes to the new PSAT in 2015.

4 Practice Tests

More practice leads to better results. This practice test compilation book includes four full length SAT practice tests.

4 Full Practice Tests

For a more authentic test-taking experience, our four full length SAT Tests are also available in *separate booklets*.

Custom Solutions – We also offer custom solutions that are tailored to the needs of schools and tests prep companies that order books in bulk. Books can be customized to include just practice tests or to solely focus on content and strategies.

Email us at publishing@ivyglobal.com or call us at 1-888-588-7955 with any questions on licensing and bulk orders, or with any general inquires.

FRESHMAN

SEM 1	SEM 2
A	A
C	B
A	B
C	B
B	A
B	A
A	A

3.14 UW   3.57 UW
3.29 W   3.71 W

* UW: 3.568
  W: 4.038
w/ APUSH & B IN CSA

SOPHOMORE

SEM 1	SEM 2
A	CR
B	CR
B	CR
A	CR
~~A~~	CR
A	CR
A	CR
	CR

3.71 UW
4.33 W

UW: 3.628
W: 4.038
w/o APUSH
& B IN CSA

* JUNIOR
WITH APUSH

SEM 1	SEM 2
B	B
A	A
A	A
A	A
A	B
B	A
A	A
A	

3.71 UW   3.71 UW
4.43 W   4.43 W

UW: 3.684
W: 4.094
w/o APUSH
& A IN CSA

* JUNIOR
W/O APUSH AND B IN CSA

SEM 1	SEM 2
B	B
A	A
A	A
A	A
A	A
A	A
A	A
A	

3.66 UW   3.86 UW
4.43 W   4.43 W

↓

SEM 1	SEM 2
A	A
A	A
A	A
A	A
A	A
B A	A
A	A
A	

4.0 UW   4.0 UW
4.57 W   4.57 W

w/ SCOTT   4.71

UW: 3.684
W: 4.15

SOPH

A → 4
B → 3 → 4
B → 3 → 5
A → 4 → 5
A → 4
A → 4
A → 4

JUN

A → 4 → 5
A → 4 → 5
A → 4
A → 4
B → 3 → 4
A → 4
A → 4

A → 4 → 5
A → 4 → 5
A → 4
A → 4
A → 4
B → 3 → 4
A → 4
A → 4

UL APPROVED

APUSH
BRITLIT
AP CSA
TRIG H
APES
AP CSA
CHEM H
AP PSYCH

UL GPA

w/ all As Junior Year: 3.9 UW
4.65 weighted
4.3 capped

w/ 1 B Junior Year: 3.8 UW
4.55 weighted
4.2 capped

Made in the USA
San Bernardino, CA
11 November 2017